WATCHES

FRONTISPIECE: overleaf

1 Andrews, London, England. *c.* 1800. Cylinder escapement. White enamel dial. Gold arrow-head hands. Translucent enamel over engine-turning with applied filigree and pearl decoration

2 Emery. London, England. See fig. 338

3 Solomon Plaivas, Blois, France. *c.* 1640. Verge escapement. Fusee and gut. Painted enamel dial with single gilt hand. Blois painted enamel case. The brilliant but delicate colouring is typical only of the earliest Blois enamelling

4 Auguste Bretonneau, Paris, France. *c.* 1640. Verge escapement without balance-spring. Fusee and gut. Painted enamel dial with single gilt hand. Blois painted enamel case. A watch of exceptional size and the very highest quality of Blois enamel painting of the school of Toutin

5 Jaquet Droz. Swiss. See fig. 325

6 Breguet. No. 4038. Paris, France. 1824. Lever escapement. Two-arm compensation balance. Spiral balance-spring with end-curve. Regulator operated through sector in dial. Going barrel. Half-quarter repeater on single gong. Engine-turned silver dial with eccentric chapter ring and subsidiary dial for seconds. Gold hands. Silver and gold engine-turned case. Breguet short chain and male key

7 Anonymous. Swiss. Verge escapement. Quarter repeater on gongs. Three-colour gold dial with eccentric chapter ring and automata to simulate striking of hours and quarters. Gold hands. Engine-turned gold case

8 Johannes Van Ceulen, The Hague. *c.* 1670. Verge escapement originally without balance-spring. Fusee and chain with long links, probably original. Painted enamel dial with blued steel hands. Painted enamel case with colours typical of the Huaud school

9 Quare, London, See fig. 243

10 Bushman, London. See fig. 255

1	4	6
2		7
3	5	8
9		10

WATCHES

Cecil Clutton and George Daniels

A Studio Book · THE VIKING PRESS · New York

© Cecil Clutton and George Daniels, 1965

Published in 1965 by The Viking Press, Inc.
625 Madison Avenue, New York, N.Y. 10022

Library of Congress Catalog Card Number: 65-15108

Made and printed in Great Britain by
William Clowes and Sons Ltd, London and Beccles

Preface

Twenty years ago the collector of watches was well provided with works of reference. G. H. Baillie's splendidly illustrated and informative *Watches* was still available at list price and Paul Chamberlain's invaluable *It's About Time* had only recently been published. The sixth and earlier editions of Britten's *Old Clocks and Watches and their Makers* were also fairly readily available, although already hopelessly out of date except as picture books and for their invaluable lists of makers.

Now, these works are prohibitively expensive and even Britten is rare. To replace them there has been little but the almost entirely new seventh edition of Britten, which is the only general history of horology currently in print; but with so much ground to cover, only sixty of the most important watch types could be illustrated. *The Story of Watches* by T. P. Camerer Cuss contains much valuable information but is partly marred by the poor reproduction of the illustrations.

It is therefore thought that the time is ripe for a new and plentifully illustrated book on watches. Moreover, in the last twenty years, collecting tastes have changed greatly. Previously, the emphasis was on external appearance rather than mechanism and it was the early, decoratively-cased watches that fetched the highest prices. Although these keep their value, the new generation of collector is increasingly interested in the mechanical side of the subject, and especially in the period when the precision watch was developed; in the half century from 1775 to 1825. Such watches already fetch high prices, and the less wealthy collectors are already being driven—by no means unwillingly—into the nineteenth century, where a mass of semi-experimental escapements awaits them, in cases which, at their best, whether severely plain or the more exuberant manifestations of four-colour gold, may be most attractive in appearance.

No apology is therefore needed if, in the historical section of the book, an apparently disproportionate emphasis is placed on the periods of watchmaking, such as the invention of the balance-spring, and the 'early precision period', when the greatest technical advances took place. Indeed, it is believed that this is the first time that a fully chronological sequence of events in the development of the precision watch has been attempted, and some problems still remain unsolved.

Almost as many problems remain unsolved in connection with the earliest period of watchmaking, prior to about 1550. The work of the various schools cannot as yet be identified with any certainty, but it is to be hoped that the researches of Philip Cool, of the British Museum, may before long produce some clearer codification.

In the section of the historical essay dealing with decorative cases, such as those in enamel or semi-precious stones, these are regarded as specialist studies in no way connected with horology, beyond illustrating a representative selection. If the reader wants technical information on these subjects he is advised to seek it in the standard reference works upon them.

In the historical sections it has been assumed that the reader has a fair amount of general knowledge of the subject, but for basic information as to how the various escapements operate he is referred either to the seventh edition of Britten's *Old Clocks and Watches and their Makers*,[1] or W. J. Gazeley's *Clock and Watch Escapements*.[2] They are further discussed in the Technical Appendix of this book.

The authors believe that every important development is covered in the illustrations.

[1] Published by E. & E. N. Spon Ltd. 1956
[2] Published by Heywood & Co. Ltd. 1956.

Contents

CONTENTS

Acknowledgment

The authors express their gratitude to the Trustees of the British Museum for permission to illustrate several watches from the Museum's unsurpassed collection. They are also particularly grateful to Mr. Philip Cool, of the Museum staff, for his personal help in photographing the watches selected.

A large number of watches is illustrated from the collection of the Worshipful Company of Clockmakers, on show at the Guildhall, and Colonel H. Quill, c.b.e., d.s.o., m.v.o., Royal Marines, took endless trouble to make them available for photography by George Daniels, who took these and nearly all the photographs appearing in the book.

Few of the watches selected from these two great public collections have been illustrated before, and for the rest, the authors are indebted entirely to private collectors, very few of whose watches have been illustrated elsewhere. A full list of owners is set out below, but particular mention should be made of the large collections which have been drawn upon so widely, namely, those of Mr. T. P. Camerer Cuss; Mr. Edward Hornby; the late Mr. H. R. Hurle-Bath and Miss W. E. Hurle-Bradley; and Mr. Robert Marryat.

Monsieur George Brown of Breguet has been most generous with help and advice, but the authors take sole responsibility for any conclusions drawn concerning the work of Abraham-Louis Breguet.

Owing to the large number of photographs of escapements it has not been thought necessary to include many line-drawings, and these have therefore been limited to the two very spirited perspective drawings by L. H. Cresswell of Josiah Emery's lever, and John Arnold's pivoted detent escapements, as being the ancestors of all modern watches and chronometers.

Finally, no modern authors can fail to acknowledge their indebtedness to those great horological historians of the past: Paul Chamberlain, Courtenay Ilbert and Lt.Commdr. R. T. Gould.

The following is a list of owners of watches illustrated, so far as they are known to the authors at the time of going to press:—

His Grace the Duke of Wellington, 529.
The Right Honourable the Lord Harris, 422, 432, 451.
Signor A. M. Almeida, 352, 395.
Mr. Sam Bloomfield, 336, 342, 360, 386, 405, 478, 499, 525, 527, 539, 561, 569, 571, 573, 592, 596.
Monsieur George Brown, of Breguet, 330, 519.
The Trustees of the British Museum, 91, 279, 283, 290, 300, 333, 514, 541, 555.

ACKNOWLEDGMENT

The Worshipful Company of Clockmakers, 85, 112, 119, 126, 133, 136, 138, 160, 163, 169, 173, 179, 185, 188, 193, 196, 205, 208, 223, 240, 243, 268, 271, 274, 276, 285, 295, 303, 305, 308, 313, 334, 338, 350, 364, 371, 391, 393, 409, 411, 416, 419, 469, 501, 546, 551.

Mr. C. Clutton, 2, 6, 9, 10, 11, 152, 203, 233, 253, 255, 282, 287, 298, 323, 345, 358, 376, 378, 380, 389, 427, 429, 434, 439, 464, 488, 523, 535, 578, 580, 594.

Mr. T. P. C. Cuss, 13, 16, 92, 102, 122, 166, 170, 210, 219, 229, 251, 292, 344, 348, 367, 369, 372, 457, 480, 495, 512, 516, 537, 566.

Mr. G. Daniels, 221, 309, 321, 490, 582.

Mrs. G. Daniels, 544.

Monsieur C. Durand-Rouel, 403, 407.

Mr. R. D. Durrant, 249.

Mr. C. Elsom, 182, 453.

Miss M. Farrer, 553.

Major R. A. Fell, 584.

Mrs. E. Flint, 347.

Mr. R. K. Foulkes, 462, 559.

Mr. E. Giles, 476.

Mrs. B. Hawkins, 587.

Mr. E. Hornby, 5, 89, 99, 106, 109, 116, 124, 140, 149, 157, 198, 200, 212, 215, 235, 301, 311, 319, 325, 448, 482, 497, 503, 548, 557.

The late Mr. H. R. Hurle-Bath, E, 1, 7, 12, 130, 217, 260, 340, 355, 400, 414, 425, 443, 455, 508.

Miss Hurle-Bradley, 104, 143, 155, 257, 446.

Musée du Louvre, 74.

Mr. R. A. Marryatt, B, K, 3, 4, 8, 14, 69, 72, 77, 82, 94, 96, 114, 146, 176, 237, 245, 262, 315, 328, 374, 382, 418, 436, 441, 459, 472, 510, 532, 564, 590.

Mr. J. F. Moon, 474.

Mr. P. Palumbo, 506.

Colonel H. Quill, R.M., 266.

Mr. R. Shermund, 575.

Sir John Soane's Museum, 226.

Mr. C. C. Yates, 493.

The Illustrations

THE ILLUSTRATIONS

THE ILLUSTRATIONS

THE ILLUSTRATIONS

THE ILLUSTRATIONS

THE ILLUSTRATIONS

1 Historical

Mechanical 1500 – 1750

The Invention of Watches

No conclusive evidence exists as to the invention of a clock with a mechanical escapement. *Horologium* may mean a sundial, a mechanical clock or a water clock, and the latter go back to a very early date. Indeed, the Chinese had very complicated and monumental water clocks with a sort of very slow escapement, not unlike an automatic flushing tank of today. It may well be that this was developed into a weight-driven clock with a mechanical escapement in the Middle East and thence travelled into Europe.

It is certain that Villard de Honnecourt, a most observant and much-travelled architect in the middle of the thirteenth century, did not know of a mechanical clock, while by 1300 it is becoming reasonably clear that at any rate some of the literary references to an *horologium* mean a mechanical clock. It therefore seems reasonable to date the invention of the mechanical clock, or at any rate its appearance in Europe, in the last quarter of the thirteenth century.

The oldest clock surviving in any state of completeness is that at Salisbury Cathedral, made in 1386. It had been converted to pendulum, but in 1956 was reconverted to its original verge and foliot escapement. By its date quite small domestic clocks existed, although none survives; but these also were weight driven.

No watch could be made until a reliable form of portable power was available, and it is once more difficult to fix exactly when a coiled spring was first applied as the motive power of a clock.

In the Bibliothèque Royale of Belgium is a manuscript copy of a fairly well-known work *Horologium Sapientiae* (the Clock of Wisdom) which can be dated between 1455 and 1488. One of its illustrations shows a number of timekeeping and allied devices, including the movement of an octagonal spring-driven clock. This is accurately portrayed and a fusee is clearly visible. Some authorities prefer a 1455 rather than a 1488 date for the manuscript and thus infer that spring-driven clocks must have existed before 1450. There are, however, objections to the manuscript being so early, and the earliest dated reference to a spring-driven clock exists in a manuscript in the Augsburg Stadtbibliothek, by Paulus Alemannus, which can be dated accurately to the years 1477–8. It describes clock mechanism and several spring clocks, and a fusee is illustrated.

There is also a letter of 21st August, 1482 from Comino da Pontevico to the Duke of Mantua, containing the following passage (as translated by Dr. Morpurgo). 'The clock is provided with a steel ribbon, hidden in a brass box around which a string is wound. . . . If this steel ribbon were missing the instrument would not be able to run, even though the string were there, the said string tied to the box around the steel ribbon, is inserted to cause the pulling of the screw or force to which it is attached; the purpose of all this is to make all the wheels of the clock turn by propelling the said screw by force of the steel ribbon; thus are my clocks made, which I showed Your Excellency, and thus all masters make them.'

In 1480, on April 4th, Jean de Paris, clockmaker to Louis XI, received 16 livres for a clock striking the hours 'to be carried with him everywhere'. This must have been a spring clock, and there are two portraits of the king standing by a table on which stands a little hexagonal clock, with a hexagonal domed top.

There seem therefore to be good grounds for dating the spring-driven clock at about 1470, but any earlier date calls for some degree of wishful thinking. No spring clock survives which can be attributed to the fifteenth century, and the oldest dated spring clock is that belonging to the Society of Antiquaries of London, made by Jacob the Czech, for Sigismund I, King of Poland, dated 1525. This is drum shaped, $9\frac{3}{4}''$ in diameter.

From the time of the first spring clocks it would not take long to compress the mechanism into a small enough case to be carried about the person, but there is no reference to a watch before 1500.

In 1511 Johannes Cocclaens writes of Peter Hele, or Henlein of Nuremburg (1480–1542): 'from day to day more ingenious discoveries are made; for Petrus Hele, a young man, makes things which astonish the most learned mathematician, for he makes out of a small quantity of iron, horologia devised with very many wheels, and these horologia, in any position and without any weights, both indicate and strike for 40 hours, even when they are carried on the breast or in the purse'. Henlein had a contemporary, Caspar Werner, who was said to have 'devoted himself with especial industry to the making of watches which he brought into great popularity as the result of continual study and the introduction of various new inventions, though he injured his memory and health thereby'.

No watch attributable to Henlein or Werner survives, and the earliest dated watch is French, of spherical shape, in the Louvre at Paris, by Jacques de la Garde, of Blois, dated 1551 (74); a similar, larger watch by him, dated 1565, is in the Maritime Museum, Greenwich. It is not known exactly when the Blois industry started, but it cannot have been appreciably later than the Nuremburg school.

4

The Nuremburg watches appear also to have been spherical in shape and Henlein is mentioned by Dopplmayer as 'a locksmith artist who gained renown through the small watchworks which he was one of the first to make in the form of the musk-balls at that time in use', and in 1524 he received 15 florins for a gilt musk-apple with a watch. Such a German watch, dating from about the middle of the sixteenth century, is in the Ashmolean Museum, Oxford. But although both Henlein's and de la Garde's watches were spherical, it is certain that drum-shaped watches existed before 1550, being miniatures of the Antiquaries' Jacob Czech clock previously mentioned.

The exact purpose of these small drum clocks, such as those of the Clockmakers' Company, is not very clear. Mostly $2\frac{1}{2}''$–$3''$ deep and in diameter, they are rather large to be worn and in any case have no pendant from which to suspend them (69). On the other hand, if they were not intended to be carried about there seems to have been no point in making them so small. They are usually quite plain, with a little simple engraving. It may be that they were therefore carried in a bag, or regarded as travelling clocks. There is one such in the British Museum with its movement pivoted between plates; and two in the collection of the Worshipful Company of Clockmakers in the City of London Guildhall, which have skeleton movements and fusees, similar to that of the Jacob Czech clock. It may be therefore that the fusee and skeleton movement comes from the south, since the Henlein watches probably, and his immediate successors certainly, used plated movements with a stackfreed (84); a most inferior substitute for a fusee.

Fusee and Stackfreed

It is a matter of common experience that when a coiled spring is newly wound up it exerts more power than when it is nearly run down, and this is the great defect of springs as against weights, as the motive power for clockwork. As has already been shown, it had been overcome no later than about 1475 by the fusee; one of the most beautiful mechanical inventions of its own or any other time. Although described in detail in the technical section, the principle of its operation is self-evident; in effect it is a progressively variable gear, in which the spring has to pull a high gear ratio when it is fully wound, and a low ratio when it is nearly run down and at its most feeble. In this way an even torque, or nearly so, is applied to the train of wheels and the escapement, throughout the day or whatever the running period of the watch may be.

By contrast, the stackfreed is a most brutal arrangement. It again is explained in the technical section, but in brief, it consists of a cam geared to the arbor fixed to the mainspring, so as to turn once in the going period of the watch. Pressing against the cam is a roller mounted on a strong spring. The contour of the cam is such that when fully wound the stackfreed spring works against the mainspring and so slows the watch; while towards the end of the run it assists the mainspring and so hurries things along.

The Movement and its Decoration up to 1675

The earliest German watch movements were made entirely of iron, although the pinions were made of harder iron (possibly steel) than the rest. After about 1580 the plates were increasingly of brass, but all-iron trains are found as late as 1625, and the stackfreed survived even longer. Where iron plates are brass-bushed this is a later repair. One very remarkable clock in the British Museum has an iron movement entirely tin-plated, to prevent rust.

The French early realised that brass is more easily worked than iron for wheels and plates, and wears at least as well.

The balance-wheel or foliot was always outside the plates and its top pivot therefore had to be pivoted into a cock fixed to the top plate. In the earliest German watches the bottom pivot ran in a hole in the bottom plate, or sometimes in a spiral-shaped cock cut out of the bottom plate. The earliest balance-cocks were S-shaped (84), so that they could safely be bent to some extent, to adjust the depth of the engagement of the pallets with the escape wheel. The cock was pinned to a pillar riveted to the top plate. It usually had a very short tail to steady it on the plate. Later, the tail was to grow into what is more properly called a foot, with steady pins to locate it more precisely. The crown or escape wheel was pivoted between two more pillars, or potences, also riveted to the top plate. In the earliest German watches there was no adjustment for depthing the escapement, except by bending the balance-cock, as above.

In even the earliest French watches, and soon afterwards in German and all others,

6

the bottom pivot of the verge had been supported in an extension of the crown-wheel potence. The outer end of the crown-wheel arbor was always pivoted in a small circular plug, fitted friction-tight in the potence. By this means, the end-float and depthing of the escapement could be adjusted within fine limits, which is by far the best way of regulating a pre-balance-spring verge watch.

Especially in the skeleton movements, the makers were at considerable pains to place the crown-wheel arbor so as to be exactly radial to the contrate wheel. In later watches, where the contrate wheel is pivoted between the plates, and the crown wheel is pivoted at its outer end in a small separate potence attached to the plate, this is no longer possible, and the teeth of the contrate wheel have to be cut on a skew so as to mesh smoothly with the eccentrically-placed crown-wheel pinion. In the early skeleton lay-out this was avoided by having one cock pierced with two holes, at right angles to each other; one carrying the contrate wheel pivot and one the crown-wheel pivot. The advantage of this is obvious; its disadvantage is the impossibility, or at any rate considerable difficulty, of providing any means of adjusting the end-float of the crown-wheel staff.

It is very unlucky that we know so little about the fifteenth-century Italian watches, since the three quite different types of watch movement found in the early sixteenth century seem to have very little in common with each other and it is therefore difficult to say which, if any of them, stems from the Italian original. However, since the cultural connections between Italy and France were so strong it seems fair to assume that the French watches followed the Italian model. The French craftsmanship is so greatly superior to that of the German iron movements—whether the fullplate, stackfreed type, or the skeleton, fusee type—that it seems quite likely that the watch was separately invented in Germany, and that the German watches owe nothing to the fifteenth-century Italian school. Nor is it by any means improbable that the watch should have been evolved simultaneously in two or even three different places.

Only in the hands of quite exceptional artists, such as Jost Burgi and Hans Kiening, was wheel-cutting in iron brought to a standard which will bear comparison with what was quite common in French watches.

7

Mean Time Regulation before the Balance Spring

A watch with a balance spring is readily adjusted for mean time, but the earliest watches had no such convenience and other, cruder means had to be found.

Fusee watches were provided with a ratchet and click mounted on the spring-barrel arbor, to which the inner end of the spring is attached (*111*). This arbor also ended in a square so that it could be turned by a key, and thus the initial tension of the mainspring could be set up by means of the ratchet. Since the amount of set-up operated as additional power, and since the rate of a verge escapement is directly related to the power applied to it, this set-up ratchet provided a rough means of regulating the watch.

In about 1640 the ratchet set-up began to be replaced by a worm and wheel (*21* and many others). The wormwheel was mounted on a long arbor pivoted in two blued steel supports, screwed to the plate. The supports had elegantly pierced and shaped tails. After a short time the wheel, mounted on the mainspring arbor, was capped by a silver plate, usually numbered 1–6, as a guide when regulating the watch.

With a stackfreed it is not quite so simple to adjust the set-up, although it is not impossible, as is generally stated. The stackfreed incorporates stopwork which predetermines the full-wind and fully-run-down positions. As the pinion which drives the stackfreed wheel is squared on to the spring arbor there is no great difficulty in setting up the initial tension of the spring by winding it up to any desired extent, before meshing the pinion with the stackfreed wheel. In this way the mainspring can be set up in just the same way as a fusee. However, an additional means was usually provided, and this consisted of a pair of bristles placed in the path of the arms of the balance or foliot; and mounted on a pivoted arm. By moving the arm, the bristles could be moved closer to or further from the centre of the balance and thus limit the arc of its swing (*91*). A smaller arc would speed up the watch and a larger arc slow it down. It was a crude and unsatisfactory arrangement, although the fusee set-up is not much better as a means of regulation.

General Characteristics and National Styles

From the earliest times, watches had a striking train, and such watches are known as clock-watches. When Florimund Robertet, Treasurer successively to Charles VIII, Louis XII and François I, died in 1532, he left no less than 12 watches (presumably all French) which were listed as follows: 'Twelve watches, of which seven are striking and the other five silent, in cases of gold, silver, and brass of different sizes; but of these I (the widow) attach value only to the large one, merely of gilt copper, that my husband had made; it shows all the stars and the celestial signs and motions, which he understood perfectly'. The latter is also the first reference to a watch with complications.

French and German watches had a somewhat different system of striking, and when English watches began to appear at the end of the century, they followed the French system.

German watches had striking trains less frequently than the French, an alarum being preferred. Sometimes a watch had both striking and alarum. Sometimes also the alarum mechanism was separate, so that it could be attached to the watch proper at will (77).

The earliest plate pillars were plain, square or round in section, and riveted to the bottom plate. The top plate fitted over them and was secured by pins, as continued to be the practice until well into the nineteenth century. Even at this earliest period watches had at any rate one screw. In stackfreed watches it secured the stackfreed spring, and in fusee watches it secured the set-up click.

After about 1580 national styles began to develop more markedly and a native school began to appear in Britain.

German watches developed slowly. Brass plates began to appear about 1580, and sometimes brass wheels; but iron trains and the stackfreed continued in use throughout the first quarter of the seventeenth century. Finally, the Thirty Years' War (1618–48) so crippled the country that Germany ceased to be an important factor in horology, and France was left in undisputed supremacy, which she was to enjoy until successfully challenged by Britain in the last quarter of the seventeenth century.

By 1600, the watch movement had reached a fairly sophisticated state, yet it remained a villainously bad timekeeper. The daily rate might easily vary by a quarter of an hour. No means of improving this being found, it was natural that attention should

9

turn to decoration, both of the movement and the case; and mechanical complications, such as calendar and astronomical trains.

In French watches, the balance-cock became larger in size and pierced and engraved in a roughly spiral pattern. Similar pierced and engraved decoration was used to cover the locking plate of the striking train, alarum stopwork and set-up ratchet. The maker's name also began to appear on the plate (*93, 98*).

The British affected a more floreate pattern of decoration for their balance and other cocks, and for a short time after 1600 put an engraved border round the edge of the top plate (*103, 111*).

In about 1620 the balance-cock began to be screwed to the plate (*121*) instead of pinned (*129*), although it continued for a time to be fitted over a pillar at the junction of the foot and the table.

As the century progressed, the cock tended to become less oval, and more circular, completely covering the balance (*172*).

Pillars became increasingly decorative, with spiral and other fancy shapes; but the Egyptian tapering form was most common; sometimes pierced and engraved. After about 1660 the very decorative tulip shape began to appear, as also did other forms of decoration between the plates, such as turned arbors, engraved spring barrels, and a pierced mounting for the fusee stop-arm.

Especially in British watches, the maker's name was inscribed on the top plate in an elegant, tall, sloping script, among which Edward East's is outstanding (*132, 151*).

Three-wheel trains and a 14-hours going period continued to be almost universal up to 1650 and quite usual up to 1675. In rare cases where 26 hours going was attempted it was sometimes achieved by the questionable practice of using five-leafed pinions instead of six; rather than introduce a fourth wheel.

During the third quarter of the seventeenth century it became fashionable to make thin watches, and some really surprisingly thin movements were produced latterly (*151*). To achieve this, the bottom plate was often cut away to allow the balance-wheel potence to be recessed into it.

Fusee chains were introduced for table clocks by about 1630 and the earliest chains have very long links. But gut continued to be used in watches, and a fusee chain is rarely found before 1670.

For the escapement, there was no serious challenger to the verge. Leonardo da Vinci invented a variant of it, with two parallel escape wheels with radial, pin-shaped teeth.

The verge lay between them, with the pallets at 180 degrees to each other. One pallet engaged with one wheel and the other pallet with the other wheel. The effect is not different from that of a verge, and it is not known if it was ever made.

More significant was the 'cross-beat' escapement invented in about 1580 by Jost Burgi of Prague (1552–1632). This had two balances geared together with one pallet on each and a single escape wheel. The balances moved in a vertical plane and each consisted of a foliot with its arms roughly vertical when at rest. Had Burgi made the lower arms longer than the upper he would, of course, have invented a very good compound pendulum escapement. But as it is, his escapement is not very much better than an ordinary verge. Several examples survive, made over a period of about half a century, including one in the British Museum. Although the escapement could have been applied to a watch, this is not known ever to have been done until a practically identical escapement was re-invented almost a century later by Robert Hooke.

Mechanically, the first three-quarters of the seventeenth century was thus a time of almost complete stagnation in watchmaking; the main interest lies in the variety of decorated cases, and for collectors more interested in the external appearance than in the mechanism, it is the most rewarding of any.

Clock and watchmakers' guilds had existed abroad from early in the sixteenth century, but despite various attempts, nothing was achieved in England until 1631, when the Worshipful Company of Clockmakers was founded, with David Ramsay (c. 1600–50) as its first master. From this time, under the leadership of such makers as Ramsay and Edward East (1602–96), the quality of British watchmaking improved steadily, until by 1675, with the development of the balance-spring, the British makers were able to take the lead from the French.

The Invention of the Balance-spring 1675–1700

The invention and development of the balance-spring marks the turning point in the history of the watch. What had previously been little more than a rich man's ornamental toy became suddenly a scientific instrument, capable of running accurately within two minutes a day. In the story of it the names Robert Hooke, Christian Huygens, Thomas Tompion and Isaac Thuret figure prominently.

Robert Hooke (1635–1703), the first 'Curator of Experiments' to the newly founded Royal Society, had an extremely enquiring and inventive mind which ranged over most scientific problems of his day, including those of horology. In 1658 he began making experiments to improve the timekeeping of watches, by using a spring to control and regularise the oscillations of the balance. In 1668 Lorenzo Magalotti, of the Florentine Academy, visited London and saw Hooke demonstrating his invention before members of the Royal Society; which he described as 'a pocket watch with a new pendulum invention. You might call it with a bridle: the time being regulated by a little spring of tempered wire which at one end is attached to the balance-wheel, and at the other to the body of the watch. This works in such a way that if the movements of the balance-wheel are unequal, and if some irregularity of the toothed movement tends to increase the inequality, the wire keeps it in check, obliging it to make the same journey'.

Evidently this was a straight spring, anchored at one end to the plate, with its free end playing between two pins set vertically on the rim of the balance. Hooke claimed to know twenty ways of attaching the balance-spring to a watch, but withheld the best until he should have derived some benefit from it. He also experimented with two balances geared together, with one pallet on each (presumably a revival of Burgi's cross-beat escapement); at another time he tried out a loadstone as a regulator.

Hooke was not alone in this field. As early as 1660 Christian Huygens van Zulichem (1629–95), the eminent Dutch physicist, mathematician and astronomer, saw a balance-spring watch being made by Martinet to the designs of Pascal and the Duc de Roannais. Huygens did not think their method practicable and said that he himself already knew of a better.

As often happened with Hooke, having had the seeds of an idea, he laid it aside before bringing it to fruition, and when someone else did so he accused them of stealing his invention. It seems that he abandoned his experiments in 1668, whereas Huygens continued his. Like Hooke, he had tried two balances geared together, but eventually chose a single balance with a spiral spring. However, it differed in one important way from what was to become standard practice. Instead of the balance-wheel and spring being applied to the verge, the balance with its spring was on a separate staff, geared to the verge in such a way that instead of having the usual verge arc of about 100 degrees, the balance described several complete turns at each vibration. To make this possible, his balance-spring had 4 turns, as against the $1\frac{1}{2}$ or 2 turns found in the earliest surviving balance-spring watches.

The year 1675 saw a splendid contest develop between Huygens and Hooke for the priority of inventing the balance spring. It seems that both were active towards the end of 1674, as on October 4th Hooke notes in his diary: 'Tompion here all day. Discoursed . . . of the ways of springs etc.' Huygens brought his ideas to finality over Christmas in Paris, and on 22nd January, 1675 explained his invention to Isaac Thuret under the seal of secrecy. Thuret worked fast to put it into practice as only two days later Huygens notes 'Thuret showed me his trials at making a watch'. On January 30th he wrote to Henry Oldenburg, first secretary of the Royal Society, telling him of the watch, and enclosing an anagram to establish the priority of his invention. On February 20th he sent the solution of the anagram which is: 'Axis circuli mobilis affixus in centro volutae ferreae' (the arbor of the moving ring is fixed at the centre of an iron spiral).

Huygens next sought a patent in France, in which he was first opposed by Thuret who, fearing that he might get left out, laid a counter-claim. This Huygens defeated without difficulty and eventually forgave Thuret, who made an abject apology. But the Abbé Jean de Hautefeuille also laid claim to the invention, and although his experiments had been with a straight spring, or alternatively with a helical spring in tension (as later used by Harrison in his first three marine timekeepers), Huygens decided that it would be too troublesome and expensive to establish his claim, and so left his invention free to anyone who might care to profit by it. However, he did not despair of getting an English patent and offered Oldenburg an interest in the invention if he could make use of it.

In the meantime, on February 17th, Hooke had been 'At Mr. Boiles. He told me of Mr. Zulichem's watch with springs' (Hooke always referred to Huygens by the second part of his surname). He at once hurried round to Tompion to make a watch which should establish his own priority of invention. It is interesting to speculate how Robert Boyle came to have this early knowledge of Huygens' watch. This may have come from Denis Papin, best known in his own right as a pioneer in the evolution of the steam engine; but also employed as an assistant by Huygens. Papin, who was a Huguenot, left France in this significant year of 1675, to avoid religious persecution. He then settled in England and was employed by Boyle who may thus have learnt of Huygens' horological experiments.

On February 20th Hooke writes: 'Zulichem's spring not worth a farthing', but unless he had received detailed information from Boyle this can be hardly more than bravado, since no watch by Huygens seems to have reached England until April at the earliest, or quite possibly until the end of June, and Oldenburg could not yet have received the solution of his anagram. Indeed, this is borne out by Hooke's diary for March 18th when: 'Saw Zulichem's Watch scheme and transcribed it' (presumably meaning the anagram). Already, on March 6th, he had been 'At Sir J. Mores. He told me of Oldenburg's treachery his defeating the (Royal) Society and getting a patent for Spring Watches for himself'. And on April 3rd 'Segnior told me of Oldenburg procuring a patent for Zulichem'.

In the meantime Tompion had been active and had produced a watch with a balance spring, though of what type is not disclosed. On April 7th Hooke was 'With the King and shewd him my new spring watch. Sir J. More & Tompion there. The King was most graciously pleased with it & commended it far beyond Zulichem's. He promised me a patent'. On April 8th the President of the Royal Society, 'Lord Brounckner and Oldenburg discovered their designe. R. Southwell told me of the King's refusing the warrant to Oldenburg after I had left the King. I vented some of mind against Lord Brounckner & Oldenburg. Told them of defrauding'. Nevertheless, on April 10th he was 'At Sir Jonas Mores who told me the King's message and that he said unless we made haste with the watch he would grant the patent'.

The watch Hooke had showed the King on April 7th was a hurriedly run-up affair in a brass case, and Tompion was thereupon set to make a finished article in a gold case for the King. It was this that the King was pressing for on April 10th, and it was finally delivered on May 17th when Hooke went 'with Sir J. More to the King who Received the watch very kindly, it was locked up in his closet'.

All this time Hooke and Tompion were at work on all sorts of springs. 'Tompion I shewd my way of fixing Double Springs to the inside of the Ballance wheel' (an impracticable idea, consisting of no more than a balance with two curved, spring steel spokes). 'Tryd perpendicular spiral spring at Tompions . . . did well' (this was probably a helical spring in tension between two balances, which he later illustrated in one of the Cutlerian Lectures) and again 'the thrusting spring did best'. So Hooke had certainly not decided at any time during 1675 that a spiral spring was best. What is equally uncertain is when one of Huygens' watches first arrived in England. Charles II seems to have had one as early as April, but in the correspondence between Oldenburg and Huygens there is no mention of it, and Oldenburg does not seem to have received one until the end of June when, on July 1st, he thanked Huygens for it. This watch was destined for Lord Brounckner and had a regulator in the form of a sliding piece for shortening the spring. Oldenburg tells Huygens that no one except the King has yet seen Hooke's watch.

No more is heard of Huygens' watch, but all the year the Hooke-Tompion instrument went backwards and forwards; thus on August 4th 'Gave Tompion King's watch' and on the 8th 'Tompion here. King's watch spring loose' and even a year later, on 14th June, 1676 'At Tompions he had mended King's watch'.

Hooke continued to vilify Oldenburg as 'a trafficker in intelligence'. Oldenburg wrote to Huygens on October 21st that Hooke, having learnt that Huygens had offered Oldenburg the benefit of any privilege granted to his watches in England, had publicly declared that this was a reward to Oldenburg for having disclosed Hooke's invention. Huygens dutifully wrote to Brounckner disclaiming any such disclosure by Oldenburg.

The last we hear of Huygens' watch is in Hooke's diary for December 14th when Sir John More told him 'of Zulichem's new watch moving $\frac{1}{4}$ turn'. Historians seem previously to have overlooked these important words, which show that by the end of 1675, Huygens had finally abandoned his pirouette balance, and fixed the balance-wheel and spiral spring on the verge itself, as has been the universal practice ever since.

Hooke continued to pester Tompion with experiments, of which Tompion, no doubt having decided that Huygens' lay-out was best, became increasingly tardy in their execution; so that over Christmas he appears in Hooke's diary successively as a 'slug', 'a clownish churlish Dog, I have limited him to 3 day & will never come neer him more' despite which, after five days 'Tompion a Rascall'. But they made it up and, so far as is known, continued friends throughout Hooke's life.

In the end, Charles II granted no privilege to anyone.

As to Huygens' priority in arriving at a practical watch with a spiral balance-spring there can be no doubt. It is impossible to say if Hooke ever had experimented with such a thing before Huygens' invention became public. The evidence as set out above seems entirely against him, and the evidence of William Derham in 'the Artificial Clock-maker' was not only written 20 years later, but is manifestly partial.

Nevertheless, in 1675 when Hooke maintained that he had 'found out' the spiral spring long previously, Sir John More and Christopher Wren supported him and they were accurate observers of the utmost integrity, who were in a good position to know the facts. Finally, there is the opinion of Tompion himself. In a biographical sketch of Hooke appearing in 1740 in John Ward's *Lives of the Professors of Gresham College*

Ward writes: 'I have lately seen a round brass plate, which was formerly a cover to the balance of one of Mr. Hooke's watches. It is cut through in the form of sprigs, and has on it this inscription "R. HOOK invenit an. 1658. T. TOMPION fecit 1675". This plate is now in the hands of the ingenious and accurate Mr. George Graham, fellow of the royal society, who informed me, that he heard Mr. Tompion say, he was imployed three months that year by Mr. Hooke, in making some parts of those watches, before he let him know, for what purpose they were designed; and that Mr. Tompion was likewise used to say, he thought the first invention of them was owing to Mr. Hooke.'

It seems unlikely that the matter will now ever be settled conclusively.

The Movement 1675–1700

An invention of Hooke's about whose authorship there is no dispute, or as to its immense utility, is his wheel-cutting or dividing engine, which he also evolved in about 1670. It is still used with little variation.

By the end of 1675, other watches had been made or commissioned on Huygens' and Hooke's principles and it is thus fairly certain that during 1676 the balance-sprung verge watch as now known began to appear in increasing numbers.

Tompion made the first improvement in the form of his regulator. The collet pins moved on a segmental rack corresponding with the outer turn of the balance-spring. This was geared to a wheel with a squared arbor, carrying a numbered plate such as appeared on the later set-up regulators (190). This was preferable to Nathaniel Barrow's regulator (195), which looked more like the old set-up regulator, with its endless worm on a long arbor pivoted on the plate. A slide moved along this with two pins spanning the balance-spring. The defect of this was that the spring had to end in a long straight section, for the operation of the regulator. Tompion's type of regulator became universal, and Barrow's type is now extremely rare.

Tompion was not of an inventive nature, but he was a very good designer to put an idea into execution. He was also a very good craftsman and later, when he had become successful, he had the ability to secure first-rate work from his employees. It was on this footing that he built up his reputation. Others, such as Quare and Knibb, might approach him at their best, and frequently their products are to be preferred to his in terms of elegance; but for consistently good work he was in a class of his own.

Undoubtedly too he owed much to Hooke for introducing him into the Royal circle. Apart from his regulator, Tompion's only other innovation in the watch field was an escapement which is illustrated in Rees's *Cyclopaedia*. It has been described as a fore-runner of the cylinder escapement, but in fact it is nothing so much as a prototype of the Virgule (to be described later) since impulse is given in only one direction. Even the idea of this may have come from Hooke who on 15th October, 1676 'taught him the way of the single pallet for watches'. Tompion took out a patent in 1695 in conjunction with Edward Barlow and William Houghton; but none of them seems to have followed it up. It is described in the patent as 'a ballance wheele either flatt or hollow, to work within & crosse the centre of the verge or axis of the balance with a new sort of teeth made like tinterhooks to move the balance & the pallets of the axis or verge, one to be circular, concave & convex'.

As soon as the balance-spring was established it became fairly difficult to make a weak enough mainspring for a three-wheel train, and four wheels with a going period of 26 hours became almost universal. Some makers, both French and English, Tompion included, at first thought they could do without a fusee, but they quickly found out that their optimism was unfounded, in conjunction with the verge escapement.

The need for a set-up regulator did, however, become superfluous except as a means of once-for-all adjustment by the maker or anyone cleaning the watch. It was accordingly moved to between the plates in English watches, with a worm drive as previously; or as a ratchet between the plate and the dial, in most French watches.

An entirely new and most useful invention came ten years later, in the form of repeating mechanism. It was invented simultaneously by Edward Barlow (1636–1716) and Daniel Quare (1647–1724) and both applied for a patent; but James II favoured Quare on the grounds that on his watch, one push-piece caused both the hours and quarters to sound, whereas in Barlow's version there were two push-pieces, one for the hours and one for the quarters. The patent was granted in 1687.

The first repeaters struck on a bell filling the back of the case, like the earlier clock-watches. A single stroke denoted each hour and a double stroke each quarter. Somewhat later, some were fitted with a 'pulse-piece'. When this was pressed and the repeater operated, the hammer and bell did not sound, but the operator was informed of the time by a series of taps on the pulse piece. In the last quarter of the eighteenth century Le Roy and Breguet substituted wire gongs for bells, and Breguet often had only a block of steel which was struck by the hammer. These are known as 'dumb' or 'à toc' repeaters.

The work of Tompion and Quare was faked in their lifetime and throughout the first half of the eighteenth century, and latterly that of Graham, almost as freely as Breguet in the nineteenth century. Tompion and Quare fakes usually come from Holland and are easily detected. Dutch fakes almost always have an arcaded minute-circle on the dial. Quare had a very thriving export business. Some seemingly authentic Quares are signed Quarré or Quaré. It is thought that these are not necessarily fakes, if the quality of the watch is up to Quare's standards; and that he was simply making things easier for foreign customers who might otherwise find the pronunciation of his name insuperably difficult.

There are fortunately a good many aids to judging the validity and date of a Tompion watch (assuming it is not hallmarked, which silver cases seldom were before about 1740).

From 1701 to 1707 or '08 Tompion was in partnership with Edward Banger and pieces are signed 'Tompion & Banger'. In about 1711 he took George Graham into partnership, but pieces with the joint signature are very rare (Tompion died only two years later, in 1713).

For Tompion's system of numbering see page 148.

The Movement 1700–1750

In 1704 Facio de Duillier and P. & J. Debaufre, foreign artists domiciled in England, discovered a method of piercing jewels for the pivot holes in watches. At first, it was used only for the balance-staffs of high-grade watches, and Graham and later Mudge used it for the balance arbors of their cylinder watches from about 1725 onwards. The jewelling of the train came increasingly into use with the development of the precision watch from about 1775. Even then it was entirely unknown abroad, and Breguet was the first foreign artist who succeeded in jewelling his watches. The French instead used polished steel end-plates for their balance arbors, called cocquerets.

Facio and his confederates applied for a patent, but were defeated by the production of a watch by Ignatius Huggeford with what was ostensibly a large jewelled bearing to the balance-staff. This watch survives in the Guildhall Museum (175). Only in 1848 was it dismantled and the jewel found to be unpierced, and decorative only.

The next improvement came from France, where the English Henry Sully (1680–1728) had the idea in about 1715 of oil sinks for retaining oil and these were finally perfected by Julien le Roy. In about 1740 le Roy also improved the method of mounting and locating the crown-wheel in the verge escapement. This he did by screw-adjusted sliding plates containing the pivot holes, whereby the escapement could be adjusted with great accuracy, both laterally and as to depth. Le Roy was an artist of the highest quality who did much to raise the standards of work in the French industry to a level at which they could again rival British watches.

In 1704 Debaufre invented an escapement which goes by his name, or is known alternatively as a 'club-foot verge'. It consists of two co-axial escape wheels operating on a single steel or jewelled pallet on the balance-staff. This pallet has 'dead' faces, on which the escape wheel teeth rest during the supplementary arc, and sloping impulse faces down which the points of the teeth slide alternatively, giving impulse to the watch at each swing of the balance. This was the first of the 'frictional rest' escapements of which the cylinder is the best known. It is not known if any example by Debaufre survives, but in any case it was little used for nearly a century, until the Lancashire makers took it up (*63*), after which it became known more generally as the 'Ormskirk escapement'. It was long supposed that the recoil inherent in the verge escapement is a bad thing; but in fact in an escapement which is not at all isochronous, recoil can provide an automatic corrective to small variations in motive power, and thus serves to preserve a constant arc. Thus, although the frictional rest escapements are theoretically better than the verge, it is only in their later and most sophisticated forms that they produce better results; while the verge, as carried to its final perfection by John Harrison, proved to be capable of an almost miraculous accuracy. In 1718 Sully devised a variant of Debaufre's escapement, which he used in his unsuccessful marine timekeeper, and in 1735 it was developed further by Julien le Roy. It differs from Debaufre in having only one escape wheel. Its use in watches is, however, exceedingly rare (*64*).

In 1725 came the cylinder escapement of George Graham (1673 or 4–1751). Graham was apprenticed to Tompion, married his niece and was for a few years in partnership with Tompion up to the time of Tompion's death in 1713. He was the outstanding British maker in the second quarter of the eighteenth century and fully carried on Tompion's standards of craftsmanship. He was, moreover, of a more original mind than Tompion, as is evidenced by his election as a Fellow of the Royal Society. In clocks he made the first highly accurate instruments, when fitted with his dead-beat escapement and mercurial pendulum. It is difficult to see quite why the cylinder escapement acquired the pre-eminence it did, since it is exceedingly difficult to make (especially as to the escape wheel); much more fragile than the verge; wears rapidly; and does not (at any rate as made before Breguet) give a greatly superior performance to the verge. Probably it was Graham's established position, and the great elegance of his work, that did much to establish the cylinder escapement (23). Julien le Roy saw it at an early date and preferred it to the verge, and Graham used no other escapement from about 1727 onwards. After his death, cylinder watches almost identical in every way continued to be made by Mudge, and then Mudge and Dutton, until well into the 1770's (287). Graham and Mudge used a brass escape wheel and a steel cylinder, but John Arnold and John Ellicott sometimes used a steel wheel and a ruby cylinder. Ruby cylinders are, however, rare in English watches. James Ashley mitigated the rapid wear of ordinary cylinders by staggering the teeth of his escape wheels at three different levels, thus reducing wear on the cylinder by three times.

Somewhat allied to the cylinder but really a development of Tompion's escapement is the virgule, which is a frictional rest escapement, like the cylinder, but gives impulse only on alternate swings of the balance (25). The impulse pallet takes the form of a long curved tail to the 'cylinder' giving it the appearance of a comma, whence the name 'virgule'. As far as can be ascertained, it was first devised by Jean-André Lepaute, but it was not much used until the last quarter of the eighteenth century, by Jean Antoine Lepine. A very rare variant, the 'double virgule', was invented by his brother-in-law Pierre-Augustin Caron, with two lots of teeth on opposite sides of the escape wheel, and two corresponding pallets, which thus secures impulses in both directions (26).

Although belonging more properly to the end of the century, and the precision period, the virgule escapement can hardly be regarded as one of precision, and it is therefore mentioned here because of its derivation from Tompion's prototype.

Another escapement of this period which did not come into use until much later was the rack lever, invented by the Abbé de Hautefeuille in 1722. This contained the seeds of the lever escapement, the escape wheel and anchor being identical. But instead of being detached, the lever was geared directly to the balance by a toothed sector on the lever, meshing with a pinion on the balance-staff (49). It is not known whether Mudge was indebted to it for the idea of his detached lever escapement, and it did not come into general use until after 1791, when a considerably different form of it was patented by the Liverpool maker, Peter Litherland.

Despite this variety of escapements, the verge continued to be used in the great majority of watches throughout the eighteenth century. Although the arc is limited to about 120 degrees at most, so that there is no need for a long balance-spring, this did gradually increase from its original 1½ turns to as much as 4. When it increased even more, during the nineteenth century, its timekeeping qualities suffered.

An immediate effect of the balance spring was to make watches much thicker. So long as they remained very inferior timekeepers there was a tendency to make them thin, and this applies particularly to enamelled watches. But it was always recognised that a large-diameter escape wheel was more conducive to good timekeeping; so that when timekeeping became the primary objective, the thickness of an average English watch increased from about an inch to an inch and a quarter, or an inch and a half for a typical French watch of the period which, from its almost spherical shape, earned the name of an 'oignon' (229). Later in the century the situation was reversed, and French verges became slimmer than the English, with detriment to their timekeeping. Otherwise, French balance-spring verges only differ from English to any important extent in having very much larger balances; sometimes the full diameter of the plate. And these are supported in a bridge cock, instead of the single-footed English cock. These bridge cocks may be pierced, but sometimes they are solid and engraved, or covered by a painted enamel plaque. Oignons are generally wound through the dial, but this is very rare in English watches, except for clock-watches and repeaters.

Decoration of the Movement 1675–1800

Soon after the introduction of the balance-spring the decoration of English watch movements became fairly standardised. The floreate-patterned cocks of the earlier period gave way to an arabesque pattern, at first bold and open, but becoming increasingly fussy and perfunctory (207, 221). The table, completely covering the balance, was circular, although not at first with a solid rim (195). The foot was more irregular in shape, but by 1690 both had acquired a well-defined rim, that of the foot following the edge of the plate. Most cocks have a mask engraved at the point where the table joins the foot, but prior to 1685 this is very small, and before about 1680 it may not exist (214). This mask survived in British verge watches until the middle of the nineteenth

21

century. Up to about 1740 the pattern of the cock decoration is symmetrical about the centre line, but thereafter, with the rococo taste, it becomes generally asymmetrical.

At the invention of the balance-spring, the application of the pendulum to clocks was within the memory of a great many people, and it was found that the newly accurate watches sold better if they appeared to have a pendulum. In France, watches were therefore made with solid cocks, with an annular slot through which a seeming pendulum bob was seen to swing, but which was in fact no more than a disk on one arm of the balance. This arrangement was applicable to French watches where the bridge cock could be made to conceal the balance-wheel completely. With the English form of cock, the illusion was not so impressive, and the matter was arranged differently. Here, the balance was generally placed between the back plate and the dial and the bob appeared through an annular slot in the latter (*218*). This silly delusion is not found much after 1690.

Pillars were made in considerable decorative variety in British watches, especially the Egyptian, baluster and tulip, and variants of them. The French seldom used anything but the Egyptian type in their *oignons*, and plain baluster pillars in their later, thin watches, where the movement did not hinge out of the case.

The cursive script of the maker's name becomes less bold soon after 1680 and, soon after 1690, increasingly appears in plain capitals; as it almost always did in France.

Dust caps fitting over the movement are very rarely found before 1715 (*232*) and seldom before 1725, after which they become usual for watches of any quality; especially Graham's and Mudge's cylinder watches (*289*). They are sometimes of silver, but generally of brass gilt.

After about 1725 the cock foot is increasingly solid and engraved, instead of being pierced (*270*). After the introduction of compensation balances in the last quarter of the century the table ceased to be circular and became wedge-shaped. Sometimes it was solid and engraved, but pierced cocks, including Arnold's, continued up to the end of the century. Verge watches continued to have pierced circular tables until the middle of the nineteenth century (*536*).

The Precision Watch
1750 – 1830

Birth of the Precision Watch 1750 - 1770

If the third quarter of the seventeenth century saw the greatest advance in the whole history of horology, with the practical application of the pendulum to clocks and the balance-spring to watches, the third quarter of the eighteenth century produced advances hardly less spectacular in the realm of marine timekeepers and precision watches. There has certainly been no time when there was greater experimental activity among the leading artists in England and France. The history of the marine chronometer forms no essential part of this book and in any case, Gould's classic work *The Marine Chronometer*[1] has stood the test of time and could hardly be improved upon. Nevertheless, it must be recapitulated briefly here, as a background to the development of the pocket chronometer. Although the detent or chronometer escapement eventually gave way to the lever escapement as the best for precision watches, the detent was first in the field and held the lead for over half a century.

The world's first successful marine timekeeper was John Harrison's 'No. 4' which came triumphantly through its tests in 1761. Its escapement was a much-refined form of verge, coupled with a train remontoire and a compensation curb. The purpose of the remontoire was to isolate any irregularities in torque from the escapement. It was mounted on the fourth wheel and was rewound every $7\frac{1}{2}$ seconds. Although this device has seldom been revived, and never in modern times, recent experiment has shown that a remontoire might usefully improve the performance of even a modern marine chronometer. In Harrison's 'No. 4', with its non-detached and not-very-isochronous escapement, the remontoire was a vital factor towards its success.

The compensation curb operated as an automatic regulator. It consisted of a straight strip of brass and steel, riveted together. One end was fixed to the plate and two pins were mounted on the other end, which closely embraced the balance-spring near its fixed end, just as is done with an ordinary regulator. In hot weather the brass expanded more than the steel, so that the curb became slightly curved. The two pins moved correspondingly along the balance-spring, shortening its effective length and thus increasing the rate of the balance. In cold weather the system operated in reverse.

Harrison (1693–1776) knew that it was not a perfect arrangement, and that ideally the compensation should be incorporated in the balance itself. This, however, he never succeeded in accomplishing, although he lived long enough to have seen it done. Nevertheless, a properly proportioned compensation curb can give a remarkably

[1] R. T. Gould. London 1923. Republished in facsimile in 1960.

23

accurate result, and in the early stages of the true compensation balance it was probably superior.

Harrison had tried out the principles of 'No. 4' in a pocket watch made for him by John Jeffreys as early as 1753, which lacked only the remontoire of the larger machine. This watch survives, although badly damaged by extreme heat during the incendiary bombing of Hull in the late war. With one possible exception to be mentioned later, this Harrison-Jeffreys watch can claim to be the world's first pocket watch with temperature compensation, and thus to be the first precision watch. Its performance was little inferior to 'No. 4'. The laminae of the compensation curb are soldered together, but in Nos. 4 and 5 they are riveted. Harrison planned to make an improved version of the Jeffreys watch at the same time as 'No. 4', but nothing seems to have come of the idea. He probably found it impossible to make a remontoire small enough for a pocket watch.

Although Harrison's work led to nothing, he at least showed that accurate marine timekeeping was a possibility, just as the 1753 prototype pointed the way to the precision watch.

So far as can be traced, ten years were to elapse before another pocket watch was made with temperature compensation. This is a verge watch by Ferdinand Berthoud, now in the Ilbert Collection (*291*). It has a compensation curb in the form of an elaborate steel and brass gridiron, covering most of the top plate.

Thomas Mudge (1715–94) probably made the next step, although unfortunately it survives only as a movement (in the collection of the Worshipful Company of Clockmakers, on exhibition in the City of London Guildhall) so that it cannot be dated. However, it is reasonable to suppose that it dates from the late 1760's, after Mudge had been present at Harrison's disclosure of the details of 'No. 4'. This watch has a very sophisticated verge escapement coupled with both a compensation curb and a remontoire, let off once a minute. It was, however, only the prelude to Mudge's final contribution to the precision watch, the lever escapement, which will be considered later.

The Detent Escapement

Pierre le Roy (1717–85) perfected a detent escapement as early as 1765, in his version of a marine timekeeper. Moreover, it incorporated a true compensation balance. The instrument survives in the Musée des Arts et Métiers in Paris. It received neither the national recognition that was accorded to Harrison and No. 4; nor was it so thoroughly tested at sea. While it contained greater promise, it is doubtful if le Roy's machine would have rivalled Harrison's highly-developed No. 4, and it was probably too delicate for extensive use at sea. Lacking encouragement, le Roy retired from the scene and it was the English John Arnold (1736–99) who carried the marine chronometer forward to substantially its modern form. His first attempt at the detent escapement was made in 1770 and it was not successful (two examples are owned by the Royal Society); but he persevered, and shortly devised a satisfactory pivoted detent escapement which he used in his first pocket chronometers. By 1773 he had developed a form of bi-metallic compensation balance. In 1774 he began using helical balance-springs and in 1776 applied terminal end-curves to them. These are essential for isochronism and are used in all modern chronometers. In the same year he finalised his pivoted detent escapement (30).

In about 1780 Arnold devised a new escapement with the detent mounted on a spring, whereas previously it had been pivoted (36). Pivoted detents continued to be preferred by many Continental makers until far into the nineteenth century, but they have the disadvantage that as the oil thickens the detent does not move so freely. At about the same time Ferdinand Berthoud (1727–1807), who had also been working on pivoted detent escapements since 1771, evolved a different version of the spring detent; but it was somewhat cumbersome, and as far as is known he never applied it to a pocket watch.

The most vociferous claimant to the invention of the spring detent was the then-unknown English journeyman, Thomas Earnshaw (1749–1829). Earnshaw was born in 1749 and by 1780 was working for watchmakers, in which capacity he said that he had 'in three or four years obtained the reputation of a most capital workman as a watch-finisher'. He produced a long and circumstantial story of how he invented the spring detent escapement towards the end of 1780 and was then vilely betrayed by everyone to whom he had shown the thing. Having explained it to the Brockbanks he then went to one Thomas Wright and suggested he should take a patent for it (which Earnshaw could not afford on his own). Wright prevaricated for three years by which time, according to Earnshaw, the Brockbanks had told the secret to Arnold, who had taken out a patent himself.

Arnold, who had an arrogant character, never even bothered to deny the story, being prepared to let his unassailed reputation defend him against the unknown

HISTORICAL

Earnshaw. Earnshaw had a well-developed persecution complex which could anyway be relied upon to lead him into spoiling his case in any argument by overstatement.

Earnshaw's arrangement is in fact a straightforward application of the spring detent to the lay-out adopted by Arnold for his pivoted detent (37). To this extent one may give him credit for an original thought, but Arnold's approach to the problem was far more radical. Earnshaw's escapement put the slender detent spring in compression; an unpleasing arrangement which Arnold was at pains to avoid. This he did by reversing the lay-out, putting the detent spring in tension. At the same time he evolved a new form of escape wheel with teeth of epicycloidal shape, as opposed to the pointed teeth of Earnshaw's and his own earlier escapement. Although Arnold's escapement is theoretically sound, and continued to be made for at least 40 years, Earnshaw's lay-out was found in the end to have the greater practical advantage and is in use to this day with only slight but important modifications to the angle between the escape wheel teeth and the impulse pallet. The modification is important because, as devised by Earnshaw, the escapement wore rapidly, which is probably one reason why so few of his chronometers (especially marine) survive.

Probably the priority of invention will never be decided, and it is very likely that Arnold and Earnshaw arrived at their conclusion separately.

Earnshaw probably must have credit for devising the modern method of fusing together the brass and steel laminae of the balance-wheel, although Rees's *Cyclopaedia* (which tends to be biased) gives the priority to Brockbank. Arnold had preshaped and soldered the arms of his balances, which is unlikely to produce such a homogeneous result. Even here, it must be remembered that Earnshaw only took the final step from ten years of experimental development of the bimetallic balance by Arnold. As against this, Earnshaw's balance-springs, usually of untempered steel, and as often as not of plain spiral shape, were inferior in isochronism to Arnold's beautiful tempered steel or gold helical springs over a long period.

A peculiarity of Earnshaw's watches is that they vary greatly in superficial finish. He was certainly capable of a very fine finish, but fairly early in his career it was suggested that his work relied upon high finish for its performance (which performance, at its best, equalled or surpassed Arnold's). After this, he asked his customers if they wanted a good working watch, or a pretty one as well. His unpolished watches are, indeed, remarkably stark in appearance, while the more highly finished examples have a coarse and unpleasing style of engraving on the balance-cock.

26

Although Earnshaw made pocket watches with bimetallic balances and free-sprung helical springs, he equally often turned them out with an uncut flat steel balance, spiral spring, regulator, and compensation curb (*456, 467*). This latter was a curious arrangement with two arms, one pin on each. Instead of sliding along the balance-spring, the gap between the two pins widened in cold weather and closed in hot, which had the same effect. Owing to its pincer-like appearance and operation, Earnshaw's curb is usually known as 'sugar-tong compensation'. It is reasonable to suppose that he supplied this arrangement to hunting-men or those otherwise of an energetic bent, where his heavy bimetallic balances might have been expected to produce a crop of broken or bent pivots (Arnold, by contrast, kept his bimetallic balances as light as possible, even if at some loss of rigidity).

Before leaving Earnshaw, it may be noted that his earliest pieces, made under the patent tardily taken out by Wright, were marked 'Wright's patent'; but it is not known to the authors if any example survives.

Earnshaw outlived Arnold by 30 years, but although he came to comfortable prosperity he never quite lost the chip on his shoulder.

The Brockbanks decided to make use of Earnshaw's disclosure in their own way, and one of their workmen, named Peto, devised an ingenious detent which used Earnshaw's form of escape wheel, but kept the detent spring in tension (*39*). In this way he theoretically combined the advantages of Arnold's and Earnshaw's escapements, but only at the expense of a somewhat cumbersome complication, of which Earnshaw remarked 'it was like a person going round a house to get in at the back door, when the front door stood fairly open to him. But when I mentioned this absurdity to Mr. Peto he said it was different from mine, and evaded the patent, and that I could not prosecute him for it'.

Peto's cross-detent escapement was never much used, and is now extremely rare; most surviving specimens are by Brockbanks.

While Earnshaw's contribution to precision timekeeping was very substantial, the authors feel that his importance has been over-rated at the expense of Arnold. It was John Arnold alone who really developed the marine chronometer and the precision pocket watch as practical commercial propositions, during the period 1776–80, with subsequent refinements up to the time of his death in 1799.

The pocket chronometers which he began making in about 1776 were unquestionably the earliest precision watches on sale to the public. Some of them were half-quarter repeaters, of such enormous size (over $2\frac{1}{2}$ inches diameter) as hardly to be capable of pocket use. The finish was of the highest quality imaginable and their accuracy was shown in 1779 when he sent a watch (No. 36) for trial at Greenwich. It was tested in the pocket for 13 months at the end of which time its total error was only 2 minutes 33·2 seconds, and its extreme variation in daily rate in six positions was only 4·2 seconds. This instrument had a pivoted detent escapement of the kind Arnold seems to have arrived at by 1776, and a balance like that described below (*). This was followed up by a protracted test carried out between 1785 and 1790 by a private customer, Mr. Everard of Lynn, which Arnold made public in 1791 in a now exceedingly rare pamphlet entitled *Certificates and Circumstances Relative to the going of Mr. Arnold's Chronometers.* Even allowing for some partiality on the part of its fond owner, the results revealed a consistency of going which would be highly creditable even today. Over $4\frac{1}{2}$ years its fastest daily rate was $+2\cdot7$ seconds and its slowest $-2\cdot5$ seconds. The watch, No. $\frac{21}{68}$, is now in the British Museum.

Arnold also experimented continuously with the bimetallic compensation balance. Pierre le Roy first had the idea of such a balance in about 1770, but he preferred the alcohol and mercury compensation of his marine timekeeper and, as has been said (and unlike his father Julien), he was apparently not interested in the precision pocket watch. Le Roy's sketch shows a plain two-arm balance without balancing-screws or weights, as a result of which it would have been difficult to adjust and its compensation effect inadequate.

The sequence and dating of Arnold's experiments have fortunately been recorded in Abraham Rees's *Cyclopaedia or Universal Dictionary of Arts, Sciences and Literature*, published in instalments concluding in 1820. (This invaluable work, published in 45 volumes, is the best record of the most interesting phase of the Industrial Revolution, but it is becoming quite rare because of the deplorable habit of booksellers of breaking it up to extract the few articles of interest to their special customers.) Rees not only gives the dates when each type was made, but also the numbers that were made of each (no doubt on information supplied by John Arnold's son, John Roger Arnold). The first had a spiral bimetallic coil on the balance, which moved two weights through a system of levers. It seems unlikely to have been satisfactory and only about a dozen were made between 1775–8. The next resembled the 'S' balance illustrated in figure 321, but the place of the S-pieces was taken by two straight bars*. Twenty of this type were made between 1778–80. Its compensation effect is unlikely to have been sufficient and Arnold therefore replaced the short straight bars by the longer S-pieces. These balances were effective and 40 were made between 1779–82. Then came the final form in which the rims of the wheel were bimetallic, and this was the parent of all subsequent compensation balances.

By the results obtained, the early types clearly worked well, but they all suffered from the disadvantage that there could be no means of adjusting their compensation effect, except by fitting a different size of weight, necessitating further adjustments for mean time; or by filing one or other of the bimetallic strips. Even in his final, almost modern form of bimetallic balance, Arnold seems to have relied to some extent upon filing to adjust the compensation effect, since the outer lamina is reduced in thickness progressively from the fixed to the free end of each arm. John Roger Arnold continued this practice. By 1782 Arnold had arrived at the beginnings of a modern balance, even if Earnshaw took the final step. Arnold's earlier balances are now extremely rare and may be accounted a great prize for any collector so fortunate as to procure one. The 'S-shaped' balance, in particular, is an object of the greatest elegance, and wonderfully light.

It is not always possible to date Arnold's watches by their balances as he frequently took watches back to bring them up to date for their owners, by adding his latest modifications. For example, the watch in figure 298, number 21, evidently started life as one of the first spring detent watches, but in 1797 Arnold recased it (as is evident by the hallmark), put on his final type of balance-wheel, and a new dial and hands.

One certain date line in Arnold's work is 1790, at about which time he took his son into partnership after serving a short apprenticeship with Abraham Louis Breguet. Earlier pieces are marked 'John Arnold', and subsequent pieces are marked 'John Arnold & Son'. In number 21 above, the former signature is on the watch plate and the latter on the dial.

Arnold's numbering is no very sure guide, especially among his earliest pieces, of which he blandly remarked that 'he had made twenty number ones'. He also used a curious form of fractional numbering. In those used on marine chronometers the difference between the lesser and greater number is always 90 but this does not apply to the watch numbers.

John Arnold died in 1799, after which his son carried on the business under his own name. He continued to make pocket chronometers of the highest grade, such as that (No. 1869) illustrated in figure 380, made in 1802. This has the characteristic gold

29

balance-spring and an escapement approximating closely to Earnshaw's, of which several other examples by John Roger Arnold exist. As if to stress that Earnshaw never invented it at all, Arnold has added on the watch plate '*Inv et fecit*'.

It quite often happens that Arnold escapements have been converted subsequently to Earnshaw's type, but it is easy to detect when this has happened. Arnold always mounted his spring detent in a slot cut out of the top plate. When converted to the Earnshaw lay-out, where the detent is mounted between the plates, the slot is either left empty or filled in. If the plate has then been re-gilt the modification may be difficult but not impossible to detect. In No. 1869 it is quite obvious that no modification has taken place and the escapement is that fitted originally.

John Roger Arnold has got a bad name, partly because of the anathemas heaped upon him by Earnshaw, and partly because he did put it on a number of second-rate watches, probably made for him in the trade. But watches such as No. 1869, which is by no means unique, showed that he was capable of the finest work, and probably continued to turn it out as long as Thomas Prest worked for him. Prest was a most able workman who also devised about the first effective system of keyless winding, examples of which were made by Arnold (*469*). Prest either left Arnold or died some time after 1820, after which Arnold, being a comfortably wealthy man, had little incentive to continue in business and in 1830 he went into partnership with E. J. Dent for ten years, during which time John Roger took a less and less active part. After ten years Dent left to set up on his own as the firm which continues to flourish. Arnold then maintained the business on his own, still at 84 Strand, until the time of his death in 1843.

Pocket chronometers in the English tradition continued to be made until well into the 1860's and occasionally even later (*559*), but by 1850 or soon after, the leading artists had developed the English lever to the point that it was generally recognised as the best escapement for pocket watches, while the increasing demand for smaller and slimmer watches militated against the continued successful employment of the detent escapement, which is not readily compressed into a small space.

In the meantime, the spring detent had not by any means driven the pivoted detent from the field. James Ferguson Cole (1798–1880) has been described as the English Breguet. The epithet is not entirely apt, though in terms of misapplied ingenuity he sometimes ran him close, or even outstripped him, and the workmanship and re-strained elegance of his pieces are almost always of the highest order. On coming out of his apprenticeship Cole chose to make for his 'masterpiece the superb pivoted detent watch of unusual calibre which is in the Ilbert Collection at the British Museum.

Continental makers also produced a limited number of pocket chronometers, both pivoted and spring, of the highest merit. A very early specimen is the pivoted example by Breguet, made in 1789 and shown in figure 319, which has the peculiarity of its balance wheel being between the plates, with its pivots mounted in friction rollers. These emphasise the reluctance or inability of Continental makers to use jewelling at even so relatively late a date, when it had long been commonplace in England. They may be seen clearly in figure 320.

Although Ferdinand Berthoud does not seem to have taken any part in developing the precision watch, several splendid examples were made by his nephew Louis Berthoud (1750–1813) and figure 425 shows a typical pivoted detent by him. Other splendid examples, showing more of Breguet's influence, were made by Jean François Henri Motel (1786–1859).

After the early specimen in figure 319 Breguet turned over entirely to using a spring detent, as might be expected of his admiration for Arnold (which Arnold no less wholeheartedly reciprocated). He sometimes used an Arnold and sometimes an Earnshaw lay-out, sometimes even a Peto cross-detent, sometimes in conjunction with his tourbillon (to be discussed later). Breguet's pocket chronometers are almost invariably of the starkest simplicity, although naturally they cannot avoid his innate sense of style, as shown in figure 342. Some have a reversed fusee, but in his slightly larger deck watches he preferred two going-barrels geared together (472).

Perhaps the last of the great individual artists, who never entered into large-scale production, but continued to do much of his own work, was the Dane, Urban Brunn Jürgensen (1776–1830). After studying with both Breguet in France and Arnold in England (1800–1), as well as having close contacts with other leading makers, Berthoud in particular, he remarked: 'While Ferdinand Berthoud enjoyed the highest reputation in France and in all Europe for his beautiful productions in the art, the chronometers which the English exported to their neighbours across the water were admirable because of the simplicity of their construction, the making of the instruments after rules most applicable, most exact and true to theory, and manufactured in much greater quantities than those of the French artists, whose chronometers as exact measures of time left nothing to be desired'. When Jürgensen came to England with an introduction to Arnold he quotes the latter as saying 'that since I had worked in the house of Breguet it would help me little to work in London, for it was well-known that he was the most distinguished artist in Europe'—which shows a degree of modesty by no means credited to him by Earnshaw.

Although Jürgensen might have been expected to follow Breguet rather than the by then relatively old-fashioned Arnold, he seems in fact to have adhered more to an English technique. His plainest cylinder escapement watches have a full-plate movement, and the very fine spring detent watch illustrated in figure 441 uses an Arnold escape wheel and gold balance-spring. Jürgensen made 72 chronometers and about 800 watches. The chronometers had a double number, the first being the chronometer series number and the latter the watch number. The chronometer in figure 441 is No. 24/58 indicating a date around 1815. Jürgensen very seldom used a gold case (probably only 23 in all). His work is of the highest possible quality, and because of this and its rarity, watches by him are very greatly prized.

His sons Louis and Jules worked more in the Continental tradition and continued to make pivoted detent watches of the highest quality. This may be regarded as the close of the chapter so far as the detent escapement in pocket watches is concerned. For marine chronometers it continues in almost universal employment, although even here it may before long give way to an electronic timekeeper.

Frictional Rest and the Duplex Escapements

Before passing on to the lever escapement it is appropriate first to consider the duplex, which was the favourite escapement for high-grade British pocket watches during the first half of the nineteenth century; and other frictional rest escapements which were in popular use in the late eighteenth and early nineteenth centuries.

The duplex escapement consists of two co-axial escape wheels (or two sets of teeth on one wheel). One set of teeth is for locking and the other set is for impulse. The longer, more pointed teeth lock by resting against a very thin roller on the balance arbor. Cut in this roller is a narrow slot through which the locking tooth may pass, when the balance is rotating in the opposite direction to the escape wheel. Also on the balance staff is mounted a long impulse pallet. As the escape wheel advances (being unlocked as just described) one of the shorter teeth attached to it gives impulse to the balance. As impulse is completed, the next long-tooth locks on the safety roller. On the return swing of the balance the escape-slot passes the locking tooth, causing a slight recoil and no impulse is given. The escapement thus has the same disadvantage as the detent escapement, in that impulse being given on alternate swings of the balance it is more prone to set; coupled with which it is never detached and involves a slight recoil. Despite this, if well proportioned and made, and regularly cleaned and oiled, the duplex can give remarkably good results (*27*).

After a tentative escapement by Dutertre, with two geared-together balances, it was brought to a recognisably modern form by Pierre le Roy in about 1750. However, it was not in France, but England, that it achieved its greatest popularity. Here it was introduced by Thomas Tyrer of London who in 1782 patented a duplex escapement, which he described as an 'horizontal scapement for a watch to act with two wheels'. Among makers of the front rank, Emery used it by the early 1790's, still with two separate wheels.

The characteristic nineteenth-century escape wheel had the locking teeth protruding radially from the rim, and the impulse teeth standing up from it. The most noted and prolific of the early nineteenth-century makers of the escapement was James McCabe who came from Belfast, was received into the Clockmakers' Company in 1781 and died in 1811. His best work was signed '*James McCabe*', second grade '*McCabe*' and a cheap line was signed '*Beatson*'. Other early makers of first-rate duplex watches were D. & W. Morice. The watch by them illustrated (*439*) is hallmarked 1815 and has an early example of what was to become the standard English compensation balance. Although there is only one adjusting screw to each arm, there are four holes into which it or others in addition can be screwed. Similar balances were being produced by Robert Pennington at the same time, who claimed to obtain better results from pre-shaped rims, soldered together, than from pre-fused blocks, subsequently turned down to shape.

The duplex escapement held its ground against the lever, certainly until 1850, and it was made until after 1900.

The cylinder escapement continued to enjoy a fair measure of popularity among English makers, but during the nineteenth century it was mostly used by the Swiss who made cylinder watches with a barred movement in enormous numbers. Some of these are exceedingly thin.

In England, the Debaufre escapement was revived in Lancashire at the end of the eighteenth century and it was made in considerable numbers during the first quarter of the nineteenth. In this form it became known as the Ormskirk escapement and had two

33

co-axial escape wheels with saw-shaped teeth operating on a circular pallet with in-clined impulse planes on the balance-staff. These were capable of a performance fully equal to an ordinary cylinder and a few were made of quite high quality.

The Lever Escapement in England 1770 - 1830

If the history of the detent escapement was easily traced, with little need for original research, the same can by no means be said of the lever escapement. The name 'lever escapement' is not found before 1820 at earliest. Previously, it was known as the 'forked escapement'.

At any rate in England (apparently with very little challenge from Continental historians) its invention and early development have been claimed as British, but there is certainly considerable evidence to suggest that it was invented quite independently in France and its early development there by Breguet had the greater influence in the long run.

To trace the course of events in England, it is undoubted that the inventor was Thomas Mudge, although the date of his invention is still in doubt. So far as is known, he made only four working examples and one rough model of the escape-ment. Of these only one was a watch, which is therefore the principal interest so far as this book is concerned. The earliest date for the invention was that given by Mudge's (at times somewhat importunate) patron, Count Hans Moritz Graf von Bruhl (1736–1809; Envoy Extraordinary from the Kingdom of Saxony at the Court of Great Britain from 1764 to his death in 1809; diplomat, astronomer and patron of horology) as 1754, For many years this date has been generally disbelieved, but as things have turned out, it may be quite accurate after all.

The hallmark on the cases of Mudge's one and only lever escapement watch was stated by Chamberlain in *It's About Time* to be 1759, and this date was accepted by all subsequent writers and generally regarded as the date of Mudge's invention.

The watch itself belongs to Her Majesty the Queen and is kept at Windsor Castle. It was apparently bought by George III and given to Queen Charlotte, from which it has ever since been known as 'the Queen's watch'. The acquisition of the watch by George III is not at all remarkable. In 1764 Arnold, then aged 38, obtained leave to present to George III a half-quarter repeating, ruby cylinder watch, set in a ring (the movement only one third of an inch in diameter). The King in fact paid Arnold well for the watch, but when the Czar of Russia offered Arnold a thousand guineas to make him a replica of the watch, Arnold refused, wishing the King's to remain unique. George III later showed his practical interest in horology by personally carrying out an extensive test of Harrison's No. 5 marine timekeeper (a replica of No. 4, now in the London Guildhall) and used all the force of his royal influence to obtain for Harrison the full reward for 'finding the Longitude' to which he was entitled under an Act of Parliament of 1714; but which the Board of Longitude, set up under the Act, was most reluctant to pay. It was therefore natural that he should acquire this first (and, as it proved, only) example of Mudge's new invention—possibly prompted by Count von Bruhl, as Mudge's patron; or it may even be that the watch was a present from von Bruhl to the Queen.

Although the watch is unique, Mudge made at least two clocks of bracket size with lever escapements, of which the more important is in the Ilbert Collection at the British Museum. It is certainly very much older than the watch, and from the style of the case it could well have been 1754, the year given by von Bruhl as the date of Mudge's invention. Nevertheless, this date was generally discarded in favour of 1759, the supposed date of the watch. However, several close students of the subject began in turn to have doubts about 1759, since not until 1772 is there any surviving mention whatever of the existence of the watch. But in this year, and then onwards, at intervals up to 1776, there starts a correspondence between Mudge and von Bruhl about the performance of the watch, indicating that at this time it was still not out of its teething troubles. It was therefore beginning to be thought that the date of the watch was more like 1770 than 1759.

There had long been a tradition of Mudge having made a second lever watch, for a Colonel Johnes, in 1785. Mudge had retired from commerce in 1771 and removed to Plymouth in order to perfect his marine timekeeper (which had a special form of remontoire escapement in no way related to the lever; it is fully explained in Gould's *Marine Chronometer*). By 1785 Mudge was 70 years old, and as early as 1776 he had resisted von Bruhl's earnest entreaties to make a second lever watch, on the grounds of age, the difficulty of the undertaking, and his preoccupation with the marine timekeeper. He might have been expected to indulge his influential patron and friend

35

sooner than anyone else, yet the most he could be prevailed upon to do was to make a rough model of the escapement for von Bruhl in about 1782. The Colonel Johnes story therefore seems a most improbable one. It rests almost certainly upon a footnote by Thomas Mudge junior to page 154 of 'Letters from Mr. Mudge to His Excellency Count Bruhl written between the years 1772 and 1787'. In a letter dated September 14th 1784, Mudge senior refers to a marine timekeeper he was experimenting upon, and Mudge junior adds the following footnote: 'This was a timekeeper made by my father with a scapement similar to that in the Queen's watch, for the purpose of making experiments on, and not with a view to any public trial. It is now the property of Colonel Johnes, member for Radnorshire, who some time since purchased it of Messrs. Duttons.' It seems clear enough from this that the instrument Colonel Johnes purchased was not a pocket watch at all, but a marine timekeeper to which Mudge had experimentally applied a lever escapement.

Nevertheless, it does seem that a replica of the Queen's watch was made, although not by Mudge himself. In the course of extensive researches during 1959, made by J. K. Bellchambers, he came across a watch belonging to the late Major Eric Flint in Devonshire, a direct descendant of Mudge; which watch had hitherto been quite unknown in horological circles. Disastrously enough, the watch had later been converted to a quite modern spring-detent escapement, but closer examination showed beyond question that originally it had been an exact replica of 'the Queen's watch'. And around the edge of the enamel dial is inscribed 'THE ORIGINAL WAS INVENTED AND MADE BY THOMAS MUDGE FOR HER BRITANNIC MAJESTY. A.D. 1770'. The hallmark on the case is for 1795, which is the year after Mudge's death (347).

The inference is that the watch was commissioned, possibly by Thomas's brother, Dr. John Mudge, as some sort of memento, and probably made by Thomas's partner, William Dutton, who was certainly capable of such a work, and slightly later (1800) made another lever watch himself, now in a private collection.

The date of Mudge's watch was thus fixed beyond doubt at 1770, but the 1759 hallmark still had to be explained. At this juncture Dr. Torrens, the eminent horological historian, suggested that the hallmark itself should be re-examined, since the marks for 1759 and 1769 are very similar and frequently mistaken for each other. This was duly undertaken by Colonel Quill shortly before Christmas 1964, when it was found beyond the slightest shadow of doubt that the hallmark is that for the year 1769. Thus at last all the pieces of the jigsaw fitted into place.

The escapement has all the essentials of a modern lever escapement except that of 'draw' (to be discussed later). It is not illustrated here as Emery's first type of lever escapement, shown on page 115, is almost identical to it. The watch and its escapement are fully illustrated in the seventh edition of *Britten's Old Clocks and Watches*. Its chief peculiarity lies in having two pins, instead of the normal one, on the balance-staff, and corresponding offset prongs on the fork of the lever; the safety action is normal. This complicated arrangement Mudge evidently devised in an attempt to obtain impulse at the line of centres. The balance is uncompensated, and has two spiral balance-springs, each of three turns and one of which is affected by a bimetallic compensation curb.

All modern lever watches have an almost imperceptible recoil, or 'draw'; just sufficient to ensure that the anchor is drawn fully into engagement with the teeth of the escape wheel at each vibration of the balance. Neither Mudge nor any of the other early makers of lever escapements with the sole exception of Leroux (see Technical Section, page 116), realised this near-necessity, and his escapement is 'dead-beat'. 'Draw' is discussed fully in the Technical Appendix.

The watch performed well enough to lead Mudge to believe that it might rival Harrison's No. 4 as a marine timekeeper. Although he did not say so, as a pocket watch, its small balance arc of little more than 90 degrees, and lack of draw, would have precluded the likelihood of accurate pocket timekeeping.

When pressed by von Bruhl to make a replica he summed up his opinion of his escapement for pocket watches as follows: 'I think, if well executed, it has great merit, and will, in a pocket watch particularly, answer the purpose of time-keeping better than any other at present known; yet you will find very few artists equal to, and fewer still that will give themselves the trouble to arrive at; which takes much from its merit. And as to the honour of the invention, I must confess I am not at all solicitous about it: whoever would rob me of it does me honour'.

Mudge's words were prophetic in two ways; firstly as to the reluctance of anyone else for many years to make another lever watch; and secondly as to its ultimate supremacy for pocket watches. As to making a replica, the most he would do for von Bruhl was to make a rough, large-scale model, from which stemmed all future development of the English lever watch.

Von Bruhl handed the model to Josiah Emery (1725–96, a Swiss workman who emigrated to England) and desired him to incorporate the escapement in a pocket watch. Emery put him off for a considerable time, protesting 'that Mr. Mudge was the properest person for such an undertaking; for to own the truth, I doubted whether it would be possible to ever make a common sized pocket watch with an escapement on so large a scale'. However, in the end he was prevailed upon and completed the first watch in 1782. What the number was, or whether the watch survives is not now known. Emery seems to have produced about three lever watches a year, which he sold at a price of 150 guineas; and as the last known specimen was apparently made in 1795 it may be supposed that he made about 36 altogether.

The early ones followed Mudge's escapement fairly closely, as to the shape of the escape-wheel teeth. The unlocking and impulse action is effected by a fork and pins disposed in two planes. They differed from Mudge in the escapement adopting the straight-line lay-out; that is to say, the lever being at right angles with the anchor, and in alignment with the escape-wheel arbor and the balance-staff. This is the lay-out adopted almost uniformly in Continental lever watches, whereas English watches mostly followed Mudge's lay-out, in which the lever is aligned with the anchor and lies tangentially to the escape-wheel. Emery broke away from Mudge and followed Arnold for his balance-wheel, which is a rather heavier and more robust version of Arnold's 'S-shaped' compensation balance; with a helical balance-spring. The proportions of the escapement were Emery's own, so that he procured a very much more vigorous action than Mudge's watch, rendering Emery's watches better suited than Mudge's for pocket use, although they still suffered from the disability of being without draw. Nevertheless, they proved capable of an excellent performance (*338*).

In about 1792 Emery redesigned the escapement and replaced Mudge's two-plane arrangement with a single cranked roller. Despite the assertions of Chamberlain and other writers subsequently he never used draw.

Twelve Emery lever watches are at present known to survive, but unfortunately the numbering of several is at variance with the hallmarks, so that it is difficult to determine in precisely what order they were made. The oldest is No. 937, hallmarked 1783. The next oldest is No. 939, which has a regulator dial like the rest, but whereas in all the others, the two subsidiary dials are occupied by the hour and seconds hands, in No. 939 the hour and minute hands are concentric and the upper subsidiary dial is a thermometer. The case of this watch, which is silver (subsequently gilt), is hallmarked 1793, so it must have been recased. The next earliest number is 947 and as this is hallmarked 1785 it may safely be taken as fairly accurately dated. There is, however, an apparent anomaly in No. 1319, which is in the Old Ashmolean Museum at Oxford. It has an ordinary English type of cock, as opposed to all the others which have bridged cocks. This points to an early date; also, there is no name on the dial, and the hallmark of the case is for 1784. Yet of the twelve survivors this watch has the tenth highest number.

The third lowest number is 1057 which suggests 1785 or 1786 as its date. This watch belonged to George IV as Prince of Wales, and in 1800 he appears to have given it to his brother the Duke of Kent, who had it recased and engraved with his own arms, the hallmark of the case being that for 1800. On his death in 1820 he appears to have left it to his brother the Duke of Sussex, in whose famous sale it was subsequently sold (2). The next number, 1087, is part of the Ilbert Collection in the British Museum, and is hallmarked 1786, which thus fixes the Prince of Wales's watch fairly well to the previous year.

Four watches survive with the crank-roller lay-out; No. 937, just mentioned as the oldest surviving Emery lever, was later converted to crank-roller, evidently by Emery himself; No. 1289, which is in the Clockmakers' Company Collection in the City of London Guildhall, hallmarked 1792; No. 1350 in the National Maritime Museum, Greenwich, which has a silver case, also hallmarked 1792 (and retains its original wooden box); and finally No. 1379, also part of the Ilbert Collection, which has concentric hour and minute hands and is a five-minute repeater. It has a later, very ugly dial, and has been re-cased, but under the dial is scratched '*R. Rippon fecit. London 1795*'. This may to some extent discount Thomas Mudge junior's remark, in 1799: 'it is a fact now very well known, that these watches, made in Mr. Emery's name, were executed by Mr. Pendleton, and Mr. Pendleton candidly acknowledges that their accuracy is owing to the escapement invented by my Father, which they all contain'. It is certainly true that Richard Pendleton was concerned with Emery's lever watches, as two watches survive with his name upon them, but unfortunately both have been recased, so that they cannot be dated. No. 172 (Ilbert Collection) is practically identical with the Emery cranked-roller escapement, but No. 180, although superficially similar, has a quite different and unusual escapement. The fork is replaced by a ring on the end of the lever, which encircles the balance-staff and has two little pins which act as the fork (*328*). Unfortunately it is not known whether Pendleton was employed by Emery, or whether Emery only put work out to him. It cannot therefore be determined whether Pendleton's two watches were made during Emery's life-time or subsequently. Pendleton died in 1808.

One other watch survives from the Emery school, signed '*Cayetano Sanches en Londres. Pensionado de S. M. Cath 1792*'. Sanches was a Spaniard sent to study the making of marine chronometers in France and England, and worked for a time with Emery, when he made this lever escapement watch. He returned to Spain in the following year but died of the plague before he could establish a Spanish industry.

Apart from this very important group, very few English lever watches from before 1800 survive, or probably were made. The Mudge replica has been mentioned, and Thomas Dutton made another in 1800. According to Rees's *Cyclopaedia*, George Margetts made lever watches with a cranked-roller escapement, and a separate safety action, of which there is a drawing; but no specimen is known to survive. They were said to perform well, but liable to stop in the pocket. One very fine watch survives by Francis Perigal, who was appointed watchmaker to George III on January 1st 1784, in which capacity he would presumably have access to the Mudge watch (*309*). The general style of his own lever watch (especially the dial and hands) is early, and thus a date about 1785–6 seems likely. Unfortunately, like so many early lever watches, it has been re-cased, so that the hallmark is no help. Like Emery's No. 939, the upper subsidiary dial is a thermometer. The escapement and its layout follow Mudge's very closely, except that the impulse pallet is a cranked roller; there is a separate safety roller. Like Mudge's, the lever is balanced, and in practice moves most firmly to the limit of its travel and shows no tendency to set. The compensation is by two parellel bimetallic compensation curbs, with one pin on each.

One very important watch by John Leroux survives in the Guildhall Collection (*305*) and an almost identical movement is in the British Museum. The former is unnumbered but hallmarked 1785–6, so the fact that the British Museum movement is numbered 3153 is no help to dating it. Little is known about Leroux except that he was admitted to the Clockmakers' Company in 1781 and died after the turn of the century. His version of the lever escapement is entirely unusual. The lever is very short and tangential to the escape wheel, of which the anchor pallets span only 2 teeth. Leroux's watches are alone among lever escapements of the eighteenth century in having draw (see Technical Section, page 116). They have a quite modern double-roller escapement, but their main peculiarity lies in the escape-wheel which has 16 teeth with hooked points. The pallets of the anchor are pointed, so that all the lift is on the teeth. In all the other English makers with one exception, the whole of the lift is on the pallet. The Leroux balance-wheels are brass and have four bimetallic arms fixed to them, lying parallel

40

with the brass rim. These are very flimsy and have stops on the brass rim, presumably to prevent their bending outward too far in case of violent shock (and not, as has been suggested, to correct middle temperature error, which came much later). The balance-springs are also most unusual, being not truly helical, but conical in shape.

Not unlike Leroux's escapement is that of a very remarkable movement by one, Taylor (48, 345). Unfortunately it has been recased so that it cannot be dated, but the style of the movement suggests a date very close to 1800. Like Leroux, all the lift is on the teeth which have very long lifting surfaces. The compensation balance is similar to Arnold's final pattern, and carries two spiral balance-springs, like Mudge's watch. The escapement is a better version of Pendleton's No. 180 (see above). Taylor does not even give his initials, so that he cannot be identified, but he was certainly an important pioneer and the movement is of high quality.

The last and latest member of the little band of eighteenth-century English makers of the lever escapement was John Grant, who was admitted to the Clockmakers' Company in 1781 and died in 1810. He was nephew and apprentice to the very eminent maker Alexander Cumming, F.R.S. At least five watches by Grant survive; two in the Guildhall; two in the British Museum and one in private ownership. They all vary widely (350). The most remarkable and apparently later form has its escape-wheel at right-angles to the watch-plates and parallel to the balance-arbor. The lever pallets are at different levels so that they enter the path of the escape-wheel teeth from opposite sides alternately, and receive impulse down their inclined faces. There is, of course, no draw. The escapement of this watch (No. 1787, made in 1803–4) closely resembles that of Pendleton No. 180. Grant's earlier type has the escape-wheel teeth standing up from the face of the wheel, thus permitting very deep locking. All the Grants have compensation balances of differing and interesting design, and helical balance-springs. There is also a most interesting movement in the Guildhall Collection, evidently by Grant. This was two balance-wheels, geared together, each with its balance-spring and regulator; but the escapement is on one balance-staff only. The plate is signed 'J.G.—May 1800' (46).

It is thus probably true to say that no more than two dozen English lever escapement watches survive from before 1800, even including Grant's, made around the turn of the century. After this, no more is heard of the escapement in England for 15 years, and when it did reappear, it was in an entirely different form. Evidently makers found that results as good or better could be obtained from the detent escapement, with less trouble, and also the duplex escapement was beginning to come into favour.

When the lever escapement was again taken up in England it was in Lancashire, in quite cheap watches, and it did not fully regain its status as a high-grade escapement until about 1850.

In the meantime, two or three exceptions may be noted. The first was Edward Massey, who in about 1815 made lever watches (commonly misnamed cranked rollers) with an ingenious and simple form of safety action. On each side of the impulse knib a vertical slot was cut out of the roller (50). As the lever had pointed ends to the fork, and as the fork embraced the knib, its pointed ends entered these two slots. Thus, if the lever tried to jump out of engagement, it could not do so until the fork points registered with the safety slots. Massey's lever watches are now extremely rare. It has been suggested that Massey's escapement is a direct descendant of the rack-lever, being in fact a rack-lever reduced to one tooth on the balance-staff and two on the lever.

In about 1820 George Savage devised an escapement which came to be called 'the Savage two pin escapement', which enjoyed a considerable following until about 1880, and certainly gave good results. In it, the balance-staff had a large roller with two pins on it, instead of a normal pin, which engaged with a wide fork on the lever. On the end of the lever was another pin which engaged with a very narrow safety slot in the roller. The two pins were only concerned to unlock the escapement, their wide spacing being so as to ensure that unlocking was completed with a minimum of friction by the centre line (a simpler way of achieving what Mudge and Emery sought with their two-plane escapement). Impulse was imparted by the safety pin and hardly, if at all via the fork. Savage escapements are characterised by a very brisk action, which certainly testifies to the efficiency of his escapement. It called for very accurate manufacture and was thus seldom used (52).

Probably the only English maker producing lever watches of the highest quality between roughly 1805 and 1830 was the little-known T. Cummins of London. The example illustrated (488) is hallmarked for 1826. He employed Massey's escapement; a jewelled impulse pallet; resilient banking pins; Massey's safety action; quite a modern type of compensation balance; and a helical balance-spring. The purchaser's name and address were sometimes engraved on the balance-cock. Of the handful of surviving specimens all but the earliest one have the very elegant form of engine-turned regulator dial (488), and all are superbly finished, and have a very good performance.

42

The first Lancashire lever watches were the rack-levers, made in increasing numbers during the early nineteenth century. The pioneer of this revival of the rack-lever was Peter Litherland who took out his first patent in 1791; but whether or not he was aware of Abbé Hautefeuille's form of the escapement already described, in the early eighteenth century, is not known. Despite their non-detachment, the Lancashire rack-levers performed surprisingly well when well made, which some of them were. All had flat steel balances and a very few had compensation curbs. The lever was laid out tangentially to the escape-wheel.

All the foregoing types—Massey's, Savage's and Litherland's—gradually disappeared after 1830. It was the single roller, or 'table-roller' lay-out which eventually established itself as the standard British lever escapement for over a century. It has something in common with both Massey's and Savage's escapement, and it is generally supposed to have originated in Lancashire; but some of the earliest surviving specimens are by London makers, although in some of these the jewelling is evidently Lancashire work. However, the probability is that it was invented by Breguet, who used it in tourbillon watches in about 1810 (without draw), from which it would have been easy for one of the English makers to copy. Following the earlier types, the escape-wheels had pointed teeth, so that all the lift was on the pallet, and draw very soon became universal. The balances continued to be uncompensated but nearly all had maintaining power, and were jewelled, often with the very large, transparent stones, which came to be known as 'Liverpool windows'.

The first London maker of note to make lever watches of this kind may well have been Thomas Earnshaw. He evidently regarded it as a good, robust escapement for medium-priced watches. The full-plate movements usually have neither compensation nor maintaining power, and only the balance-wheel arbors are jewelled. It is hallmarked 1829, the last year of Earnshaw's life. There is a rather more sophisticated watch by him, with maintaining power and bimetallic balance, in the Guildhall collection.

All the English lever watches mentioned so far had full-plate movements. Only the balance-wheel was outside the plates, pivoted in a separate cock. This made for a very thick watch, and Breguet's watches were already creating a demand for something thinner. The British answer to this was the three-quarter plate movement, which continued until well into the twentieth century. In it, about one quarter of the top plate is cut away and in this space are the balance-wheel and escape-wheel, each pivoted in a separate cock. A most interesting transition between the full and three-quarter plate layout exists in a fine watch by the London maker Richard Webster, hall-marked 1823 (474). At first sight it appears to be a three-quarter plate, but closer examination reveals that it has a full-plate, the top plate being recessed to house the balance-wheel so that the latter is flush with the rest of the plate. Under the plate, the escape-wheel is carried in a large potence. Three-quarter plate movements are not found at all commonly until after 1830.

From this stage the lever escapement gradually revived in favour until by 1850 Frodsham and some others were once more using it in watches of the highest quality.

In collecting English lever watches of the early nineteenth century extreme caution must be exercised against watches which have been converted to lever at some date subsequent to their manufacture, usually from duplex, but sometimes from cylinder. A fairly sure sign of conversion is when the lever has concave-curved sides. Original levers nearly always had straight sides. Other indications of different jewelling, and regilding of the plate, etc. may also be found. But any single-roller English lever hallmarked 1820 or earlier is to be regarded with the utmost suspicion. No genuine specimen is known to the authors.

The Lever Escapement in France and the Work of Breguet prior to 1795

We must now turn to follow the development of the lever escapement in France where the starting point apparently is the remnant of a watch shown in figure 282 which must be one of the most, if not the most enigmatic piece in the whole history of watches. It was found in a Paris street market by Dr. Gschwind, the well-known Swiss collector, a few years ago, and bought for a few francs. It then consisted simply of the escapement and wheels; no fusee or spring barrel, and most of the temperature compensation curb missing. Round the edge of the plate is inscribed '*Julien le Roy Ivenit et Fecit à Paris 4757*'.

Julien le Roy, the most celebrated French maker of his day, and father of the equally famous Pierre, was born in 1686 and died in 1759. His pioneer work for the improvement of the French industry has already been described.

The movement is consistent with his other known work, and the number suggests a date towards the end of his life. The '*Ivenit*' (so spelt) means very little, as he generally put it on his watches.

The escapement is a detached lever; experimental certainly, but a lever indubitably and despite examination by the most expert judges, no sign of any modification can be found in it. It is just possible that it could have started life as a rack-lever; but Julien le Roy evidently regarded it as being of great importance, since it was certainly made originally with temperature compensation and is thus either the first or second pocket watch so fitted (the alternative being the Harrison-Jeffreys watch of 1753).

It thus antedates the Mudge watch on any reckoning, and the extraordinary thing is that there should have been no contemporary mention of it. That it is not mentioned by the prolific Berthoud is perhaps not remarkable, as no love was lost between him and the le Roys. Berthoud himself twice came within measurable distance of inventing a lever escapement (on plates XXXIII and XXXV of his *Essai sur l'Horlogerie*) but he never quite arrived at it. Berthoud knew of and described Mudge's lever escapement, but necessarily all at a much later date, having regard to Julien le Roy's death in 1759.

Like Mudge's escapement, the fork is a continuation of one arm of the anchor and the whole lever is counterbalanced. Instead of a fork there are two pins standing up from the end of the lever, which are engaged by a cranked roller on the balance-staff. There is a safety dart of quite modern design. The most remarkable part of the escapement is the anchor which has steel rollers instead of fixed pallets. The escape-wheel has 12 pointed teeth so arranged (unavoidably with roller pallets) as to have a slight recoil or draw, on the exit pallet only. The balance-wheel is steel with a number of gold inserts, presumably to increase its weight. A long lever pivoted near one foot of the bridge-cock, passes under the balance and acts as an ordinary compensation curb, with an indicator marked 'ch' and 'fr' for hot and cold. This was operated through a system of levers by some form of bimetallic arrangement of which there are puzzling vestiges, but, from the lay-out, almost certainly comprised a gridiron. These have been conjecturally completed by George Daniels, together with a fusee and spring barrel, and mounted in a brass box.

There are no writings of either Julien or Pierre le Roy which in any way tie up with the escapement, except that Julien was the first to use a miniature anchor escapement to control the speed of a watch repeater train. Presumably therefore the watch was an experiment which Julien decided not to pursue, and published nothing about it;

45

or death cut off his experiments, which Pierre did not carry on, being already fully engaged upon his marine timekeeper.

The case for Julien le Roy having anticipated Thomas Mudge in inventing the lever escapement must probably remain non-proven, lacking more corroborative evidence; but the possibility of their having arrived at it independently certainly cannot be ruled out, with le Roy a good ten years ahead of Mudge. Nor does it seem quite certain that le Roy's work remained completely unnoticed, when we come to consider the work of Breguet, who was otherwise almost certainly first in the field with the lever escapement in France.

Abraham Louis Breguet (1747–1823) was born in Neuchâtel in Switzerland and in 1762 was sent to France and apprenticed to a watchmaker in Versailles. He there attended night-classes at the Collège Mazarin and attracted the attention of the Abbé Marie, who brought him to the notice of Louis XVI, himself a keen horologist.

Very little is known of Breguet's early history, up to 1787, when the books of the firm commence and have continued in unbroken sequence to the present day.

It has been generally supposed that he set up in business on his own account in the late 'seventies, but this theory does not seem to stand up to examination. Far more likely is an ancient tradition that he worked for Berthoud until about 1782 or 1783, which ties up with the date of the earliest known Breguet watch to have survived. This is a self-winding watch that belonged to the Queen, Marie-Antoinette. The case is engraved '*Inventé, perfectionné et exécuté par Breguet*' and '*Breguet à Paris No. 2—$\frac{10}{82}$*'. Of these, No. 2 is the serial number of the watch, and the $\frac{10}{82}$ signifies that it was completed in October (the 10th month) of 1782.

This form of fractional numbering seems to have been used exclusively by Breguet before 1787, and is thus a most convenient means of dating his earliest watches of which exceedingly few survive.

The nature or whereabouts of No. 1 is not known, but as No. 2 dates from October 1782 it seems reasonable to suppose that Breguet set up in business in that year. The next known survivor is No. 8 $\frac{10}{83}$, which was made for the Tsar Nicholas of Russia. It also is a perpetuelle and like No. 2 $\frac{10}{82}$ has a quite ordinary cylinder escapement.

The next survivor known to the authors was only recently discovered by Cecil Clutton, despite its having been for many years in the Guildhall Museum where, however, it had been relegated ignominiously to a case of 'fakes'.

The earliest Breguets have the signature in an elegant cursive hand on the dial, very

46

seldom found in later watches; and it was this that first attracted attention to the watch, which in every other way looked most unlike a genuine Breguet. The movement could not be seen without removing the dial, but this accomplished it transpired to be a quite ordinary French cylinder movement with a decoratively pierced bridge-cock which may have been made by Breguet himself, but could equally well have been bought from the trade. To this ébauche Breguet had then attached a highly finished minute-repeating mechanism. On the back plate is engraved *'Breguet à Paris $\frac{5}{85}$ No. 128'*. The only externally visible signature (other than that on the dial) is on the dust cap: *'Breguet No. 128'*. The very rare 'fractional' numbering has never been faked and the authors have no doubt at all that the watch is genuine (*305*).

It is widely stated that any watch signed *'Breguet à Paris'* is a fake, and on any watch manifestly dating from after about 1795 this is almost always true. But up to 1793, so far as is known, all his work was signed *'à Paris'*. In some cases, especially on clocks, the final 's' of 'Paris' is an antique French form, closely resembling an 'a'. It is also significant that all the Breguet certificates have written large along the margin *'Breguet à Paris'*.

These early cylinder escapement watches are relatively unsophisticated in design and execution, giving little indication of what was to come. With three other, very different watches, they are the only specimens known to the authors to have survived from the pre-1787 period, although with little doubt there are others.

These other three watches were made for the Duc d'Orléans, the Duc de Praslin, and the Queen, Marie-Antoinette.

The latter is probably the most famous watch in the world, perhaps after the English, Mudge lever, 'Queen's Watch'. It was ordered in 1783 by an officer of the royal guard as a present for the Queen. It was to have every known refinement and complication and contains the following: self-winding; minute repeater; perpetual calendar; equation of time; thermometer; up-and-down indicator; independent seconds. The escapement is a detached lever with a helical spring and compensation balance. The perpetuelle weight is of platinum. All parts are of gold except where they have to be of steel. The movement is sapphire-jewelled and rollered throughout. The workshop costs were 30,000 francs (equal to almost as many pounds today). This watch, however, is no very sure evidence of Breguet's pre-1787 style, since it was not completed by the outbreak of the Revolution, and was not finally completed until 1800. It is not known how far it had progressed when it was put on one side, and it has the high number of 160.

47

The Duc de Praslin watch was said to have been made between 1783 and 1785, but it may not have been completed until much later, as it was not sold until 1805, and it has the fairly high number of 92.

The first 30 watches appearing in the books from 1787 are all perpetuelles, with lever escapement, helical balance-spring, and compensation balance. They differ completely from the two early perpetuelles, Nos. 2 and 8, mentioned earlier. In them are seen all the characteristics of Breguet's work for the rest of his life. It therefore appears reasonable to suppose that it was some time between the years 1783–7 that Breguet reached his horological maturity. There is, however, a very curious and contradictory feature of the Orléans watch. When Breguet made some autobiographical notes in about 1820, he stated that he had made this watch in 1780 and probably at about that time there was engraved on the perpetuelle weight '*Fait par Breguet pour le Duc d'Orléans en 1780*' (*330*).

As has already been indicated, all the weight of evidence previously cited is quite against the possibility of so early a date. If Breguet could produce so superlative a watch in 1780 it is most unlikely that he would have fobbed-off such important clients as the Queen and the Tsar with such relatively second-rate cylinder watches as Nos. 2 and 8 in 1782 and 1783 respectively. Moreover, as in the Marie-Antoinette and the Praslin watches, the number, 62, suggests a substantially later date.

One can only suppose that Breguet's memory for dates had somewhat failed him or, just possibly, that he was indulging deliberately in a mild deception to establish himself as the inventor of the self-winding watch (although this is not at all consistent with his known character). In fact, it is now fairly well established that the self-winding watch was invented in about 1780, but by Abraham-Louis Perrelet, in Switzerland. Again, it is possible that Breguet made two perpetuelles for the Duc d'Orléans, one very early, and the inscription was put on the wrong watch.

If the 1780 date were to be established it would open up new difficulties as to the independent invention of the lever escapement in France. Mudge's invention of 1770 remained a complete secret for 12 years, when he gave von Bruhl his rough model from which Emery made his first lever-escapement watch in 1782. If therefore Breguet made the Orléans watch in 1780 he would have had to invent the lever escapement for himself, unless he was acquainted with the Julien le Roy watch already described. This possibility cannot be ruled out entirely, since the fork ends of the le Roy, and of Breguet's first form of lever, are remarkably alike.

However, assuming the arguments put forward against the 1780 date for Breguet's lever escapement are valid, it is still possible that he had seen the le Roy version. Whatever its date, Breguet's first lever was in every way different from the English lay-out, except as to broad principle. He could never have accepted the cumbersomeness of the Mudge-Emery escapement, but having once seen it (as well he could have done by 1783) he might easily have developed the form he did; especially if he had also seen the le Roy version. In any case, Breguet never claimed to have invented the lever escapement; and he was not usually backward in laying claim to inventions.

The authors therefore suggest that Breguet matured his style in general, and his lever escapement in particular, during the years 1785–7. Whether their appraisal of his early work will stand the test of future research must remain to be seen, but they hope it is at least of value as being a good deal less indefinite and illogical than any previously published attempts at this admittedly very obscure subject.

However one looks at it, Breguet was very early in the field as a maker of the lever escapement, and his form of it had a far greater influence on future development than had that of his predecessors, Mudge and Emery.

As to the escapement; it is laid out in a straight line, like Emery's, and has no draw. Instead of the impulse knib on the balance-staff engaging with a fork on the end of the lever, it does so with two vertical pins on the end of the lever, just as in the Julien le Roy watch. Having no draw, Breguet foresaw the possibility of the lever jumping out of engagement prematurely, and to reduce the evil effects of this happening he used a safety roller of very small diameter. To reduce the risk of its happening at all, he made the lever itself as slender and light as possible, and balanced it.

Having got through his experimental period, as it seems, Breguet started his famous books in 1787 and the first 30 watches to appear in them follow closely upon the Praslin-Orléans prototypes. They are perpetuelles, with lever escapement, helical balance and beautifully light compensation balance not unlike Arnold's 1782 balance, but much lighter. As far as is known, all had enamel dials and most were signed 'Breguet à Paris' round the outside edge of a rim immediately below the dial, revealed to view when the front bezel is opened. Many were fitted subsequently with silver or gold engine-turned dials (382).

There is no means of key-winding this first batch of perpetuelles, and the movement can only be got at by taking off the dial. Breguet made a great point of this, saying that as the movement was completely sealed, it needed cleaning much less frequently than other watches.

All were repeaters and all, unfortunately, had an inadequate arrangement for locking the heavy platinum weight when the spring was fully wound. The effect of this was that under adverse conditions winding might continue until there was a major explosion and a much damaged watch resulted. In later years, Breguet recalled or modified as many of the early perpetuelles as he could.

In addition to the early, fractional numbered watches, Breguet seems to have made about 220 watches by 1793 when his position in relationship to the Revolution became so hazardous that he was forced to flee the country. He went first to Switzerland and then to England where he was kindly received. It is not known how much new work he accomplished during his exile, and he may have continued his fractional numbering during this period, as there was a plain lever watch in the Chamberlain collection numbered $\frac{2}{94}$. By 1795 conditions in France had become sufficiently stable once more for him to return to Paris and rebuild his shattered equipment and business.

Robin, Pouzzait, Tavan and the Lever Escapement

Since the progress of the lever escapement on the Continent was almost solely with Breguet, it seems reasonable to consider next the rest of his work, which is exceptionally well recorded in the books of the firm. There are, however, one or two minor pioneers who must first be considered.

Robert Robin of Paris, having seen one of Emery's watches, devised in 1791 a form of the escapement in which the lever was used for locking, but the escape-wheel gives impulse on alternate beats, like a chronometer. This escapement was later used occasionally by Breguet and subsequently by others. It is the nearest thing to what is somewhat vaguely referred to as a 'half-chronometer' (61).

In the Physics Museum of the University of Geneva there is a model of a very crude form of lever escapement, made by Pouzzait in 1786, which may well be an independent invention so far as it goes. Later, Pouzzait or some very similar maker added an exceedingly bad form of safety action, involving quite excessive friction if brought into play. Watches of this kind are found with very large balance-wheels, the full diameter of the watch, beating seconds (58). Several survive with Breguet's early type of signature, and the possibility cannot be ruled out that he bought them from the trade, before he had perfected his own lever escapement. Antoine Tavan (1749–1836), a distinguished Geneva maker, also made lever watches from about 1785 onwards, but his versions of the escapement are more curious than useful and added nothing to its development. Other Swiss makers experimented with pin-toothed escape-wheels in connection with a lever.

The Work of Breguet after 1795

The following consideration of Breguet's post-revolution work may seem of excessive length in relationship to the book as a whole, but it is nevertheless necessary in view of the quantity, diversity, and horological importance of his watches. Most leading makers have brought one type to a high level of perfection and done little else (such as John Arnold and his chronometers) but Breguet ranged over the whole field of pocket horology. His work is no better than, for example, Arnold's and his superficial finish was seldom better than it needed to be. It is his impeccable taste, coupled with an inexhaustible fund of mechanical inventiveness which has given him his unique place in horology, and secured for his watches the very high prices they commanded when new, and have done ever since.

Breguet's cases and dials, and his famous 'secret signature', are discussed in the chapter on 'Decoration'.

Breguet mostly used three watch escapements; the cylinder, lever, and spring detent. He occasionally used the verge (but only very rarely and in special circumstances, and in some early carriage clocks), virgule, two-wheel duplex, Robin lever and (very rarely) his own highly complex, and strangely-named 'échappement naturel'. His constant force escapement was unsuited for pocket use and was used only (and that rarely) in marine chronometers, and one or two special clocks.

The English cylinder has the defect that the cylinder being part of the balance-staff, the latter is fragile and expensive to replace. Breguet overcame this weakness by outrigging the cylinder beyond the bottom bearing of the balance-staff. The bottom bearing of the balance-staff is therefore mounted on a very slender steel arm, round which the cylinder moves (21). The balance-staff has a crank continued past the bottom bearing, on to which the ruby cylinder is cemented. The steel escape-wheel has teeth of

51

triangular shape, considerably easier to make than the English pattern. Breguet's cylinder escapements have an outstanding performance and are practically indestructible. He seldom fitted them with compensation balances, but with a very light gold balance and his compensation curb. This consists of one fixed pin and one mounted on a U-shaped bimetallic curb, whose movement opens or closes the gap through which the balance-spring passes. The fixed pin and curb are mounted on the regulator so that both are moved for mean-time regulation. Breguet's curb works remarkably well.

As in most of Breguet's watches, the escapement lies between the dial and dial-plate and so is not visible except by removing the dial.

The cylinder escapement watches always have a going barrel, but here again, Breguet did everything to mitigate its faults. He used the largest possible barrel, limiting the going period to a small percentage of the spring, so as to have as even a torque as possible. Breguet's stopwork is practically always invisible. Only in exceptional circumstances did he mount it on top of the barrel. In some small Breguet watches the chapter ring is placed eccentrically on the dial. This was done to make possible a large spring barrel (6).

For spring-detent watches Breguet used either Arnold's or Earnshaw's escapement, but with an increasing preference for the latter. Occasionally, too, he used the Peto cross-detent-arrangement, especially in tourbillons (405, 407). These watches were made entirely for accuracy, with no concessions to slimness and therefore had a free-sprung helical balance-spring and compensation balance. Breguet's compensation balances, always commendably light, may have two, three or four arms. The rims are sometimes recessed so that the screws do not project, which was presumably done for improved streamlining. These watches often have a reversed fusee and usually a three-quarter plate lay-out.

Breguet's first form of lever escapement has already been described. In about 1814 he revised it considerably, to the almost completely modern lay-out shown in the Technical Appendix. The two ears of the lever are partly for balance and partly for banking, which they do against the escape-wheel arbor. This escapement has divided lift, and the teeth of the escape-wheel are drilled to retain oil. The early perpetuelles generally had helical balance-springs, but in later watches he used a flat spiral spring with his own 'Breguet overcoil' (described in the Technical Appendix). Lever watches have usually one, and very occasionally two going barrels; but all perpetuelles have two.

52

Breguet only used the verge escapement in some early carriage clocks, watches for the Turkish Market, and watches which he sold but which were not made in his own workshops. The ones he did make were of very high quality. The verge pallets do not project from the staff, but the latter is very much thicker than usual, and at the two points opposite the teeth of the escape-wheel, half the staff is cut away to form the verges, and the impulse faces are jewelled. To this extent the escapement resembles the Flamenville and other varieties of dead-beat verge, but Breguet wisely did not use the verge in this way, realising that its recoil is an important factor in successful verge time-keeping. The watch illustrated (378) has a verge escapement of this form and may be regarded as one of the most sophisticated verge watches to be found, with its parachute, reversed fusee, and jewelled holes for the balance-staff and crown-wheel pivots. It will be mentioned again under the heading of 'Breguet Mixte'. The British Museum has a remarkable Breguet movement, combining the verge and lever escapement. Here the impulse is given as in a verge, but the escape-wheel is locked on a lever at other times, so that it is practically a free escapement, without recoil.

Breguet evidently regarded the verge escapement as suitable for watches and carriage clocks which might expect rough treatment, or unskilled maintenance.

There is a recorded use of the virgule escapement by Breguet in a watch in the Salomons collection, in which it is No. 26. It is a quite high-quality and complicated watch, made in 1797. It was certainly a special order throughout. Another virgule, 'à tact', was sold to Madame Murat in 1802.

Breguet did not often use the duplex escapement, but he evidently thought highly of it, as he only used it in high-grade watches with compensation balances. He always used two separate wheels, that for locking being of steel and that for impulse of gold.

Despite Breguet's faithful support of the lever escapement he evidently liked escapements where impulse was delivered direct by the escape-wheel, and it was therefore natural that he should use Robin's escapement, usually in fairly high grade watches, including one fairly late perpetuelle. He also developed it a stage further into his 'échappement naturel' which is in effect a double Robin, giving impulse at every beat instead of only on alternate beats. This he did by having two escape-wheels geared together, and the lever lay between them. The lever locked alternately on one and the other and impulse was also given alternately by each wheel. As they revolved in opposite directions impulse can be given at each swing of the balance. In order to avoid undue inertia loadings, in its final development the second, driven escape-wheel is very much smaller than the other, having only three pairs of locking and impulse teeth (*403*).

Breguet probably regarded this escapement as the ultimate in pocket timekeeping, and as the appendix on rating old watches shows, his confidence was fully justified. The escapement has survived in one marine chronometer, two pocket tourbillon watches (one in the Salomons collection) and in one quite small watch, in obviously a prototype or experimental form. It was also used at least once after Breguet's death, in a very fine watch made in about 1840 for the Turkish Market. It seems therefore to have been used only in very important watches.

It is next appropriate to consider Breguet's more important inventions, and their dates as fixed by the present firm from their records.

It is now generally agreed that the self-winding watch was not invented by Breguet, but by Abraham-Louis Perrelet (1729–1826) of Neuchâtel, in about 1780. But Breguet was the first person to make self-winding watches in any quantity. The first 30 watches in the books are perpetuelles, but the books start in 1787 and as had already been indicated, Breguet was certainly making such watches in 1782.

The following is a list of Breguet's more important inventions, and their probable dates.

1789	'Echappement naturel' (see earlier, page 53).
1789	Breguet 'tipsy' key. This has a spring-loaded ratchet which frustrates attempts to wind the watch in the wrong direction (*432*).
1790–93	(and again, for some reason, in 1796) Breguet's version of the ruby cylinder (see page 51).
1790–93	'Parechute', shock-proof mounting of the balance-staff.
1795	Perpetual calendar.
1795	'Regulateur à Tourbillon' (however, the date of the 'Brevet d'Invention' is 1801).

This latter is Breguet's method of avoiding position errors and is typical of his radical approach to mechanical problems. By mounting the escapement on a revolving platform he repeated all the position errors once in every revolution of the platform (varying, in his watches, from one to six minutes according to the lay-out). He thus had no need even to try to correct the position errors, although, owing to the good propor-

tions of his escapement and its consequently lively action, his watches are less suscep-
tible than most to errors of position.

In his patent Breguet refers to 'the extreme difficulty, if not impossibility, of securing
that the centre of movement of the balance and its spring should coincide with their
centre of gravity'.

The mechanism consists of a platform which carries on it the balance and escape-
wheels, and is driven by the third-wheel. In the 4 and 5 minute versions the fourth-
wheel is also mounted on the platform.

Some Breguet tourbillons are of the plainest construction and finish, though always
with all his most advanced devices for timekeeping. The escapement may be spring-
detent, lever, or *échappement naturel*. The finest specimens have a cartouche on the dial
engraved '*Regulateur à tourbillon*' or, in one sold to an English customer 'Whirling
About Regulator'.

1793–5	'*Pendule sympathique*'. This was Breguet's most advanced flight of mis-applied ingenuity. It consisted of a pair of timekeepers, the one a very accurate chronometer of about the size of a very large carriage clock; the other an ordinary, uncompensated pocket watch. On top of the clock was a watch-stand in which the watch was placed at night after being wound. A key in the stand registered with a hole in the watch-case and by devious means set it to time by the parent clock and moved the regulator according to the previous day's error (*519–22*).
1795–6	'*Echappement à force constante*'. A form of remontoir escapement in which impulse is imparted to the balance by a spring, retentioned by the train after each impulse. It was used in some marine chronometers, without outstanding success; it was too bulky and subject to position errors for use in watches.
1796–1800	'*Montres à tact*'. These are commonly and erroneously known as blind-men's watches, because the time may be ascertained by touch. In fact Breguet regarded the device as an alternative to the repeater (than which it was very much cheaper to make) and sometimes referred to as '*répéti-tion à cuvette*'. In his catalogue he writes: 'one thus easily distinguishes the hour by touch, in the darkness and, with a little practice, the quarters and lesser intervals'. The 'tact' consisted of a stout arm, pivoted at the centre of the watch, with its outer end secured to the bezel round which it is free to travel. The centre-wheel of the watch, rotating once in 12 hours,

has mounted upon it a ratchet of one tooth with which a catch on the 'tact' engages. If the 'tact' is rotated in an anti-clockwise direction it rides over the ratchet and can be turned round indefinitely. But if it is turned in a clockwise direction the catch will engage with the ratchet and further movement will be prevented. The 'tact' arm will then point to the time, and ease of establishing this in the dark is secured by touch knobs spaced at hourly intervals round the case (*433*).

The merit of the 'tact' is that when worn in the pocket, the 'tact' arm imposes no friction upon the train.

1798	Independent seconds.
1805–10	*'Pendule sympathique remettant à l'heure et remontant la montre'*—the crowning folly to the first sympathique, by which the watch is not only set to time and regulated, but wound up as well.

Finally, the types into which Breguet divided his watches:

'Montres Simples'. These have one or two hands, with or without simple calendar-work and with or without a seconds dial. They include small and medium-sized ladies' watches. Dials may be enamel, gold or silver and the case plain or engine-turned.

This type includes the *'montre à souscription'*. In his 'notice' Breguet writes: 'I have thought that the Public would receive favourably some watches good enough to be in the front rank, second only to Astronomical and marine timekeepers, if they could be had at a reasonable price. . . . They are distinguished by their simplicity and by a lay-out which guarantees the escapement from the worst of accidents, even being dropped. . . . Repairs can be done in any country and will be easier and cheaper than those to common watches. . . . The mainspring has twice the duration of any other watch, so that in driving the watch for 36 hours there is hardly any falling off in power, and there is no risk of its breaking. . . . The watches will have only one hand. . . . The size (25 lignes; about $2\frac{5}{16}''$) of the dial gives ample room to put 12 divisions between each pair of hours so that the hand passes one every five minutes, and it is quite easy to tell the time to about a minute. . . . It will be necessary to make a certain number of watches at a time, in order to endow their construction with the desired degree of uniformity and perfection. But for this an outlay of cash is necessary. The means of procuring this by borrowing involves such an enormous payment of interest which, in the present state of things, no honest trade can afford. I therefore thought that a subscription would be preferable and that the subscriber who makes a partial advance payment will find his indemnity in the moderate purchase price. The price of the watches will be from 600 francs, of which a quarter is payable in advance.' (*429*).

Breguet goes on to refer to the secret signature which, in subscription watches, takes the form of the words '*souscription*'; the number of the watch; and '*Breguet*' (*431*).

The watches are wound up through the centre of the hand. They are set to time by manually pushing the hand. This should be done with some fairly soft pusher, such as a match, and not too far from the centre; otherwise the delicate pointer may snap off. If the hand is pushed by something pointed, like a pin, the enamel of the dial will be scratched, as has only too often happened in surviving specimens.

At their most handsome, the cases have a silver body and back, simply engine-turned, with gold bezels and loose-fitting gold pendant ring. In this form a Souscription is indeed a most handsome object. It is said that some 150 were made, but from the number of survivors this seems likely to be an underestimate.

Souscriptions are occasionally found with gold or silver dials, when they usually have a quite plain, pointed hand.

The second class is '*Montres à répétition*'.

These come in three classes of which the best may have cylinder or duplex escapement, compensation curb, fully jewelled, with gold cuvette. The second and third classes, which are not easily distinguished, have only the escapement jewelled, and the cuvette is gilt. The push-piece may be either in the pendant boss (*330*) or in the side of the case (*400*).

The repetition may be on blocks or gongs, and Breguet's gongs are characterised by a remarkable tonelessness; perhaps attributable to his (latterly complete) deafness. In the best watches, with gongs, an intermediate piece is placed between the hammer and the gong, thus softening the blow. Many Breguet repeaters have what is known as a 'jump hour hand'. In these, the hour hand only moves at each hour, when it jumps forward to the next hour.

The third class is '*Montre de fantaisie et de luxe, sur les principes de chronomètres*' and includes a number of types including the perpetuelles of all sorts; complicated watches of all sorts; very thin repeaters with a free escapement (usually lever) with or without complications; *Montres à tact*—which is difficult to understand since they are among the simplest. The calibre of an *à tact* was usually that of a *souscription*. For daylight reading, a small eccentrically placed dial was usually placed on the opposite side of the watch to the *tact* lever, driven off the centre wheel. However, some *montres à tact* have a full normal dial on one side and the *tact* on the other. In others, the watch has a plain open dial, with a close-fitting outer case, making it look like a full hunter, known by Breguet as a '*savonette*', which carries the *tact* lever. *Montres à tact* are the only watches carrying Breguet's name, and made in his own workshops, with any amount of superficial decoration. These, however, may have transparent enamel over gold engine-turning, with the *tact* lever and the touch-knobs decorated with pearls and diamonds. In all other watches, the most decoration which Breguet would supply was buff or grey-coloured transparent enamel over an engraved or engine-turned back cover.

Also under this heading, even less understandably, come the '*montres mixtes*, plain or repeaters, made outside our workshops, but to our design, and under our supervision. The escapement and regulator are finished in our workshops'. '*Montres mixtes*' may be of a very high quality, indistinguishable from Breguet's own, and as they carry the correct signature the best of them cannot be distinguished from the '*pur sang*'; except that they do not usually appear in the books so that no certificate can be obtained for them, and the secret signature is '*Breguet. Et. Mixte*'. For example, the watch with verge escapement, made for the Turkish Market illustrated earlier (*378*), has for its secret signature first a hieroglyphic, which is presumably Breguet's name in Turkish; then '*Et Mixte*' (i.e. *Etablissement mixte*) '*Breguet*' and '*No. 898*'. See also fig. 422.

Finally comes '*Seconde Division pour la Marine, l'Astronomie et la Physique. Instrumens destinée spécialement à la MESURE DE TEMPS*'.

These include marine chronometers, and deck watches with two going barrels; also '*chronomètres de luxe et inventions diverses*'. These include chronometer repeaters; chronometers à tourbillon; split independent seconds observation watches; chronometers with equation of time; chronometers with two complete independent movements in the one case (Breguet maintained that the two kept each other to time by sympathetic effect and so halved any errors; examples were owned by George IV and Louis XVIII); and various types of regulator clock.

With the foregoing information, it should not be difficult for anyone to detect a faked Breguet. The most obvious evidence of faking is the signature '*Breguet à Paris*', unless the circumstances are such as to suggest that the date of the watch may be before 1795, in which case, other things being equal, it is almost certainly genuine. However, by way of confusing the issue, one quite late perpetuelle has

'*Breguet*' only in secret signature on the dial, and as the only visible words on the dial, '*à Paris*'!

Fakers sometimes put an accent on the name thus: '*Bréguet*'.

Much mystery surrounds Breguet's system of numbering his watches, but in fact the exceptions which produce the mystery are relatively few in number and most of them can be accounted for quite easily.

In the first place, when a low number has a late date according to its certificate it will generally be found that the date on the certificate is not the first sale of the watch. For example, No. 1977 was sold to General Junot in 1807, bought back in 1813 and resold to the Queen of Naples in 1814.

Breguet quite frequently bought back watches in this way, sometimes modernising them considerably before reselling them, in which case he frequently gave them a new number. For example, No. 153, a very early pivoted detent watch, undoubtedly dating from just after the Revolution, was bought back and resold in 1810 and again bought back in 1826, rebuilt and resold as No. 4570 (*336*).

Breguet seems sometimes to have added a digit to a low number, below 1000, so as to make it appear to be of later date. This certainly happened to No. 267, a most interesting watch in the British Museum, which may be the prototype *Souscription*. The movement is a three-quarter plate lay-out, quite unlike the standardised *souscription* and unlike them it has a little wheel on the back plate for setting the hand. Its date is 1796. But at some date, probably about 1810, the watch returned to the shop and Breguet prefixed a 2, making the number 2267. He did it rather badly, the prefixed 2 being not quite in line with the rest. As if to emphasise this he subsequently engraved a new number (the original one is stamped) on the plate 'No. 2267'. But what he could not alter was the secret signature on the dial, which remains 'No. 267'.

Breguet used three series of numbers. The first series comprises the very early 'fractional' numbers. The second series starts with the books in 1787, with the first 30 perpetuelles. A third series was started later, but its purpose is difficult to establish and so far as the authors have been able to ascertain it does not seem greatly to upset an overall chronology. Upwards of 300 dated numbers are known to them, from which they feel able to give the following rough guide to dates and numbers, with some confidence that all or nearly all exceptions can be explained in one of the above-mentioned ways.

	Number		Year
up to	220	up to	1793
	500		1800
	1000		1803
	1500		1805
	2000		1809
	2500		1812
	3000		1818
	3500		1820
	4000		1823

It is noticeable how the war years slowed down sales, but as a rule, Breguet seems to have made about 150–200 watches a year. This is consistent with the known size of his establishment. Salomon's estimated output of 17,000 watches during Breguet's life-time is manifestly grotesque.

Other broad guides as to date are that in about 1807 Breguet took his son into partnership, after which the watches are generally (but not invariably) signed 'Breguet et Fils'. However, when an enamel dial got damaged and was replaced by a metal dial after 1807, the 'Breguet et Fils' may appear on a much earlier watch.

In 1815 Breguet was appointed 'Horloger de la Marine' after which these words frequently appear on the cuvette of high-grade watches. The signature 'Breguet et Neveu' was used only for a short time, after Breguet's death, in about 1830.

Apart from these clear indications, the best training of all is to see and handle as many Breguet watches as possible. An invaluable work also is Breguet by Sir David Salomons (London 1921) which is still occasionally available from horological booksellers in English, or more easily in the French edition. Although the book is confusingly arranged, and much has been learnt about Breguet since it was written, it is indispensable for its mostly excellent illustrations of 100 Breguet watches or travelling clocks.

No one knows much about the watches which Breguet obtained from the trade and sold without having any part in their construction. But whether or not they come in this category, or are complete fakes, is not particularly significant, as in neither case have they the quality or value of the real thing.

Little inferior to Breguet's work, but much in value, are watches by the best of his pupils after they set up on their own. The example illustrated (*464*) might be a genuine Breguet to all outward appearances, except for the hands, but it is signed on the cuvette '*Lopin, élève de Breguet*'. Equally, when an ex-pupil set out to fake a Breguet, the result may be very difficult to detect.

The following is a list of pupils or workmen of Breguet who subsequently set up on their own, but it is probably not complete:

> J. R. Arnold, Audemars, Benoit, Fatton, Firche, Ingold, Jacob, Urban Jürgensen, Kessels, Laissieur, Lopin, Moinet, Mugnier, Oudin, Rabi, Renevier, Robert, Tavernier, Winnerl.

Breguet regarded Michel Weber as his most gifted pupil and he was made responsible for furnishing the Marie-Antoinette watch, No. 160. George Brown, the present head of the firm, is descended from Weber.

The ultimate test of authenticity is to refer to the firm for a certificate. On Breguet's death in 1823 his son and grandson continued to control the firm, but in 1880 no member of the family was prepared to continue. The business thereupon passed to the English foreman, Mr. George Brown whose grandson, of the same name, now has it, at 28 Place Vendôme, Paris, where are all the books of the firm. Any watch taken there can be identified if genuine and a certificate granted, on payment of a reasonable fee. Mr. Brown himself is a trained watchmaker and a very great admirer and expert concerning the work of Breguet. The date on an old certificate may, however, not be the real date of a watch. Breguet often bought watches back and resold them; sometimes with a new number. The date on the certificate would then be the date of this re-sale but research in the books might reveal the true age of the watch.

Certainly no other maker in the history of horology has produced a greater number and variety of masterpieces, nor had more effect on the development of the precision watch.

However, other French firms; Berthoud & Le Roy particularly; and various pupils of Breguet, were doing excellent work, which would be much more considered if it was not so overshadowed by his tremendous reputation. This is the more pity, because the ordinary '*Breguet simple*' is not a particularly interesting or exciting watch, and less valued watches by other makers may in fact be more horologically desirable. Various makers, such as Antoine Tavan, Sylvan Mairet, and Ferguson Cole, produced watches of the highest quality, often with strange experimental escapements, which are most desirable when they can be found; but in the end they had no effect upon the history of horology. It was in Switzerland, towards the end of Breguet's life, that the stage was being set for the mass-produced watch, which was eventually to give the supremacy in horology to Switzerland and, finally, produce watches whose accuracy would even surpass the finest work of Breguet or Arnold.

The Modern Watch
1830 – 1960

To a collector concentrating on the post-1830 period a great many avenues are open.

The variety of lever escapements alone, produced during the second and third quarters of the nineteenth century, would itself afford a lifetime's study. Many of them were drawn by Chamberlain and are illustrated in *It's About Time*. Many such watches had gold cases which have subsequently been broken up, but this may be considered an actual advantage by the collector, who is thus spared the expense of buying a lump of gold he may not want.

A collector who appreciates quality before all else may still obtain the finest work of the nineteenth century at a remarkably modest price; partly because so much of it survives, and partly because it is not yet in great demand. But the possession of a watch by such artists as Sylvan Mairet, Victor Kullberg, Louis Audemars, Jules and Louis Jürgensen, James Ferguson Cole, or such firms as Frodsham, Dent, Waltham, Vacheron & Constantin, or Patek Phillipe, may soon come to rate almost as high as the finest artists of the early precision period; and for the finest work, they are and will remain unsurpassed. Probably a Frodsham or Smith Tourbillon, made by Nicole Nielsen, is as fine a watch as has ever been made, and one whose performance can hardly be bettered (*584*). These instruments are already appreciated to the full by collectors.

At the other end of the scale of revolving escapments, the cheap Waterbury had many variants, and to own a complete run of these is the aim of some collectors, particularly in America (*566*).

Yet another revolving escapement whose performance surpasses that of most tourbillons, and is not unduly rare, is the Karrusel. The minute revolving tourbillon produces inertia problems of its own, owing to its high speed of rotation. Bahne Bonniksen evolved his karrusel to avoid these, and patented it in England in 1894. The wheel of the revolving platform is driven off the pinion of the third-wheel, and the third-wheel drives the pinion of the fourth-wheel, which is concentric with the platform. The platform revolves in $52\frac{1}{2}$ minutes and thus avoids heavy inertia loadings. Breguet himself achieved much the same result on some of his best tourbillons by mounting his fourth-wheel on the tourbillon carriage which then revolved in either four, five or six minutes (*408*).

Bonniksen produced an improved model in 1903, in which the rotating carriage was pivoted at both ends, instead of being supported on a single bearing only. It was driven by a separate train from the centre wheel and rotated in 39 minutes. This he called a 'Bonniksen tourbillon'.

Karrusel watches were made, or at any rate signed, by Bonniksen, H. Golay, Nicole Nielsen and Rotheram & Sons Ltd. It is not always easy to know who may have made any particular specimen, but it is not important, as they are all much alike, and if a karrusel has been properly cared for, an outstanding performance is assured. In the early years of the century they swept all before them in the Kew trials, and their manufacture probably continued until about 1923.

With such a variety of choice, it would be impossible to illustrate and describe a comprehensive coverage in this book. A more or less random selection has therefore been chosen, to give some idea of the extent of this latest hunting ground for the collector of watches.

Decorative

Types of Decoration

There are three principal ways of decorating a watch case.

The great majority of cases are made of metal, which may be decorated in a variety of ways. Otherwise, cases may be enamelled, or they may be made of, or decorated with precious or semi-precious stones. Cases may also be covered with leather, and decorated with pinwork; or they may be covered in tortoise-shell and inlaid with patterns in gold or silver.

Metal cases may be decorated in five ways: (1) casting; (2) chiselling; (3) engraving; (4) repoussé; (5) engine-turning.

(1) As a preliminary, a decorative shape or pierced pattern may be cast, but this will need finishing by chiselling or engraving.

(2) Chiselling is carried out on the surface of the metal by a hammer and punches (*124*).

(3) Engraving is a finer form of decoration, executed by a 'graver' which produces fine V-grooves on the surface of the metal (*77*).

Chiselling and engraving are often combined as, for example, in 'champlevé engraving', where the background is chiselled back to a common level and then engraved with fine grooves or punch-marks all over, to give it a dark appearance. The foreground, or pattern, will also be finished with engraving (*85*).

(4) Repoussé is a very ancient art, but it does not appear much in watches before the end of the seventeenth century. It is sometimes difficult to distinguish on the surface from casting, since both produce a moulded surface. But repoussé is executed in fairly thin, pliable sheet metal (almost invariably silver or gold), worked on by hammering it out from the back into the desired shape (*245*).

(5) Engine-turning, or guilloche, dates from about 1670 but is rarely found on watch-cases before 1780. It is done on an engine-turning lathe which can produce a variety of repeated patterns. 'Barley-corn' (*530*) is the most popular and usual form for watch-cases.

Enamel

Enamel is a glass composed of silica, red lead and potash. It is coloured with various metal oxides, but very occasionally it is used without colouring, when it is a transparent flux called 'fondant'.

Enamel may be hard or soft, according to its composition. Hard enamel retains its surface and colour indefinitely but can only be applied to metal with a high melting temperature. It cracks much more easily than soft enamel which, however, is more readily scratched.

Enamel decoration may take six forms:

(1) Plain enamel
(2) Painting in enamel
(3) Painting on enamel
(4) Basse-taille
(5) Champlevé
(6) Cloisonné

(1) is self-explanatory and is hardly ever found alone.

(2) Painting in enamels was developed during the sixteenth century after which it is seldom found. It was hardly applicable to curved surfaces, such as watch-cases. It is however found in its simplest form on watch-cases, which are some of the most beautiful enamelled cases in existence. In these, small blobs of enamel were deposited on the enamel base, in the form of a pattern, usually floral. After firing the blobs remain in relief. It is found on English watches as frequently as any, and perhaps the finest example is the watch by Edward East in the Victoria and Albert Museum, where a light blue ground is decorated with applied enamel flowers in white and pink. Another specimen is in the British Museum.

(3) The technique of painting on enamel was evolved in about 1630 by Jean Toutin, a French goldsmith (1578–1644). The painting is applied on a plain enamel ground. The colours are metal oxides with a little fondant to make them vitrifiable. After firing, the picture was covered with a layer of fondant and again fired.

Blois was the centre of enamel-painting throughout the seventeenth and eighteenth centuries after which it moved to Geneva. Early Blois masters who painted watch cases were Henri and Jean Toutin (sons of the original Jean) and Isaac Gribelin. Pierre Chartier and Christophe Marlière specialised in flower painting. The early painted enamel cases are of the greatest splendour as to design, technique, and colour (*3, 3a, 4, 4a*). Many of them are miniatures and the colours are very brilliant. After about 1650 the quality fell off noticeably and the colours used were less brilliant. The favourite subject then became fat women in négligé attire, closely observed by eager-looking old men or satyrs. The most renowned artists of this style are the Huaut family (*8, 8a*). The members of the family who painted watch-cases were Pierre, Jean and Amy. Pierre, the eldest, signed himself '*Huaut l'aisné*', '*P. Huaud primogenitus*', '*Pierre Huaud*' and '*Petrus Huaud major natus*'. Jean signed himself '*Huaud le puisné*' but mostly worked with Amy when they signed their work '*Les Deux frères Huaut les jeunes*' up to 1686. They then moved to Berlin after which they signed themselves simply '*les frères Huaud*'. In 1700 they settled in Geneva after which the signature might be '*Les frères Huaut*' or '*Peter et Amicus Huaut*' or '*Frères Huaut*'. It will be noticed that the terminal 'd' appears only in the German period. The Huauds' signatures have been retailed in some detail because they are so renowned. Many other competent artists specialised in watch-cases; but since enamelling is a quite separate subject, the watch-collector who wishes to specialise in it is recommended to study the standard works on the subject, rather than it should be dealt with superficially here. The Geneva school continued throughout the eighteenth century while the Blois school declined. Latterly the Swiss artists specialised in scenes of an intimate nature, delicately referred to in their accounts as 'salacious', whose verisimilitude was sometimes heightened by moving automata. That very high prices are paid for these need not be a matter of concern to the horological collector, as they are invariably found in pieces of no horological interest or quality.

(4) Basse-taille is perhaps the most elegant form of enamel decoration as applied to watch-cases. It consists of a coloured, transparent enamel on a chiselled or engine-turned gold ground. Examples over chiselling survive in very small numbers from before 1650, but basse-taille did not become fashionable until after 1780 and surviving examples are mostly Swiss (*158*).

(5) Champlevé is the commonest and earliest form of enamelling found in watches. It consists of cutting cells out of the metal and filling them with enamel (*94 & Colour A*).

Allied to champlevé enamel is the technique known as Niello, which is found, rarely, in early seventeenth-century cases. Here the cells, instead of being filled with enamel, are filled with an alloy of silver with lead and copper and various sulphides.

Champlevé chapter-rings are found even in sixteenth-century watches. It was a popular form of case-decoration during the seventeenth century. The cells may be so close together that the walls between them are so thin as to be hardly visible, in which case champlevé is quite difficult to distinguish from:

(6) Cloisonné in which the pattern to be followed is outlined in thin strips of metal, or 'cloisons', almost always gold, fixed to the metal ground, and filled in with enamel. The enamel is then ground down to the level of the cloisons and polished.

Watches decorated with precious and semi-precious stones cover such a wide field of the lapidary's art that to cover it comprehensively here would not be practicable. It is sufficient for the horologist to recognise the principal types.

The earliest and commonest form is the case of rock crystal. This consisted of two parts, one of which was hollowed out to take the movement; and the other formed a lid. Each was mounted in a narrow metal frame, or bezel, of which the two parts were hinged together (*112*). The crystal was decorated by faceting in a variety of ways. Very rarely, there was no metal frame, as in the case of a watch by Michael Nouwen (1582–1613) in the British Museum. In this type a simple hinge is riveted to the crystal body and lid (*94*). The crystal of this superlative watch is smoky in colour and the dial is decorated in red and green champlevé enamel. During the seventeenth century, the cases of small watches might be made of semi-precious stone or larger watches might have panels of cornelian and similar stones (*Colour B*). Lapidaries' work is seldom found during the eighteenth century, but during the early nineteenth century, Swiss watches in particular, were often decorated in brilliants or split pearls, usually in conjunction with basse-taille enamelling (*393*).

Styles of Watch-Cases and Dials up to 1750

Having thus covered the main forms of decoration as applied to watch-cases, and briefly described the techniques involved, they may now be considered in chronological sequence. This is important horologically up to 1650 in particular, as during this early period it is generally easier and safer to date a watch by the style and decoration of its case, than by its mechanism.

Cases other than plain metal are practically never found before 1600. It is known from records that cases were made in gold and silver, but none of these survives, and only brass-gilt cases are found. These cases may be cast, or made of soldered sheet-metal. The latter is obviously applicable to simple shapes, such as the plain, flat-sided drum; and engraving (and, to a limited extent, piercing) is the only form of decoration which can be applied to it.

The commonest use of sheet-metal was in the small drum-shaped clocks or large watches, already discussed, which usually have a pushed-on back and no cover to the dial (69). However, it is only by a slight stretching of the imagination that these can be regarded as watches at all, and nearly all other sixteenth-century watches had a hinged cover to protect the hand. It might be solid; or pierced so that the hand and numerals could be seen through it (82).

Since most watches were either clock-watches or alarums the case, as well as the lid, had to be pierced, to let the sound of the bell out; and these were usually cast. Apart from the very early French and German spherical watches (of which any modern collector is most unlikely to find an unknown specimen); and the very early, tall drum-shaped clocks or watches; the mid- and late-sixteenth-century watches had circular, flat-sided cases (82). The bell was fixed inside the case, and the movement fitted inside the bell, and was hinged to the case. Since the bell was a fixture, the movement had to be swung out of the case for winding (winding through the dial or drilling a hole through the bell, did not come until the second half of the seventeenth century). The dial-cover was also hinged to the case.

As has been said, the case and cover were cast and pierced and chiselled in quite high relief (82). As the century drew to an end the chiselling became less deep and engraving began to take its place (96). During the last quarter of the century, the cover began to take on a slightly domed contour, and the sides became curved, instead of flat in section (89). It is very rare for a sixteenth-century watch to be anything but circular, but in the last quarter, octagonal and elongated octagonal watches were occasionally made (90).

The dial was almost invariably engraved gilt-metal. An applied silver chapter ring is seldom if ever found before 1600. Bohemia, Italy and south-west Germany used a 24-hour day, and calibrated their dials accordingly (69). The first 12 hours were marked in Roman numerals, and prior to 1650 these are always so stubby that the IIII is wider than it is tall. From the very earliest times, IIII was used instead of IV. This was done for purely aesthetic reasons. The IIII is heavier in appearance than IV and is thus a better balance for its opposite number, the VIII. (The truth of this is seen in the rare late-seventeenth-century clocks with Roman striking. These chapter rings, necessarily using the IV, have a distinctly lop-sided appearance.) The second 12 hours were marked in Arabic numerals and of these, the 2 invariably appears as a Z (*69*). When English watches began to appear after 1600 they had a normal 2, but the Germans continued to use Z for another quarter-century.

The centre of the dial is usually decorated with a star-shaped pattern, of which the centre may be embellished with a little champlevé enamel.

So long as the watch had to be set to time by pushing round the actual hand, this was nearly always of iron or steel. It might be quite elegantly shaped and rounded, but it was always sufficiently robust to withstand direct handling. Despite their robustness, the early hands are seldom clumsy in appearance; and when they are, usually of unrelieved square section, it is almost certain that they are replacements. Practically the only exception to the iron hand is found in enamelled watches, when the hand is always gilt-metal.

Prior to the first appearance of pockets, about 1625, pendants are usually fixed, and pierced from front to back, and fitted with a loose-fitting ring-shaped pendant (*90*). This was therefore at right angles to the watch, indicating that the watch was worn suspended on a cord, round the neck.

Surviving watches of the sixteenth century are very rare, and the majority of them are already in museums. But after 1600 they become increasingly common, and are found in the greatest variety of shape and decoration. For the first three-quarters of the seventeenth century there was no significant technical advance in the watchmaking, and the timekeeping of watches continued to be of the most casual nature. Interest was therefore concentrated upon decoration, and it is during this period that the greatest variety of high-quality decoration is found, both in the cases of watches, and in the movements. So far as the decoration of movements is concerned, this has already been dealt with in the mechanical section.

In casework, the most curious development during the first half of the seventeenth century was that of the 'pair-case'.

As soon as watches began to have expensive and delicate cases it became a sensible precaution to provide them with a protective outer case for use when travelling or when not in use. At first these were made of stiffened leather, with its outer side sometimes decoratively tooled.

As time went on, it apparently became usual to wear the outer case. This practice probably started with the introduction of pockets, but by the middle of the century, outer cases are found increasingly which are definitely part of the watch and meant to be worn with it. For this purpose, the dial side is open and the back of the case becomes increasingly decorated, generally with a pattern of silver or gold pinwork (*146*). Thus, the emphasis moved from the decorated inner case, to its protective outer, so that by 1670, especially in English watches, the inner case had generally become completely plain and it was the outer case that was completely decorated. Sometimes this decoration was of such a delicate nature as to need a third case to protect it, thus turning full circle. In the ordinary watch such as most people owned, from 1680 onwards, both inner and outer case were perfectly plain, the outer serving merely to prevent dirt entering the winding hole in the inner case; and to make the watch a good deal thicker than it need have been. The French rarely used this illogical arrangement, preferring a single case which was wound through the dial (*229*).

This trend was therefore one which was continuous during the whole of the seventeenth century, but other fashions came and went more quickly. A very early appearance after 1600 (or possibly just before) was the 'form' watch, made in a number of irrelevant shapes such as those of books, skulls, dogs, birds, crosses, flower-buds and the like (*99*). Particularly popular were forms in the *memento mori* class, such as the skull, and the cross. The skull was hinged at the jaw to open and reveal the dial. With such trivialities did early seventeenth-century watchmakers amuse themselves, and keep their customers' minds off the lamentable performance of their watches. It must be said, however, that British makers did not go in much for these frivolities, but concentrated on trying to make their watches keep time; for which they were rewarded in the last quarter of the century by finding themselves in a position of unassailed supremacy.

The traditional sixteenth-century round, octagonal, and increasingly, oval, watches were made throughout the first quarter of the seventeenth century. Flat-section sides continued, but the rounded section became increasingly popular. In British watches, particularly, this trend eventually developed into an almost unbroken, oval egg-shaped watch, quite devoid of decoration.

Brass-gilt remains the most usual metal, at any rate in surviving watches, but silver survives increasingly, and gold very occasionally, although at first only in conjunction with enamel decoration.

French watches employed increasingly the elongated oval or octagonal shape, and Swiss watches begin to appear, closely following the French style.

After the third quarter of the century, German watches become rare owing to the disastrous impact of the Thirty Years' War and thereafter, surviving German watches become relatively rare and unimportant, although there is a surprisingly large number of fine German hexagonal table clocks from about 1660 onwards; a highly decorative and functional instrument that never caught on much in other countries.

For plain metal cases after 1600, engraving fairly rapidly ousted chiselling; no doubt as watches became more widespread as items of normal attire, and so were required to be smaller and lighter. Engraved landscape scenes containing figures and animals are more usual than hitherto, and generally fill the space inside the chapter ring; unless the watch is an alarum, when the setting dial may be decorative, in the form of pierced gilt metal over blued steel; or pierced silver over gilt (*152*). The applied silver chapter ring becomes usual as the 24-hour dial tends to disappear.

Mechanical complications, in the form of astronomical movements and calendar-work, become fashionable for more luxurious watches after 1600, and this brought in a fashion for multiple subsidiary dials (*147*). One of these might be what amounts to a minute hand, especially in quarter-striking watches, when it was easy to fix a hand to the quarter-striking wheel, which revolves once an hour. However, the dial is not marked in minutes, but only in quarters. True minute hands are seldom found before 1680. But the fashion for multiple dials continued until after 1680 after which, like so many seventeenth century watch fashions, it was revived in the early nineteenth century.

During the first quarter of the seventeenth century enamelling is pretty well confined to champlevé decoration (occasionally also champlevé niello), but either side of the middle of the century saw the very finest period of enamel-painting. This was short-lived, and after 20 or 30 years there was a marked deterioration in taste in the form already described. The enamel cases are single, painted inside and out.

Glass covers over the dials appeared during the second quarter of the century. The first move in this direction was a round window of rock crystal, held to the case cover by tabs, but plain glass appeared soon after, held by either tabs or split bezels (*122, 147*). It is, however, difficult to say with certainty that an ostensibly early glass has not been added at a later date. When the cover is engraved it is often quite clear that this has happened.

At about the middle of the century developed the completely plain, almost egg-shaped British watch, already mentioned, and now generally known as a 'Puritan watch'. These are almost always of silver (only one gold case is known, in the Ashmolean Museum, Oxford). The dial cover always has a round glass window and the dial is also plain, usually with an applied silver chapter ring and fairly plain, but elegantly shaped steel hand, with a tail. The only decoration is on the plate of the movement, although the dial may sometimes be engraved (*144*).

These egg-shaped puritan watches are quite different from the so-called 'Nuremburg Egg'. This meaningless term used to be loosely applied to any big old watch, pretty well regardless of its shape. The term is never met with before the eighteenth century and is now happily quite discontinued, except among the most ignorant.

During the third quarter of the century tastes sobered down and the watch assumed increasingly the form it was going to retain for the next hundred years. A few form watches were still made, and enamel-painting continued in profusion although in deteriorating taste. The pair case became usual for British watches, the outer case being either plain, or covered in shagreen or fish-skin, with patterns of silver or gold pins (*206, 149, 171, 194, 269*).

The matt-surface silver or gold dial began to appear, and the figures of the chapter ring rapidly grew in length; by 1675 to such an extent that very little room indeed was left for the hand in the centre (*170*).

Hands in general became simpler; sometimes a perfectly plain pointer. They continued to have tails, although not such long ones as previously, and it is quite common to find no tail at all.

The pendant-hole gradually changes from its old back-to-front position, to one where the pendant ring is parallel with the watch (*144*). This no doubt followed the introduction by Charles II into England of waistcoats and waistcoat pockets.

The case-piercing of alarums and clock-watches became increasingly floral in pattern and attained a very high standard of design and engraving. Watch glasses became universal and the snap-in bezel began to appear by about 1660, although the split variety may be found almost until the end of the century.

In French watches especially, a perfectly plain white enamel dial, with plain black roman numerals, is very occasionally found (*176*).

The commercial application of the balance-spring to watches from 1675 brought about a rapid change in decorative styles. As watches suddenly became capable of sensible timekeeping, the emphasis moved rapidly from exterior decoration to mechanical superiority. From now on for the next 100 years, by far the commonest form of British watch has a paircase completely devoid of decoration. Before 1675, the finest decorative cases contained the finest movements, but by soon after 1680, the finest movements usually have the plainest cases, and by after about 1750 it is almost certain that an extravagant case will have an inferior movement, or at best, one of no horological interest.

During the third quarter of the century, watches had become surprisingly slim; especially the enamelled cases; but as soon as the emphasis shifted to good timekeeping they plumped up wonderfully; the French watches particularly so, to the extent that they rapidly earned for themselves the name of '*oignons*'—and indeed, they have the almost spherical shape of a large onion. By far the most common form of French case after 1680 is a plain, single case of brass-gilt, decorated all over in an arabesque pattern. This might be formed by chiselling, or possibly in some cases by casting, simply cleaned up with a chisel. There is rarely any engraving and indeed, at this time engraving almost disappeared as a form of watch decoration.

The usual French dial was of brass-gilt, decorated similarly to the case, with the hour numerals on separate enamel plaques stuck on to the dial. Sometimes there is a narrow enamel ring inside the hour plaques, with hours and half hours marked on it (*253*). Minute hands were unusual and did not become at all universal until well after 1700. When there is a minute hand, there is sometimes another, outer enamel chapter ring for minutes. The hand or hands long continued to be moved by hand, and even after 1700 they may be found without motion work, so that the two hands are not positively geared together, but have to be set separately. Winding is through a hole in the dial plate; occasionally through the centre of the hand.

However, some French watches had silver dials with a champlevé chapter ring, not unlike the British, and as already stated, a very few had plain white enamel dials.

Hands might be of steel, but equally often of brass-gilt, usually pierced, of rather clumsy design.

In fact, although French watches of the just-post-balance-spring period are by no means devoid of a certain robust charm, they are manifestly inferior, certainly in accuracy of performance, to their British rivals.

There ought to be some very fine Dutch watches of this period, but for some reason very few seem to have survived, and such as have either follow French styles, or British, to the extent of claiming British authorship. Tompion and Quare being great favourites for this purpose.

But without question, the outstanding watches between 1675 and 1750 were British.

74

As has been said, the finest watches have the plainest cases. Gold watches are hallmarked and were of 22 carat gold. Silver cases were seldom hallmarked before 1740. Case-makers stamped their initials, so these should be identical on inner and outer cases. Watchmakers also took to numbering their products and the watch number was usually repeated on the cases.

Repoussé began to appear as a decoration, but before about 1715 it is usually confined to such simple forms as radial fluting. Repoussé figures and scenes hardly appear before 1715 and rarely before 1725. The great period of repoussé was 1725 to 1750 (*245*) after which it again declined in favour, until by 1770 it is rarely found. At its most exuberant the repoussé became so deep that it could not be worked out of one sheet, but a second sheet had to be worked and then soldered to the main case (*261*). Some of the finest repoussé cases are signed by the embosser.

A new metal used for watch cases was 'pinchbeck', so-called after its inventor, Christopher Pinchbeck. It is an amalgam of three parts of zinc to four of copper, but the secret was jealously guarded from the time of its invention, about 1720, throughout most of the eighteenth century. It was described as 'so naturally resembling gold, as not to be distinguished by the most experienced eye, in colour, smell and ductibility'.

Pinwork leather and tortoise-shell cases continue, but the tortoise-shell may also be decorated with an inlaid pattern of very thin silver or gold strips (*213*). The shape of these is cut out of the shell which is then heated and the strips pressed in while still hot. This decoration may take the form of an arabesque, or sometimes a scene in the new Chinese taste (*201*).

Outer cases were also covered in shagreen. Real shagreen is the skin of a shark, but in commercial form it consisted of the skin of a horse or donkey, treated by pressing hard, round seeds into it until the skin is perfectly dry. It is then rubbed down to a smooth surface, polished, and stained green (*206*).

Otherwise, apart from a few enamel cases, any other form of decoration was quite unusual from the century from 1675 to 1775.

Pendants continued to be loose-fitting rings until about 1690, and sometimes after 1700 (*223*), but soon after 1690 a hinged, stirrup-shaped pattern became almost universal (*198*). The hinges of the outer cases underwent a change at about the same time. The earlier ones are square-ended (*204*), but by about 1690–1700 the ends became curved to merge less sharply into the rim of the case (*197*).

Some Unusual Forms of Dial

Dials became standardised by 1700, after a most interesting formative quarter century, almost wholly confined to British watches. This arose from an uncertainty as to how best to indicate minutes as well as hours, now that the new standards of accurate performance rendered this information of practical value.

Although the concentric hour and minute hands had appeared by 1680 their acceptance was by no means universal, and four other principal variants were tried out, admittedly not in very large numbers; which makes them a considerable prize for any collector, especially as all of them are highly decorative. The four variants are:

(1) the six-hour dial (*204*)
(2) the wandering hour dial (*255*)
(3) the differential dial (*237, 252*)
(4) the sun-and-moon dial (*219*)

The first three seek to tell hours and minutes with a single indicator, each in a most ingenious way.

(1) In the six-hour dial, a single, centre-pivoted hand rotates once in six hours. The dial is divided from I to VI in Roman numerals. Therefore, starting at twelve o'clock, the hand has performed a complete circle by six. Super-imposed over the Roman numerals are a set of smaller Arabic numerals from 7 to 12. So from 7 to 12 the owner must read the Arabic numerals. Owing to there being only six hours, instead of twelve, to the full circle, the space between each pair is twice as large as on an ordinary dial. This gives enough room for a minute-ring round the edge of the dial with two-minute divisions. Also, between the hour and minute rings is another circle divided into quarters and half-quarters. The time can therefore be read with considerable accuracy, although not without a good deal of practice for a modern owner, since none of the divisions appear in their accustomed positions. He must also decide whether he is in the 'Roman' or 'Arabic' sector.

(2) The 'wandering hour' achieves its objective rather more effectively. An annular slit extending through half a circle appears in the upper half of the dial. Round its outer edge, on the dial plate, are numbers 0–60, usually in five-minute intervals, and minute graduations. Under the dial-plate is another, rotating plate, the full diameter of the dial, usually engraved and gilt as to the visible part. Two holes, the size of the annular slit, are cut out of the rotating plate, exactly opposite to each other. Pivoted to

the rotating plate are two smaller rotating plates, one carrying the odd numerals from I to XI and the other the even numerals II to XII. These numerals appear each through one of two circles. By means of a detent, the numbered plates are advanced once an hour. Thus, at one o'clock, the figure I will appear through the hole in the large rotating plate opposite the O of the minute markings. XII will be visible at 60 through the other hole. The I and its hole then advance round the slot, the XII almost immediately disappearing from view, under the fixed dial-plate. As it advances, the I will successively pass all the minutes of an hour, so that the hours and minutes are simultaneously visible at any moment. When I comes to the end of its journey the other hour plate will have advanced and will appear again as II, opposite O.

A peculiarity of the wandering hour watches is that nearly, if not quite all, surviving English specimens have a royal attribution, such as a royal portrait (James II, Mary, or Anne; no Charles II is known to the authors) on the dial; or the royal arms engraved on the cock; or both. Also a considerable majority have a fluted repoussé outer case, which is rare at this time.

These distinctions have never been explained, and are additionally mysterious since several makers produced the type, not all of whom held a royal appointment. As one surviving example has the portrait of Queen Anne it is evident that what is, after all, a very sensible arrangement, continued in production well after the turn of the century.

(3) The differential hour arrangement is very rare indeed. An ordinary minute hand goes round once an hour. The centre of the dial is occupied by a revolving disk with the hours from I to XII numbered on it in the ordinary way. This is geared to rotate $\frac{13}{12}$ of a full circle in an hour. Thus, the current hour is always immediately under the minute hand.

(4) The sun and moon indicator is not quite such a serious affair as the rest. A minute hand revolves once an hour and is concerned with the minutes only. A semi-circular hole is cut out of the upper half of the dial plate, numbered VI to XII, and then I to VI, round its outer edge. Visible under the hole is a disk which rotates once in 24 hours. One half is decorated with the moon and the other with the sun. The sun first appears at VI and moves round the twelve hours and eventually sets again at the opposite VI, at which time the moon appears at the left-hand VI and moves in turn across the visible area. Apart from the questionable utility of distinguishing (within broad limits) between night and day, the arrangement is more decorative than useful; but decorative it certainly is, the moon and stars usually being silver against a blued ground, while the

sun and his rays are gilt on a silver ground. It is a troublesome dial by which to tell the time.

In addition to the above, there were some 'false pendulum' watches. These have an eccentric chapter ring, and what appears to be a pendulum (but is really a disk attached to the balance-wheel) swings through an aperture in the lower half of the dial. As the significance of this arrangement is mechanical, it will be found discussed in the mechanical part of the book (*218*).

Apart from these elegant flights of fancy, the modern arrangement of two concentric hands quickly came into general use, and fairly soon with motion-work under the dial (by which they are positively geared together. To set to time, it is then only necessary to apply a key to the square on the end of the minute hand arbor, and on turning it both hands will move progressively). Even seconds dials, in the ordinary modern position, are occasionally found from an early date (*208*). The hands are either of the 'beetle and poker' variety (from a fancied resemblance of the hour hand to a beetle and the minute hand to a poker) (*188*), or else, the hour hand may be of the more elegant 'tulip' pattern (*208*). The 'tulip' did not survive long after 1715, but the beetle and poker went on until after 1800.

Dials were silver or gold, with a matt ground, and champlevé hour and minute numerals. The maker's name appears on a polished cartouche in the centre part of the dial (*235*).

Enamel dials appear on English watches very occasionally, very early in the eighteenth century or possibly even earlier; but they are not at all common before about 1725, at which time Graham adopted them as standard (*268*). They exactly follow the layout of the metal dials, but in Graham's and, later, Mudge's extremely elegant cylinder watches, they are further embellished by a polished steel, sweep-centre-second hand.

Styles of Watch-Cases and Dials 1750 - 1830

After Graham introduced the cylinder escapement about 1725, the century became one of stagnation almost as complete as the century before, until the last quarter, which again was a time of tremendous activity in the development of the true precision watch.

This stagnation is reflected in watch-cases and dials which continue the old fashions in an increasingly perfunctory sort of way. This applies both to Continental and British watches.

Once the balance-spring had been fully mastered and its improved timekeeping taken as a matter of course, watches once again became smaller and thinner, although the British makers would never go so far as the Continent in this direction, which contributed to their eventual downfall.

Enamelling continued, occasionally of high quality, especially when heraldic. But it was usually confined to a framed panel in the back of the watch (277). Such enamelled, or highly repoussé watches, sometimes had an additional outer case, with the back glazed, through which the repoussé or enamel was visible (261).

Dials remained with little alteration, but the old concentric circles gradually disappeared; and as people increasingly read the time at a glance, without having to look at the numerals, the minute numerals almost completely disappeared by about the turn of the century (374).

Engine turning began to appear quite generally from about 1790, probably owing to Breguet's influence, and this led to a wide use of basse-taille enamelling, in superb translucent red and blue enamels over an engine turned gold base. It sometimes appears in conjunction with a small central painting on enamel; either heraldic or a miniature; and it may be further embellished with diamonds or split pearls (356, 383, 393).

As the new school of precision makers (predominantly Arnold and Emery in England and Breguet in France) put a new life into watchmaking, so did they instil a new look to the visual parts. As at the birth of the balance-spring, so again an elegant severity became the keynote. In England, Arnold's early dials and hands have an almost brutally functional quality. But they have so much character that they make a strong aesthetic appeal despite their lack of superficial elegance (*322*). For his new lever escapement watches, from about 1784, Emery used a form of dial copied from the 'regulator' clock, in which only the minute hand sweeps the whole dial, with subsidiary dials at 12 and 6 o'clock for hours and seconds (*339*). These, with Emery's special form of spade-ended hands, have an elegance seldom if ever surpassed, and were much copied in precision watches for the next 40 years. Both Arnold and Emery, and some of the other early precision makers, used the 'consular' case, in which the front bezel and back cover meet on the centre line of the watch, so that no body is visible at all (*322*).

In common watches, the pair case remained current in England until the extreme end of the nineteenth century. Enamel dials had painted centres, often of some topical scene relevant to the owner, such as ploughing, or a railway train. These honest, unassuming, ungaudy watches, have an endearing quality quite their own (*535*).

In the semi-precision class of watch, generally with a cylinder or duplex escapement, a heavily handsome form of dial became fashionable in England from soon after 1800. This consisted of a perfectly plain matt gold dial with highly polished gold numerals, either Arabic or Roman, applied on to it. At their most elegant, these dials had serpentine, or wavy hands, either of gold or blued steel (*412, 516*). The cases were plain or engine-turned.

With the increasingly florid tastes of the time in England, the last type of watch later developed a heavy, cast and engraved case, with a heavily encrusted body (*443*). The matt dial had applied decorations and figures in four-coloured gold (*477*). These watches, which may be found roughly through the 'twenties and 'thirties, have a ponderously handsome quality, allied to superb workmanship, which is by no means without appeal.

On the Continent, tastes generally were as uncertain as in England, with the exception of the basse-taille enamelling already mentioned. Painted enamel dials of poor quality became usual, but they can have a certain charm when allied to simple automata, such as a revolving windmill. Automata movements were often coupled with repeater mechanism, whereby a figure on the dial strikes a bell in time with the strokes of the repeater (*7*). Sometimes these watches have a slide which, when moved aside, reveals some rather less innocent occupation being energetically prosecuted.

Cheap watches, especially Swiss, sometimes have a case of transparent horn, pleasingly painted on the inside with a delicate pattern of flowers or ferns.

Better quality Swiss watches are sometimes of an alarming thinness, not surpassed at any subsequent time (*506*).

Form-watches also came back into fashion in Switzerland soon after 1800, and have remained so, in varying popularity, ever since. Most of them are no sillier than their seventeenth-century predecessors (*Colour K*).

Breguet's Watch-Cases and Dials

But the great influence on the appearance of continental watches was Abraham-Louis Breguet (1747–1823) who set up on his own account in about 1782; and at once established an entirely new conception of restrained elegance achieved through the perfect proportioning of every part, and a strict regard for functional treatment.

Breguet used three sorts of case. Perhaps the most elegant was also the cheapest, used especially for his '*souscription*' watches. This had a flat-sided body, and plain rim bezels (*429*). The glass snapped into that at the front, and the almost-flat back snapped into the back bezel. In the *souscription* watch, the body and back is usually silver (either plain or engine-turned) and the bezels and pendant-ring gold.

For his 'fashionable' watches, often very thin, Breguet used a fairly ordinary case, with a narrow, rounded body and curved bezels. These cases are almost invariably engine-turned (*490*). The most enamelling Breguet would countenance was a small heraldic cartouche in the centre of the back covered with transparent enamel. It seems that only in his 'montres à tact', and in his considerable output for the Turkish market, would he consent to put a movement of his into an enamelled case (*387*). Nevertheless, not every enamelled watch signed '*Breguet*' is necessarily a complete fake, as is usually supposed. It is known that Breguet put his name on a lot of watches that he had not made, quite apart from the '*Etablissement mixte*' where he merely did the finishing and usually made the escapement. The trade-bought watches did not go through the books, so that there is no record of the extent of this side of his business.

For his self-winding, or 'perpetuelle' watches, and his highest quality of time-keepers, such as the tourbillons, where thickness was no objection, Breguet used very wide bezels, which met along the centre-line of the watch, so that no body was visible at all (*354, 403*). These watches might either be almost flat-sided (as in the case of the earlier perpetuelles) or curved. This form of case is known as the 'consular' case and really stems from the earlier French 'oignon'.

81

Like most late Continental makers, Breguet used a gold with a fairly high copper content, to give it a markedly reddish colour.

Inside the back cover, there should be stamped a capital B, the number of the watch and the number of the case. The French equivalent to English hallmarks are complicated to interpret and only approximate as to date.

Breguet's dials may be of enamel, gold, or silver. It is believed that the metal dials were first introduced in about 1805, but the presence of a metal dial does not preclude an earlier date, since the enamel dials were subject to damage and may therefore have been replaced by metal ones. The enamel dials have a grainless surface and almost invariably the hour numerals are in sloping arabic figures (*429*). Roman numerals on an enamel dial are exceedingly rare in Breguet's lifetime and for several years afterwards, and therefore to be regarded with suspicion. The signature is usually below the minute ring at 6 o'clock, in capital letters; either *'Breguet'* or *'Breguet et fils'*. The latter does not appear before about 1807, but not invariably even then, while its appearance need not preclude an earlier date if the watch has been redialled. *'Breguet et fils'* is not therefore much help in dating a watch. In early watches the signature on the dial is sometimes in a flowing script not unlike the signature on the cuvette (*330*). But in general such a signature may be regarded with slight suspicion. It was probably used a good deal by Louis Desoutter in the present century, who had very skilled workmen of all kinds, necessary for the restoration of Breguet watches, including dial-making.

The seconds dial is painted on the enamel. The later practice of cutting a hole out of the dial and mounting a separate seconds dial beneath, and showing through it, with the seconds hand turning in the shallow well so formed, did not become current in Breguet's life-time. However, he did very occasionally grind a well out of the dial, leaving a surprisingly rough finish to the operation (*328*). The seconds dial on a Breguet watch may appear at any point on the dial; symmetry of this kind had no compelling interest for him. Enamel dials are always secured to the watch by a single screw, usually below the 12.

Breguet's hands are of a quite standard pattern shown clearly in many of the illustrations. They are known as 'Breguet' hands, or sometimes as 'moon' hands. On enamel and gold dials they are always of blued steel but on silver dials they are frequently of gold.

Metal dials are signed in the same way as the enamel ones. The chapter ring is smooth and has Roman numerals. The centre has a plain, fine form of engine turning.

The seconds dial, when present, is always sunk, and backed with a separate small plate (*400, 403*).

Soon after Breguet returned to Paris after the Revolution in 1795 he found that his name was being pirated by a number of other inferior makers, and he therefore devised the famous 'secret signature' to protect his good name, and intending purchasers of his watches. This was produced by a diamond-pointed pantograph and consists of the word 'Breguet' and usually the number of the watch, in a sloping cursive signature (*395, 431*). The word Breguet is about $\frac{1}{8}''$ long and $\frac{1}{32}''$ high (the B slightly more). On an enamel dial the signature will be found below the 12 and above the fixing screw. It may sometimes be so shallow and faint as only to be visible in a strong cross light. On metal dials the signature (not always accompanied by the number) appears twice, on the chapter ring, between XI and XII, and XII and I. The secret signature has occasionally been reproduced, and Desoutter could certainly make it, although not so as to deceive an experienced observer. However, the presence of a secret signature is a pretty sure proof of authenticity, though its absence is no proof of the reverse. Breguet did not always apply it, while it is very rarely found on silver dials. These tarnish in the course of time so that the chapter ring has to be stoned, and in the course of this operation the delicate secret signature has almost inevitably disappeared.

The restoration of silver dials presents special problems. Originally they had a whitish, mat surface, but in course of cleaning this generally takes on a certain amount of polish, which is not at all authentic and detracts from their appearance. Various 'trade secrets' exist which are more or less successful in recovering the original mat surface; but where the dial has been deeply scratched, as is so often the case, little can be done about it.

Breguet's ordinary watches set a standard of thinness, elegance, simplicity, robustness and good timekeeping that make them sought all over Europe, including Russia. His tourbillons, his perpetuelles, his complicated, and his very thin watches; and the endless variety of his mechanisms and escapements make him unquestionably the greatest watchmaker of all time.

PLATE II

11 Breguet. No. 5. Paris, France. 1787. Lever escapement. Four-arm balance with two bimetallic affixes. Helical spring with end-curves. Screw-operated regulator at edge of dial. Pedometer winding by platinum weight. Two going barrels. Dumb repeater. Silver engine-turned dial with subsidiary dials for seconds, up-and-down, and moon phases. Blued steel hands. Engine-turned gold case with Breguet-type plunger for repeating. This watch is one of the series of 30 watches described by Breguet as 'perpetuelles' and with which his surviving books commence in 1787

12 Alexander Hare, London, England. *c.* 1780. Verge escapement. Fusee. White enamel dial. Gold hands. Gold pair case, the outer decorated with a garland of translucent enamel over engine turning with central painted cartouche

3a Solomon Plaivas. *c.* 1640. See fig. 3

13 P. Gregson, Geneva and Paris. *c.* 1795. Virgule escapement. Going barrel. White enamel dial. Gold hands. Gold case with translucent enamel over engine turning

4a Auguste Bretonneau. *c.* 1640. See fig. 4

14 J. Mellie, Châtellerault, France. *c.* 1620. Verge escapement without balance-spring. Fusee with ratchet set-up regulator. Gold dial with champlevé enamel floral decoration. Single gilt hand. Gold case with champlevé translucent enamel floral decoration. Outer case of black leather with gold pinwork, possibly of later date

15 Ellicott astronomical. See fig. 262

16 Allman and Mangaar. No. 354. London, England. *c.* 1765. Verge escapement. White enamel dial. Hands not original. Pair case, the outer of Bilston enamel. The use of English enamel for watch cases was extremely rare

17 Frodsham, London. 1914. Lever escapement. Compensation balance. Going barrel. Keyless wind. Silver engine-turned dial with gold cartouche for signature and gold seconds ring. Blued steel hands. Engine-turned gold case. A late example of high quality English work in the style of Breguet

18 Simpton, London. See fig. 260

8a Johannes Van Ceulen, *c.* 1670. See fig. 8

19 Probably by Ilbury, London, England. *c.* 1800. Chinese Duplex escapement. Going barrel. The movement of Lepine calibre decorated over all with floral patterns in three-colour gold. Gold case with painted floral decoration, the pendant and borders inset with pearls. (For dial see dust jacket (F). For movement see fig. 418)

11	4a	17
12	14	18
3a	15	8a
13	16	19

2 Performance of Early Watches

Performance of Early Watches

There is not a great deal of contemporary evidence as to the performance of early watches when they were new, although all the figures survive of the trials of the earliest marine timekeepers. Thus, we know that in the trial of Harrison's No. 5 by George III its total error on mean time during a trial of 10 weeks was only $4\frac{1}{2}$ seconds. Mudge's first timekeeper was tested at Greenwich for 29 weeks from April to October, 1777, during which time the difference between the greatest and least daily rate was only 1·62 seconds, and the vast majority of days come within one second's variation. As against these, the performance of two of John Arnold's early pocket chronometers shows up favourably. No. 36 was tested at Greenwich over 13 months, in 1779–80, during the whole of which time it was worn in the pocket. Its total error amounted only to 2 minutes 33 seconds, and its daily rate never varied by more than 3 seconds on two consecutive days. Its position errors, too, were remarkably small. In the normal positions in which a watch operates, between IX, XII and III-up, and horizontal, dial up, its daily rate varied only 1·43 seconds. If the never-used positions of VI-up and horizontal dial down were added the error went up to 3·5 seconds. This watch had Arnold's 's-shaped' balance and pivoted detent escapement.

Another watch of Arnold's, No. $\frac{21}{68}$, made in 1780, was tested by Mr. Everard of Lynn pretty regularly between 1785 and 1790, and during the whole $4\frac{1}{2}$ years its fastest daily rate was +2·7 seconds and its slowest −2·5 seconds. This watch forms part of the Ilbert Collection and also has an 's-shaped' balance. It originally had a pivoted detent but now has a spring detent. This conversion may well have been carried out by Arnold before the Everard trials.

Some of Earnshaw's early watches also put up fine performances, but over long periods they tended to suffer from the inferiority of his balance springs.

Against this background it is interesting to see how a number of old watches have performed in daily wear when between 150 and 250 years old. At this age a good deal of wear has inevitably taken place and this shows up particularly in position errors. Therefore it is not fair to test old watches in positions, and in all the tests they were restricted to the positions likely to be gone through in the pocket. Compensated watches are likely to show up relatively worse than others, since their delicate compensation balances are sure to have suffered some violence during their life, and in no case were they subjected to fine readjustment equivalent to the adjustments certainly carried out by their makers before they were first sold.

The oldest watch tested was a verge by Quare, No. 4465, hallmarked for 1713. In the course of one month the difference between the greatest and least daily rate was two minutes, and if the five worst days were excluded, it ran within one minute. This performance is not exceptional and disproves the widely-held belief that early verges are hopelessly bad timekeepers. Curiously enough, no nineteenth-century verge tested has approached the above performance. For some reason, too, verges are surprisingly little affected by temperature changes, especially the early ones with short, untempered springs. A watch by Andrew Dunlop of about 1710 was tested fairly continuously over a year, and the average midsummer and midwinter daily rates varied only by half a minute.

Next in date was a cylinder watch by Mudge & Dutton, No. 580, hallmarked for 1762. The duration of the test was again one month during which the difference between the greatest and least daily rate was $1\frac{1}{2}$ minutes. If the five worst days were excluded it ran, like the Quare, within one minute. This performance is not exceptional, one way or the other, and both the Quare and the Mudge & Dutton were in as good condition as could be hoped for considering their age, not much inferior to new. It bears out how little superior the typical English mid-eighteenth-century cylinder escapement was to a verge of 1700.

Arnold's pivoted detent No. $\frac{17}{67}$, with 's-shaped' balance, probably dates from 1781 (it has been re-cased so that it cannot be dated by its hallmark). It was tested for three weeks during January and subsequently for a fortnight in a very hot June. During the June test the greatest variation in daily rate was six seconds, but excluding one exceptionally hot day it was only four seconds. During the January test the greatest variation was as much as 16 seconds. Taking January and June together the greatest difference between daily rates was still only 16 seconds. It is noteworthy that the June test came after the January one, when it had only recently been restored after coming over from America where it had been grossly abused, and it is the experience of the authors that where compensation balances have been mis-handled, or even not used for a long period, they take quite a long time to settle down again. The June run may therefore be regarded as more typical and matches up reasonably with the original performances of Nos. 36 and 68, allowing for the passage of 180 years.

Twenty years on bring us to John Roger Arnold's spring detent chronometer No. 1869, made in 1802. But this showed disappointingly little improvement, the greatest difference in daily rate over a month's trial being 13 seconds. But after further adjustment, over a subsequent fortnight, this came down to five seconds. On yet a further test, not worn, the difference came down to $2\frac{1}{2}$ seconds a day.

A 1799 Earnshaw pocket chronometer which once belonged to Neville Maskelyne, and is in good condition, was able to be tested for only a fortnight, during which time its maximum variation in daily rate was 8 seconds.

Urban Jürgensen's pocket chronometer No. $\frac{24}{58}$, dating probably from 1813, had a greatest variation in daily wear of eight seconds over a month, and in a further three weeks, not worn, the greatest variation was only four seconds.

Breguet was represented by two specimens. A souscription in fine condition, tested over a long period, showed maximum daily variations up to one minute, and the difference between the average winter and summer rates was 45 seconds per day faster in the summer, showing that the compensation curb was acting too strongly. Despite its single hand a Breguet souscription watch can be read accurately to within 15 seconds and despite these not very remarkable figures, its average performance over a long period of wear is always found to be a good deal better, and well up to the requirements of modern life.

At the other end of the Breguet scale is the four-minute tourbillon No. 1890, with 'echappement naturel', made in 1807, which may be regarded as Breguet's last word in pocket timekeeping. This has been repeatedly tested, and in daily wear regularly shows a maximum variation in daily rate of five seconds, but generally very much closer, seldom exceeding two seconds. Over one period of three weeks during which it was not worn, its daily rate never varied by so much as one second. However, even this performance was exceeded by one of Breguet's ordinary lever-escapement tourbillons, No. 2572, which was tested in daily wear for a month, during which time the difference between the slowest and fastest daily rates was only three seconds.

Eighteenth-century English levers have been disappointing on the whole, doubtless owing to their lack of draw, but an Emery lever tested in May kept within seven seconds a day. When again tested in August it ran within five seconds a day. The difference between the May and August average was 12 seconds a day faster in August.

The best modern results to be obtained from any watch known to the authors were achieved by a Barraud pocket chronometer, No. 183, hallmarked for 1797, and owned by Cedric Jagger. This was John Arnold's type of escapement and balance, and over a period of 302 days, with one or two unavoidable gaps, it was timed on 211 days. Of these, 55 days showed no variation; 92 days showed plus or minus one second; 64 days showed plus or minus two seconds. The above excludes two periods of two or three days when the instrument appeared to become deranged and then settled down again; a malady not unknown even in the best regulator clocks. It thus is about the equal of the Breguet tourbillon No. 1890, but the tests are more conclusive for having been carried out over such a long period.

3 Technical

Technical

The counting of the hours has been of interest since men found the need for regulating their affairs. The advent of the first mechanical means of achieving this started an almost continuous exercise in the development of an improved mechanical timekeeper and to this day the process continues and will always continue. The difficulty of indicating exact seconds inspired many talented men to devote their lives to the development of a mechanism to control exactly the energy of the prime mover.

The prime mover of the watch is its mainspring. It is well known that the torque of the spring varies directly as the angle of winding and, conversely, proportionately, diminishes as it unwinds.

The verge escapement is particularly affected by variation in power and the first developments in timekeeping were directed towards smoothing out the power of the mainspring. One method, employed by early German makers, was the Stackfreed. This device is extremely crude and cannot have had very much, if any, improving effect on the rate. In brief it consists of a cam geared to the arbor of the mainspring, so as to turn once in the going period of the watch. Pressing against the cam is a roller mounted on a strong spring fixed to the plate. The contour of the cam is such that when fully wound the stackfreed spring works against the mainspring and so slows the watch; while towards the end of the run it assists the mainspring and so hurries things along.

The earliest watches had unprotected springs hooked to a pillar between the plates at the outer end and to the great wheel arbor at the inner end. The great wheel was mounted freely on the arbor and the power transmitted to the wheel by a pall and ratchet. Turning the arbor wound the spring and stopped the train in the process. To protect the spring, or more probably to protect the movement in the event of breakage of the spring, it was enclosed in a barrel or pierced cage screwed to the plate. This is known as a 'resting barrel'.

It is not known who invented the fusee, but its use spread rapidly for it gave the watchmaker a sound and practical method of controlling the power of the mainspring. It is used in conjunction with a barrel mounted freely on an arbor locked to the plate. The outer end of the spring is attached to the barrel and the inner end to the arbor. Wound round the barrel is a cord the free end of which is attached to a spirally grooved pulley of constantly decreasing diameter fixed to an arbor running in the plates. Freely mounted on the arbor is the great wheel and the power is transmitted to the wheel by means of a pall and ratchet. Turning the fusee arbor winds the cord from the barrel on to the spiral pulley and in so doing winds the mainspring so that the increasing power is matched by the decreasing diameter of the pulley. By careful shaping of the fusee curve it was possible to make a reasonable approximation to uniformity of torque at the pinion engaged by the great wheel, but beyond this the power would fluctuate to an amount depending on the uniformity of the wheel cutting.

In order to make the first turn of winding equal to the subsequent turns it is necessary to put a little power on the barrel before winding commences. The amount of this 'set up' as it is called depends entirely on the torque of the spring when wound into the barrel. A spring requiring to be wound through six turns to get it into the barrel will require less set up than a spring requiring only four turns to achieve the same end.

With the rapid deterioration of the torque curve of early springs the watch soon began to lose on its rate so that it was necessary to re-set up the first turn of winding of the spring. Embarrassed by the frequent appearance of his customer to have this adjustment made, the watchmaker devised a worm and wheel set up and fitted a dial to the wheel with a pointer fixed to the plate so that the owner could make the necessary adjustment himself. Thus when the watch began to lose it was only necessary to screw up the adjuster and the original charmingly erratic rate was restored.

The gut line used to couple the fusee to the barrel was in about 1675 replaced with a chain. The only other improvement in the system was the introduction of maintaining power to prevent reversal of the train during winding. This was done by placing between the great wheel and the fusee cone a ratchet-toothed wheel of the same diameter as the fusee cone. The power was then transferred to the ratchet-wheel instead of the great wheel by means of the pall and ratchet. Between the ratchet-wheel and the great wheel is a spring coupling the two together and kept in tension by the pull of the cord on the fusee. During winding the ratchet-wheel is held by a pall pivoted in the plates so maintaining the coupling spring in tension and ensuring the continuous rotation of the great wheel.

To prevent overwinding a projection of the last turn of the fusee is caught by a pivoted steel arm raised into its path by the cord or chain.

If the great wheel is fixed to the barrel and the fusee dispensed with the arrangement is called a 'going barrel'. The power at the great wheel decreases continuously during unwinding but this defect is kept to a minimum by the use of stop work which restricts the winding to the middle turns of the spring. Thus, if the watch requires four turns of the great wheel to maintain the action for 30 hours and the mainspring is capable of six turns, then it is 'set up' one turn with the stop work in the locked down position. Winding the watch four turns brings the stop work into the locked up position and so the sixth turn is never wound. This system was used extensively by Breguet, who found it convenient to dispense with the fusee in his thin watches. With the detached escapement it is not so important to maintain a constant spring torque since the effect of escapement errors is confined to the escaping arc, leaving the supplementary arc free. With the cylinder escapement locking and impulse are conducted at the same radius of the wheel, and so the effect of the stronger turns of the spring is countered by the increased friction of the locking and vice versa.

In figure 473 can be seen an arrangement by Breguet using two going barrels without fusee. This arrangement was used mainly in his marine chronometers and deck watches of which this is an example. There are examples of timekeepers by Breguet using two barrels and a double grooved fusee and at least one example using four barrels without fusee but these were not, so far as the authors are aware, used in watches. By using two barrels a reduction in the thickness of the springs can be achieved and the number of turns in the barrel can be increased to eight; so that by setting up the mainsprings two turns and using the middle four turns a more even torque results. By placing the barrels one each side of the centre pinion the couple relieves the pivots of the burden of resisting the spring torque and reduces the wear from this source. The reduction in arc during the last few hours of running is only a few degrees and amounts to no more than is found in fusee watches caused by the friction of the thick spring during the early and middle turns of unwinding. Sometimes two barrel systems are fitted with geared arbors and are wound by a common square.

The necessity for keeping the spring torque within reasonable bounds is important if the rate is to be at all constant. It is well known that the verge escapement gains with an increase of power and loses with a decrease in power and the reasons for this are easily seen. The same species of error occurs in detached escapements, but the cases are more obscure. A complete analysis of the functioning of detached escapements is beyond the scope of this work but the following may help in an understanding of the problems of ensuring a close rate.

Consideration will be given to the lever escapement, but the chronometer is, to a lesser extent, affected in the same way.

The line of centres of the escapement is drawn through the centre of motion of the balance-staff and the pallet-staff. The unlocking takes place before this imaginary line is reached by the impulse pin and, depending on the angle of movement of the lever required to complete the unlocking, a certain proportion of the impulse will also take place before the centre line.

If the escapement is set exactly in beat the quiescent point of the spring will also coincide with this line.

Consider now what happens when the free oscillation of a balance and spring meets a disturbing force. If the force momentarily impedes the approach to the quiescent point the vibration will be slower. Conversely, if the force momentarily impulses the balance the vibration will be quicker. The reverse takes place after the quiescent point so that a force impeding the balance will quicken the vibration and an impulse will slow the vibration. These forces occur continuously in escapements, and from this it can be seen that in the lever escapement the effect of unlocking is to slow the vibration. This is then quickened by the impulse before the quiescent point and again slowed by the impulse after the latter point is passed. This variation in the time of vibration occurs, however, only during the actual escaping arc, and the balance is left free to continue its natural period for the supplementary arc. Since the escaping arc remains constant any variation in the forces of unlocking and impulse can affect only the supplementary arc. Since these forces tend to slow the escaping arc it follows that a decrease in balance amplitude must result in a decrease in rate. The same variation is found in the chronometer in which it is necessary, to reduce the risk of setting, so to adjust the position of the unlocking stone that almost all the impulse is delivered after the quiescent point.

From the foregoing it can be seen that the watch will lose in the short arcs. Since it is impossible to maintain the arc constant other means must be found of maintaining the rate irrespective of the arc.

John Arnold's plan of incurving the ends of the spring has never been improved upon and is still used today as a means of equalising the long and short arcs. Breguet adapted the device to his spiral springs by raising the outer turn of the spring and curving it to a smaller radius above the main body of the spiral. By manipulating this curve so that more or less of the outer coil is included it is possible to equalise the time of vibration for small changes in arc. In Arnold's helical springs the effect is achieved by bending the curves at either or both ends of the spring. It is more difficult to maintain the centre of the helical spring after adjustment and as a result this sometimes appears to wobble; but this is not detrimental.

Breguet was disinclined to use end curves in his two barrel chronometers with helical springs but usually did so when the fusee was used. His stud and collet are machined with curved clamps for fixing the spring, and the stud with its three adjustable legs and central fixing screw can be set to make the spring true with the staff. The arrangement gives a very close and constant rate and shows uniformity of two barrels to be as good as a fusee and chain. The very large balances used by Breguet may also have contributed to the excellence of the rate, for a large diameter balance is affected to a greater extent by centrifugal force, and this would tend to slow the long arcs and diminish the effects of the escapement error.

One of the most disturbing influences on the rate is change in temperature. A watch without temperature compensation will lose about 10 seconds per degree centigrade per day and even if worn this might make a difference of one and a half to two minutes a day between summer and winter. Since the error lies mainly in the balance-spring it was not unnatural that early attempts to equalise the hot and cold rates should have been directed towards varying its length to effect a correction. The earliest system used with effect in a watch was a bimetallic strip made of brass and steel riveted together. At one end were two pins embracing the spring and the other end was screwed to a plate with the brass side nearest the stud. As the temperature rose the brass with its greater rate of expansion curled the strip away from the stud and the pins effectively shortened the length of the spring. To effect a permanent change in rate the plate carrying the strip was moved bodily along the length of the spring by a rack and pinion. Because the freedom of the spring in the curbs is essential to allow free movement of the curb, and the concentricity of the movement of the curb with the spring cannot be certain, the effect was erratic and introduced isochronal errors which produced an erratic change of rate for a change in temperature. Transferring the compensation to the balance left the balance-spring free of disturbance and made the effects of the compensation more certain.

Early balance compensations suffered from frailty through insufficient rigidity of the compensating laminations. The effects of centrifugal force caused conflict between the rate for change of arc and the rate for change of temperature, so that it was difficult to achieve a precise adjustment. The want of uniformity in the dimensions of the bi-metallic strips tended to put the balance out of poise with temperature change so that the compensation was unpredictable. The steady development of the laminations from riveting to soldering, and finally fusing the two metals, produced an increasing uniformity in the rate of compensation. Forming the laminations into curves and screwing them to the arms to make the rim of the balance increased the rigidity. This reached its final development with the arms and rim turned from one piece of steel with the brass fused on to the outer edge. In this form its performance is quite predictable but it cannot be adjusted to compensate uniformly, for the change in elasticity of the spring, and the displacement of the bimetallic strips is proportional to the change in temperature; but the inertia of the balance will vary as the square of the radius of gyration which is determined by the displacement of the bimetallic strips. With the rate for temperature adjusted at the two most likely extremes, say 40 degrees and 80 degrees Fahrenheit, there will be at 60 degrees an error of $1\frac{1}{2}$ to 2 seconds a day. Watches are not usually subjected to such extremes of change in temperature, being kept for the most part at a uniform temperature in the pocket, and so the error is not important. The 'middle temperature' error, as this is called, is difficult to determine, for with change of temperature the condition of the oil will affect the balance arc and isochronal errors may confuse the rate. The adjustment for temperature is made by moving a weight to or from the free end of the rim to cause a larger or smaller change in the radius of gyration. Provision for mean time adjustment is by screws in the rim at the point nearest the arms least likely to be affected by temperature.

Although, for precision watches, the compensation curb was abandoned, it was still used, especially by Continental makers, for watches of quite high quality where an exact compensation was not important.

Breguet's compensation curb carried only one pin, and the spring, passing between this and a fixed pin, was allowed more or less free play according to the change in temperature. His cylinder escapements were always fitted with this device and for this escapement it works very well. Earnshaw used a similar curb in some of his watches, and these employed two curbs with a pin at the free end and the fixed end screwed to a regulator rack. With change of temperature the pins opened or closed like pincers and altered the play of the spring to compensate. The lever watch by Perigal uses this system and, within the limits of change to be found in wear, works well enough to give a good average rate over a long period.

Damage to the balance pivots is one of the most disastrous things that can happen to a precision watch. If the watch is dropped flat the pivot will spread at the tip and if dropped on edge the pivot will either bend or raise a burr. Whatever damage occurs it can be certain that the rate will be ruined. When it is considered that dropping a heavy watch a height of two inches, so that it lands on edge, will usually break the staff, it is surprising that the development of shock-proofing was so neglected. The danger of this happening is far greater than that of the fusee chain breaking, but to protect the escapement in the unlikely event of a chain failure a guard was usually fitted. This was either a pin fixed in the plate close to the barrel or a curved plate separating the barrel from the escapement.

Only Breguet seems to have appreciated fully the advantages of protecting the pivots against damage. Not only does the rate suffer, but with it goes the maker's reputation, for it has always been universally understood by the owner that any deterioration in the going is entirely the fault of the maker. Breguet's 'parachute' was a long steel spring screwed to the cock with the jewel hole and end stone set into the free end. Strong enough to hold the balance firmly upright, it was nevertheless thin enough to flex if the watch were jarred and thus relieved the staff of the extra burden. When pointed pivots were used the parachute was fitted to the cock only; but with conical pivots another was screwed to the front plate to serve the bottom pivot. The system is extremely efficient and a *souscription* known to the authors to have been dropped from a height of three feet on to concrete suffered no ill effects.

The difficulty of maintaining a steady rate in the pocket is due in the main to the constant change of position to which the watch is subjected. To bring the piece to time in the 12 up, 9 up and 3 up positions requires the most careful adjustment to the escapement, balance and balance spring. The adjustments are complex and inter-related. In the final stages they are tedious and costly in time and the effect is not permanent.

The solution to the simplification of the problem was supplied by Breguet with his tourbillon or rotating escapement. With the escapement mounted on a platform fixed to the fourth-wheel arbor, and the fourth-wheel fixed to the plate concentric to the arbor, the 'scape pinion is rotated as a consequence of the rotation of the platform rolling it around the fixed fourth-wheel. By this means positional errors were eliminated leaving only temperature and isochronal adjustments to be made. The rotation of the platform every 60 seconds called for a powerful mainspring to overcome the inertia of the platform, for it must be started from rest at every vibration of the balance. To reduce the effects of stopping and starting the platform Breguet introduced four-minute and six-minute periods of rotation so that the spring detent escapement could be used, although the use of Earnshaw's detent was prohibited by reason of the detent being insufficiently rigid to withstand the locking force of the platform. Breguet found the solution to this in Peto's cross detent escapement in which the detent is kept in tension by the locking of the 'scape-wheel. The performance of Breguet's tourbillons is phenomenal, for the positional errors are averaged at every rotation so that even change of balance arc has no effect. Any difference in rate between the dial up and edgewise positions is corrected by adjustment to the balance spring and the shape of the balance pivots and such adjustment is permanent.

The construction of the tourbillon requires the most careful and costly workmanship and for this reason production was limited. No other French maker seems to have produced any and it was not until the end of the nineteenth century that any were produced in England. At that time Nicole Nielson applied the device to a series of watches for Frodsham and Smith. The development in the proportions of the lever escapement with club-tooth wheel and the improvement in uniform production of the compensation balance assured these one-minute tourbillons of success, and their rate, excepting for metallurgical improvements to compensation in modern watches, has never been beaten for uniformity. The success in trials of these watches attracted the attention of Bonniksen, who devised an extremely ingenious method of constructing a rotating escapement which eliminated the extra precision of construction that made the tourbillon so expensive. This mechanism he called a karrusel. Excepting for the continuous rotation of the escapement it is in principle quite different from the tourbillon, for the rotating platform is not mounted upon an arbor of the train. The fourth-wheel arbor passes through the centre of the carriage which is located in a large plain bearing in the front plate. The top pivot hole of the fourth-wheel is cocked to the carriage which can be rotated concentrically with this arbor. The escapement is mounted upon the platform above the fourth-wheel, which engages the 'scape-pinion in the conventional manner. Thus, excepting that the escapement is above the fourth-wheel, the going of the piece would be no different from any common watch. However, screwed to the under side of the platform is a toothed-ring concentric with the platform and engaged by the third pinion. With the going of the watch the platform is rotated by the third pinion so that it completes a revolution every 52·5 minutes. Watches employing this device kept a very close rate and were extremely successful in trials.

Improvements in the technique of watch manufacture and new metals with special properties for the elimination of temperature effects improved the rate far beyond anything the pioneers of precision watches could have hoped for. With the escapement reduced to its bare essentials and the final rate determined by the chemist and metallurgist the modern watch has not the interest of its predecessor. Although the rate of one is still occasionally vied with the rate of another of different make, the trend of manufacture is such that watches are becoming so accurate with the development of new techniques in electricity that soon even this individuality will cease.

From the foregoing general comments we can now pass to a consideration of the principles of the various types of escapement.

Verge

Until the application of the balance-spring no fundamental change had taken place in the watch from its earliest beginnings. So long as the balance formed part of the escapement and directly controlled the unwinding of the main spring the timekeeping was at the mercy of every variation in power delivered to the balance. Its only moderating influence was its inertia, and to make use of this it had to be kept oscillating; and without the balance-spring recoil was essential. Thus the verge escapement combined the two greatest escapement faults—restriction of balance freedom and excessive reversal of the train. When it is considered that the balance spends roughly a quarter of its working life winding up its driving spring through a hand-divided train with no pretensions to constant velocity ratios, it is easy to see that the verge escapement is severely tried as a timekeeper. That it is capable of maintaining a reasonable rate without the controlling influence of a spring when properly made is evident from its daily average. Only by the most careful adjustment of fusee curve to spring torque can its rate be brought even within the bounds of consideration as a check on the passing hours. With the relatively poor mainsprings available, and the wheel engine yet to be invented, it is not surprising that the watchmaker turned his efforts towards case forms and decoration. With the introduction of the balance-spring and the steady improvement of the train and mainspring the verge began to keep a much closer rate, so that it was possible by experiment to make improvements to the escapement. Such experiments were directed to increasing the supplementary arc, and reducing the recoil by opening the pallet angles to between 100 and 115 degrees; an increase of some 20 degrees. It soon became apparent that if the recoil were reduced without reference to the total arc the rate began to deteriorate. Excessive end thrust to the crown wheel pivot caused rapid wear and the watch was liable to set during winding or would not be inclined to start if wound after running down. With the pallets finally set at 100 degrees to 105 degrees the escapement continued in use for a further 200 years and resisted all efforts at refinement. If jewelled and very carefully made it would, for a few months, show a fairly consistent rate; but with the thickening of the oil the rate deteriorated so that it was inferior to that of a plain unjewelled escapement which would, by virtue of its many compensating inefficiencies, keep an indifferently close rate for many years without any attention. The usual arrangement of the escapement between the watch plates is shown in figure 20.

Cylinder

The development of the cylinder escapement by George Graham introduced a new era of timekeeping. The absence of recoil and the inherent ability of the escapement to compensate to a large extent for variations in impulse due to its frictional rest, produced rates that were consistent enough to warrant the application of correction for temperature. Encouraged by these results makers devoted much labour to improving the escapement. Early examples were prone to self destruction due to the heavy brass 'scape-wheel cutting the impulse lips of the cylinder. By curving the impulse face of the wheel teeth its velocity was more constant, and the pressure on the lips of the cylinder was reduced during the latter half of the impulse; this helped considerably in reducing wear. With a reduction in velocity at the beginning of the impulse and the consequent increase at the end of impulse it was soon discovered that the increased velocity of the wheel at the moment of leaving the impulse lips was sufficient to cause pitting of the resting surface at the point where the wheel tooth dropped on to the cylinder. The introduction of the lighter steel wheel almost completely cured these faults which were finally overcome by making the cylinder of ruby.

Once the difficulties of producing the 'scape-wheel with its elevated impulse teeth had been overcome the cylinder watch was produced in large numbers both in England and on the Continent. The best proportions for the diameters of the wheel and cylinder were proposed by Breguet, who also used a higher number of vibrations for the balance and always, after about 1790, his ruby cylinder of unique design in which the half section of ruby cylinder was suspended below the balance-staff on a cranked extension of the balance-seat. No doubt the object of the design was to simplify the manufacture of the ruby but, as with so many sound mechanical designs, it offered additional advantages. The thin crank to which the cylinder is attached allowed a considerable increase in arc before banking occurred and since the weight of the balance is taken on a separate staff the robustness is not impaired as would be the case if the more conventional cylinder were used. The teeth of the wheel do not require undercutting at the root to give banking clearance and so are stronger and very much easier to produce. The oil cannot creep away along the cylinder, the recess into which the ruby fits being too great a hurdle to overcome. The balance-wheel is attached to the staff midway between the pivots and so more evenly distributes its weight between the pivots and helps smooth away positional errors. The one disadvantage in the arrangement is the difficulty of placing sufficient oil in the bottom pivot hole. This hole and its end stone are mounted in a steel tube attached to the plate by a thin arm against which the ruby suspending crank banks if the arc is excessive. The tube is small enough to give adequate clearance to the inside of the ruby cylinder, and the jewel hole and end stone are correspondingly smaller and so there is very little space for oil. Oiling these holes requires a special oiler mounted in an uprighting tool so that the oiler cannot touch the inside of the tube. If any oil gets to the inside of the tube it will quickly run up the staff and ruin the rate of the watch. Figure 21 shows the arrangement of the Breguet ruby cylinder and pivot hole in which the end of the pivot can be seen. Figure 22 shows the form of the 'scape-wheel teeth. Figure 23 shows the arrangement of the English cylinder as produced by Graham. Note the form of the teeth and the excessive cutting away of the cylinder to give banking clearance.

Occasionally a cylinder escapement is met with having a flat 'scape wheel, see figure 24. These escapements do not perform very well since the arc of the balance must be kept small if the cylinder is not to bank against the root of the wheel tooth. The oil soon creeps away along the teeth and leaves the acting surfaces dry resulting in rapid wear. This probably accounts for their almost complete disappearance.

Virgule

Since the virgule offers no advantages over the cylinder escapement it is difficult to see why it should have been made at all. It is quite incapable of retaining any oil at its working surfaces and soon sets if not oiled frequently. At first sight it would appear to have the advantage of being easier to construct so far as the wheel is concerned since it can be seen from figure 25 that the impulse teeth are removed from the stalks of the wheel and replaced with a single impulse curve on the balance-staff. The construction of the staff, however, gave rise to fresh difficulties because it involved a certain amount of freehand work in filing and polishing the impulse curves to shape. For this reason, and the realisation that it would never perform so reliably as the cylinder, it was soon abandoned, although it did enjoy considerable popularity on the Continent for about 20 years.

To reduce the tendency to set, Beaumarchais introduced a further set of pins to the other side of the 'scape-wheel and an additional impulse curve to the staff. Figure 26 shows the form of this staff which was extremely difficult to construct so that very few were made. The double virgule, as this escapement was called, did have the advantage that it was disinclined to set for want of oil but would if neglected wear its pins away.

Duplex

Although of French origin this escapement was not much employed on the Continent except by Breguet, who used it in some watches but mainly in small clocks. The principle of using the long teeth of the 'scape-wheel for locking with reduced power and the shorter vertical teeth for impulsing proved most satisfactory and appealed to English makers who used it extensively. It is said that the French preferred the cylinder as this enabled them to produce a thinner movement. The Englishman took a more practical view of his watch as a timekeeper and the construction of English watches as a whole at this period shows that he was content to be conscious of the machinery in his pocket. The escapement does require the 'scape pinion and staff to be rather long if the effect of play in the bearings is not to affect the rate, which is extremely close when properly constructed. The frequent employment of this escapement in England led to great experience in its construction and proportions, so that it was not uncommon to find watches running for years to within a few seconds a day.

In common with other single impulse escapements it is inclined to set, but English watches with their high mainsprings supplying greater power could maintain a large balance arc and a high number of vibrations, sometimes as high as 21,000 per hour, and so failure from this fault was almost eliminated. When constructed in this manner the most careful workmanship was essential. The long locking teeth need to pass through the passing slot as nearly at the centre of motion of the staff as is practicable if the side thrust is to be kept to a minimum; and since the diameter of the locking roller must be kept as small as possible to reduce the friction, the allowable tolerance in pitching the escapement is extremely small. The intersection of the impulse pallet with the vertical teeth is of necessity very shallow. The clearance required by the pallet on its return swing still further reduces the engagement of the teeth during impulse. Any variation in the depth of this engagement resulted in a variable impulse and a bad rate. It was in this department that the escapement eventually failed, for the power required to maintain a good rate caused considerable wear of the 'scape-wheel teeth so that the escapement would trip. The difficulty of making a new wheel prompted many repairers to convert the escapement to the, by then, well developed lever. Figure 27 shows the arrangement of the escapement in its most common form. The passing slot for the locking teeth can be seen below the impulse pallet. Figure 28 is of the original form of the escapement with two wheels, one for the impulse and the larger wheel for locking. This escapement is from the Breguet watch shown in figure 400. Figure 29 shows the fairly common Chinese duplex in which two oscillations of the balance are required to pass the double locking tooth, the impulse being delivered at each alternate oscillation. These were used to obtain jump seconds. The extra power required to drive the balance through the second locking vibration was so great as to render the escapement practically useless as a timekeeper. The curious horned weights attached to the balance-rim were, the authors are assured, intended to ward off the devil. It is not known whether they were any more effective than the escapement. This escapement is from the watch illustrated in Colour 19 & F.

Chronometer

The development of the pivoted detent escapement soon fulfilled the expectations of its makers, especially Arnold, who was convinced of his ability to produce at a moderate price a watch that would exceed all others in its superiority of rate. His escapement, seen in figure 48 in plan and in the perspective drawing (page 107) by Cresswell, makes no concessions to beauty or style and yet possesses a curious mechanical charm that truly reflects its maker's love of the mechanical sciences. In marine pieces it performed extraordinarily well and most reliably. In the pocket its performance was not always so good. In retrospect it is easy to see that the design is faulty. The arc described by the impulse roller is too small. This reduced the escaping angle, which Arnold realised was important but necessitated greater power to maintain the balance arc of some 280 degrees in the hanging position. Because of this, and notwithstanding the lightness of the 'scape-wheel, the drops are heavy. The detent is particularly heavy and the long thin arm terminating in the relatively heavy safety horn and table for carrying the passing spring banking pin, causes the detent to bounce on its stop screw which, itself, is badly positioned and does not meet the detent at the centre of percussion. The detent return spring is screwed to the plate and returns the detent by pressing against the locking arm. It requires to be oiled at this point of contact and the motion is excessive. The length of passing spring projecting beyond the banking pin is too great and by deflecting causes the angle of unlocking to vary with the power at the wheel. All these factors contribute to variation in rate as the oil thickens but more particularly if the watch is worn in the pocket, when, because of the small radius of the impulse pallet and the slow vibration of the balance, setting is also likely to occur. Arnold does not seem to have made any serious attempt to eradicate the faults in the escapement, but presumably believed the variations to be caused primarily by the necessity for oil at the detent pivots and abandoned the arrangement in favour of his spring detent. Examples of this pivoted detent movement are rare and collectors who own one can count themselves as extremely fortunate in possessing one of the first really serious attempts at producing a uniform precision pocket timekeeper. The escapement shown in figure 30 is from watch No. 64 shown in figure 322 and is particularly interesting as being the only one of five such watches examined by the authors that carries on the balance an isochronal curb. This can be seen in figure 31

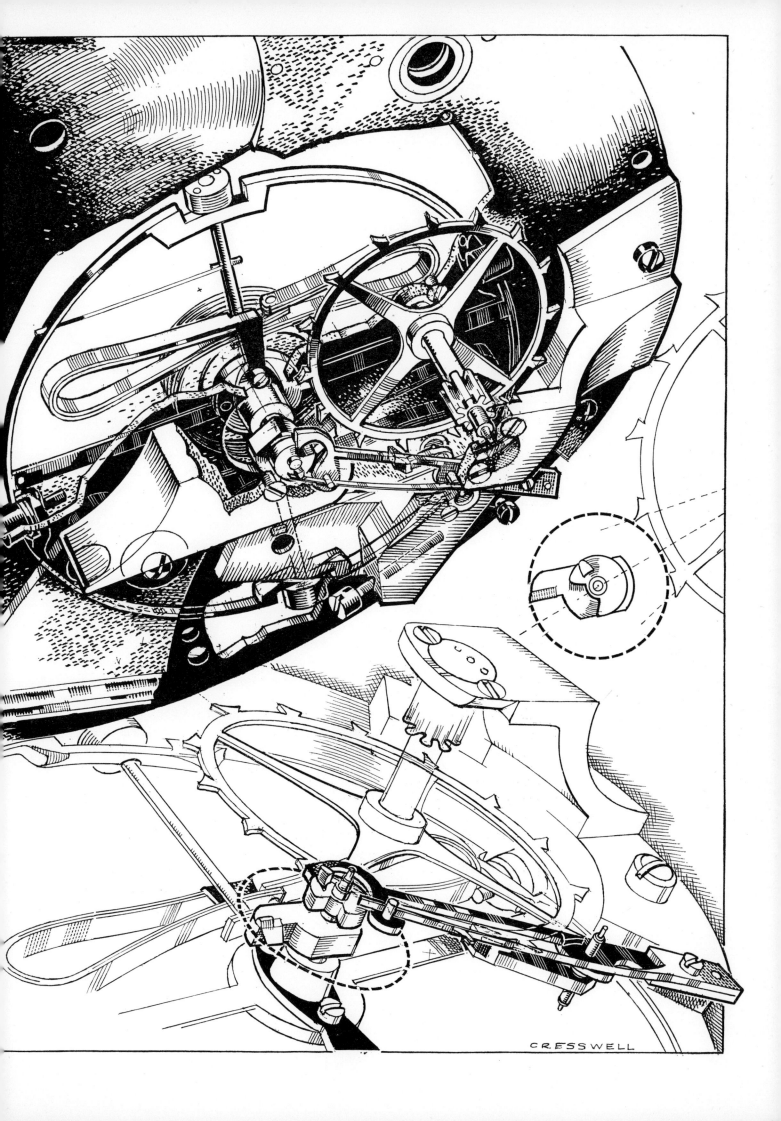

CRESSWELL

attached to the rim above the arm nearest the spring stud and terminating in a clevis screwed to the hub of the balance. The terminal curve of the balance-spring passes through a hole in the curb and is restricted during very long arcs, thus effectively shortening the balance-spring, probably to compensate for the effects of centrifugal forces on the compensation.

Berthoud's pivoted detent escapement shown in figure 32 is much superior in design and therefore more certain in its action. The relatively larger impulse radius reduces the risk of setting, for the 'scape-wheel has an increased mechanical advantage; thus the power required to impulse the balance is smaller and the action of the whole escapement becomes lighter and more delicate. The detent is again relatively shorter and very much thinner and lighter in construction. Considerable weight is removed by eliminating the safety dart and using a roller to carry the impulse pallet and supply the safety action. The excessive overhang of the passing spring is still to be seen, but the lighter lockings tend to reduce considerably the effects of this fault. Banking is effected by a screw rigidly mounted in a bracket screwed to the plate and meets the detent as nearly as possible at the centre of percussion. The inclination of the passing spring together with the short detent ensures a greater inclination of the detent during unlocking, and this makes the action more certain and in the case of the passing spring reduces the friction on the return vibration. The rate of a small marine chronometer in the possession of Cecil Clutton entirely fulfils the promise of the design.

Breguet, always seeking and often making improvements in escapements, devised the pivoted detent escapement shown in figure 33 in which the detent, of diminutive proportions, performs the sole function of locking the 'scape-wheel. The passing 'spring', in the form of a pivoted pall, is mounted on the balance roller and returned by a spring screwed to the roller. The slight advantage gained by this system in reducing the weight of the detent is completely swamped by the effects of oil at the passing spring pivots and the friction of the return spring. As with all Breguet's escapements the proportions are admirable. He did, however, have some blind spots. He seemed to make little or no attempt to eliminate the necessity for oil in his escapements and whenever possible mounted his balance-wheel at one end of the staff so that the positional errors were more difficult to eradicate. Arnold and Berthoud always put the balance in the middle of the staff and thus divided the weight of the balance equally between the two pivots. Figure 34 shows another of Breguet's escapements which is in principle an exact copy of Berthoud's and shows in what high regard Breguet held this arrangement, and rightly so, for its proportions have never been improved upon. It represented the final word in pivoted detent escapements.

The escapement shown in figure 35 is by Kendall. Its chief interest lies in the unusual design of the detent and clearly shows what can happen when an attempt is made to achieve an object without understanding fully the principles involved. The radius of the impulse pallet is far too small and is exceeded by the unlocking radius which is far too large. There is no passing spring but the effect of this is achieved by thinning the length of the detent (except for the tip) into a thin spring. The tip is formed to the shape of an incline on the underside. It can be seen in the illustration that the unlocking stone has moved aside the detent allowing a tooth to fall on to the impulse pallet. The angle of the tooth face is radial and causes a considerable change of velocity in the wheel as the two surfaces meet, and then transfer the impulse from the tip of the pallet to the tip of the tooth. On the return vibration the unlocking stone meets the incline at the tip of the detent and deflects it up and so passes underneath. The vibration caused by the detent recovering its shape is a most disturbing influence and causes the detent to move against its banking, which in any case is inadequately rigid. The greatest variable factor in the escapement, however, is the depth of the unlocking stone with the detent during the passing action. This is governed entirely by the position of the watch affecting the end shake of the balance-staff and detent, and must change many times a day if the watch is worn. The hook-like projection is a safety device and in the event of tripping returns the detent so that a tooth can safely lock. This escapement is from the watch shown in figure 314. Figure 32 is from the watch illustrated in figure 425. Figure 33 is from the watch illustrated in figure 448. Figure 34 is from the watch illustrated in figure 319.

Although Berthoud or Earnshaw may have been first in the field with the spring detent it was Arnold who, quickly perceiving the advantages of the system, made the fullest use of it. He abandoned his pivoted detent and concentrated his efforts towards the development and production of the spring detent. To protect the thin spring against buckling he arranged it so that the detent was held in tension by the 'scape-wheel when locked. To accomplish the unlocking it is necessary to move the locking stone towards the centre of the 'scape-wheel, which has vertical extensions to the impulse teeth, thus enabling the detent to pass over the rim of the wheel during unlocking. Figure 36 shows the arrangement of the escapement and is taken from the watch shown in figure 298. That it is a later development of his spring detent escapement is apparent from the short detent employed. In earlier models the detent was half as long again and extending to the edge of the plate. The longer the detent the more uncertain is the action between the passing spring and the unlocking stone, due to freedom at the balance-pivots. Arnold seems not to have been very sensible of this for his early spring detents were far too long and he never did achieve a sufficient reduction in their length. To be certain of the action at this point it is necessary with a long detent to increase the depth of contact of the unlocking stone with the passing spring, and this results in an excessive displacement of the detent to effect the unlocking. Greater misery is to follow for it now becomes necessary to increase the stiffness of the detent spring in order that the detent may be returned in time to catch the next tooth. To displace the stiff detent without reducing the balance-arc requires a stronger mainspring and now the drops are so fierce that the teeth of the 'scape-wheel are pitted by contact with the impulse pallet and the locking stone must be heavier and stronger to withstand the blow of the locking tooth.

By direct comparison with the mechanical grace and style of his pivoted detent escapement the arrangement is cumbersome and unconvincing, but its performance was superior when used in marine timekeepers. As to its use in the pocket it suffered from small variations in rate due mainly to the long detent and the still too small impulse radius of the pallet, now mounted on a roller to supply the safety action. The gradual development of the proportions of the components culminated in the shorter detent and a lighter 'scape-wheel working with a larger impulse roller. In this final form it worked very reliably and showed great consistency of rate.

Earnshaw's spring detent escapement shown in figure 37 taken from the watch shown in figure 455 is the same basic arrangement as used in Arnold's pivoted detent with the exception that the thin spring at the foot replaces the pivoted detent axis. The proportions are altogether superior to Arnold's in that the ratio of impulse radius to 'scape-wheel diameter is smaller and the detent is shorter and lighter in construction. It can be seen that the impulse face is so severely undercut that wear must result from the transfer of pressure from the tip of the impulse face to the tip of the wheel tooth. However, notwithstanding this fault (later corrected by Earnshaw) it is altogether a more attractive arrangement than Arnold's, being easier to manufacture and requiring less motive power so that a thinner watch could be produced. At its best and with a compensated balance its rate was superior to Arnold's and proved so successful that with only very minor alterations it was universally adopted. One such alteration was a still further increase in the relative size of the impulse roller. An example of this is seen in figure 38 taken from the watch shown in figure 559. Here the roller (made of sapphire in this instance) is half the diameter of the 'scape-wheel. The detent length is still shorter than Earnshaw's but finally remained at this proportion, since excessive shortening merely increases the resistance to unlocking. Watches fitted with the escapement made to these proportions were unexcelled as timekeepers when properly adjusted. The Peto cross detent is shown in figure 39 taken from the watch shown in figure 340. Its advantages are illusory. The cockling of the detent spring that this system was said by its inventor to overcome never in fact existed, for had the spring been made thin enough for this to happen it would have been insufficiently strong to return the detent. For the same reason the Peto detent cannot be made weaker, for such weight as would be saved by thinning the body of the detent would be more than counterbalanced by the weight of the curved horn. This further increased the inertia of the detent since it is formed at the most rapidly moving part of the detent. The friction between the passing spring and the horn of the detent is undesirable and, like the escapement as a whole, contributed nothing to the science of chronometer construction. It was, however, used occasionally by Breguet in his tourbillons where it is of prime importance to keep the detent in tension to withstand the effect of the kinetic energy of the rotating platform during the locking of the 'scape-wheel.

An interesting variant of the escapement is the very rare James Ferguson Cole Double Rotary Detached Escapement. It is seen in figure 40 taken from the watch shown in figure 532. The impulse in this escapement is delivered in the normal way to the balance roller, whilst the unlocking roller is carried on a separate arbor pivoted between cocks mounted on the plate. The two are geared together in the ratio of 2 : 1 so that the angular velocity of the unlocking roller is half that of the balance. Thus the balance is enabled to make more than a complete revolution without tripping the 'scape-wheel. The angle of the passing spring is ingenious for it allows the full length to flex during the passing vibration, but uses only the short rigid end for unlocking. This is essential, for with the reduced velocity of the roller the action of the stone with the passing spring must be very positive if the detent is to be released in time to catch the wheel tooth. The disruptive influence of the extra mobile completely swamped the advantage gained by the greater angular velocity of the balance, as also did the greater number of turns required in the balance-spring, for such springs are difficult to make isochronous. The escapement is no exception to the rule that the fewer and more con-

constant are the mobiles the better will be the rate. The authors have seen only two of these escapements and presumably Cole was not encouraged to continue with their manufacture in quantity.

Lever

When compared with the production of chronometers the number of lever watches produced in England up to the end of the eighteenth century was very small. Representative examples of the escapements used in surviving watches by the known makers are illustrated in figure 41 by Emery from the watch shown in figure 2, figure 42 by Pendleton from the watch shown in figure 323, figure 43 by Perigal from the watch shown in figure 310, figure 44 from the watch shown in figure 350 and figure 47 from the watch shown in figure 303 by Leroux. The arrangement used by Emery in which the 'scape-wheel, pallets and balance axis form a straight line is that which is preferred in modern watch construction. Apart from ease of lay-out it offers no advantage over that of Perigal, which system was used by Mudge in his first lever watch and was preferred in the later production of lever watches by English makers. It can be seen from a comparison of the illustrations that Emery's escapement was of somewhat robust construction. The inertia of the pallets and 'scape-wheel is considerable and absorbs a good deal of the energy in the balance so that, in conjunction with the loss of power occasioned by the high impulse angle made necessary by the long pallet arms, the action of the escapement is not very vigorous, even though the mainspring is most generously proportioned. In the earliest examples the inertia was still further increased by the use of the heavy impulse cams devised by Mudge and necessitating a double elevation for the horns of the lever. This curious method of transferring the impulse to the balance has no mechanical advantage excepting that by twisting the rollers on the balance staff the point of contact can be adjusted to give proper freedom in the notch of the lever. The probability is that Mudge relied upon the periphery of the disengaged impulse cam to ensure the correct position of the notch of the lever prior to the unlocking. The reversal of engagement of the cams during impulse then takes place and the periphery of the unlocking cam ensures safety from tripping after impulse. During the supplementary arc the safety dart would ensure the retention of the locking. The necessity for this could arise out of the use of the small safety roller with its reduced angular velocity making a proportionately larger passing hollow necessary. In modern watches this extra safety action during escaping is achieved by adding horns to the notch of the lever.

In his earliest watches Emery used the same system of double elevation to the fork. Later, by using a slightly larger safety roller, he obviated the necessity for the system and changed to a single stone impulse pin. In its final form the pin was of steel pivoted in jewel holes. Unlike Mudge's wheel the 'scape teeth are undercut so that only the tip bears upon the locking face of the pallet. The effect of radial faces to the teeth is to cause the wheel to recoil as the lever completes the run to the banking which, in an escapement without draw, and with the added disadvantage of a wheel with radial teeth, can become very uncertain. The troubles experienced in the wearing of Mudge's watch can almost certainly be attributed to this cause. The movements of the watches of Emery, Pendleton and Perigal are derived from the same *ébauche* but show considerable diversity of opinion in the details of their escapements. Thus the Perigal employs a right-angle lay-out in the style of Mudge; and the Pendleton, using the straight line lay-out of Emery, employs the curious arrangement of impulse pins set in a loop so that the action of the impulse stone takes place diametrically opposite the lever. This ungainly method of reducing the friction must have been difficult to achieve in construction. The resulting benefits were so marginal as to be completely swamped by the poor impulse angles of the pallets and the large 'scape-wheel—the first absorbing power by friction and the second by inertia. In fact more power was required to offset the increased ratio of lever length to roller diameter. In the Perigal escapement the 'scape-wheel, although smaller and lighter in construction, employs radial teeth. It only just avoids the faults of the Mudge escapement by having crescents cut into the face of the teeth for the retention of oil. Similar crescents can be seen in the drawing by Cresswell of the Emery lever, page 115. None of these escapements has draw, and the want of this small angulation of the locking faces to ensure that the lever is drawn positively against the banking pins causes their rate in wear to be unreliable. The many points of similarity in these escapements is worth noting and shows that if the makers did not actually work together they were at least in very close touch with each other's work, Pendleton in fact being credited with the construction of all of Emery's lever watches. The 'scape-wheels of Emery and Perigal are, excepting for weight, identical in style. The pallet stones are identical in texture, finish and fitting. The fork, safety dart and impulse pin, when compared with Emery's second single-stone type, would seem to have been made by the same hand, although in adopting a right angle arrangement Perigal shows how much he was influenced by the Mudge watch, to which he may well have had ready access, being at that time watchmaker to the King. The Pendleton exhibits a complete change in style and finish but uses Emery's balance. The Perigal also uses an Emery balance but of an earlier pattern such as he used on his cylinder watches. The prime virtue of these watches in comparison with the chronometer lay in the impulsing of the balance at each vibration for a relatively small escaping arc. Thus the danger of tripping was eliminated and that of setting almost so. Had the escapement been of lighter construction and made to closer limits this irritating source of failure would also have been eliminated. Whilst these makers were producing their heavy machinery Grant and Leroux, working independently, produced watches of the most extraordinary merit in their respective ways. Grant exhibited in his escapement a lightness and delicacy of construction that ensured its success from the beginning. Figure 44 shows an arrangement where the impulse is given by the inner faces of the upraised teeth of the 'scape-wheel. Figure 45 shows the teeth more clearly, and an opposite arrangement where the impulse is delivered from the outer faces of the teeth in the more conventional manner. Grant was at considerable pains to see that his escapement was truly dead, and to achieve this curved the locking faces of the stones which, like Arnold's spring detents, pass over the rim of the wheel during locking. With such light components the action is very vigorous and enables the use of a longer lever; this lessens the unlocking force at the roller and, for a given displacement of the lever, reduces the lifting angle of the pallets, thus further minimising the friction. The action of the escapement is scintillating and shows what can happen when a clever mechanic is left to play with a good idea. His work was marred only by his determination to avoid recoiling the 'scape wheel and so ensuring that his lever stayed firmly against the banking during the supplementary arc. In wear the watch shows daily variations in rate for the want of this device although these represent a minute proportion of those achieved by Emery & Co. with their escapements. Grant seems rarely to have made two escapements alike and his work is always interesting. Figure 46 shows an arrangement of his escapement using two balance-wheels geared together. Each has a balance-spring, but impulse is delivered to only one balance and is transferred by the toothed wheels to the slave balance. The watch is obviously experimental and is unjewelled. The fork and roller are typical of Grant as also are the

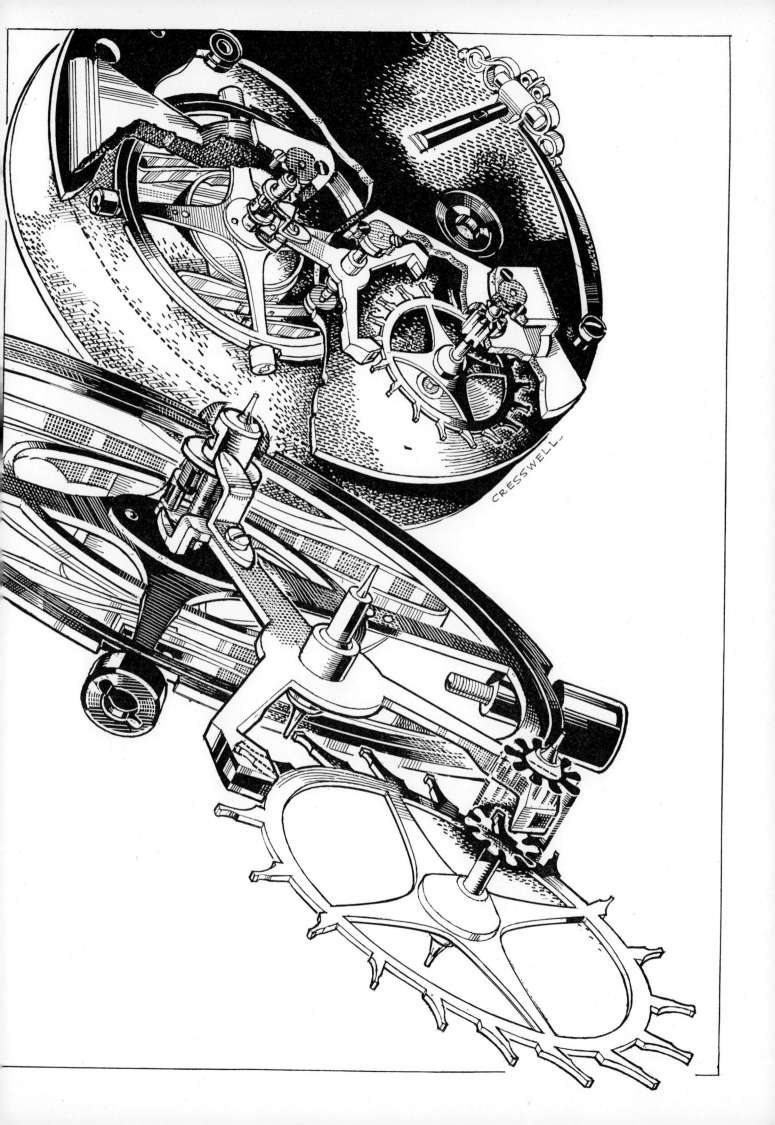

upraised teeth of the 'scape-wheel. The object of this curiosity was to keep the balance arc constant whilst the watch was moved about in wear. It performs its intended function so well that without actually starting the escapement by a touch of the balance it remains inactive in spite of the most vigorous agitation and, conversely, when vibrating, the balance amplitude is indifferent to the most energetic actions of the wearer.

The one remaining watch examined by the Authors and made during this exciting period of development of the lever is that of Leroux, and this is perhaps the most remarkable of all for it is the only escapement to possess the all-important draw. Figure 47 from the watch shown in figure 303 shows the arrangement in which the impulse is given by inclines on the 'scape-wheel teeth, to thin pointed pallet stones sandwiched between the plates of a subframe screwed to the lever. The locking faces are so inclined as to give a positive action to the lever after impulse and hold it against the banking jewel seen at the end of the lever. The jewel is banked against screws mounted in a bracket fixed to the underside of the top plate and the run can be so finely adjusted that the clearance between the safety dart and the roller need be little more than that necessary to allow for the shake in the pivots. The pallets embrace only two teeth of the 'scape-wheel so that the lift, as can be seen, is at a minimum and likewise the friction from this source. The extremely high ratio of lever length to pallet radius helps to overcome the power absorbed in reversing the train during unlocking. The watch in wear exhibits none of the fluctuations of rate to be found in the watches without draw. The proportions show that the maker had a sound knowledge of the requirements of the escapement and it is curious that so few could have been made, for only two are known to exist. Since no other watch with draw of earlier manufacture has yet been found it would seem that Leroux must receive the credit for the last remaining principal development of the escapement. Emery, who has until now received this credit, most certainly did not use it in any of his watches examined by the authors and Breguet, who also has been credited with its introduction, used, at least until 1814, circular pallets without draw. The workmanship, like that of Grant's escapements, is without peer.

An interesting lever escapement is shown in figure 48 taken from the watch shown in figure 345. Its arrangement is a composite of all the features discussed in the escapements illustrated. The date of the watch is not known for it came into the possession of Cecil Clutton as a movement which was restored and re-cased by George Daniels, but it may be presumed to date from about 1800. It can be seen that the circular termination of the lever is derived from Pendleton, whilst the pallet stones are curved like Grant's but with pointed acting tips to allow of the impulse from Leroux's 'scape-wheel. The balance wheel, which can be attributed to Arnold, is controlled by two balance-springs, one above and one below the arms, the lower one being affected by the regulator curb pins as by Mudge: a watchmaker's interpretation of the quotation, 'If you can't beat 'em—join 'em'!

By the end of the eighteenth century the detached lever in England had virtually ceased to be made. Examples are rare enough to be highly prized by their owners. They are, with Arnold's early detent watches, the most exciting of English pre-nineteenth-century watches. If their makers were on the whole not sufficiently practised in the mechanical principles of their art this detracts nothing from their honest endeavours, and we are the richer for the interesting speculations they afford us in discussing their work.

The work of Litherland ensured the continued production of the lever watch in England but the escapement was no longer detached. The action of the unlocking and impulsing was affected by a toothed rack engaging a pinion on the balance staff. Figure 49, taken from the watch shown in figure 501, shows a typical arrangement. There are widely spaced bankings and the balance can make a full turn in either direction, the locking faces being long enough to accommodate the increased movement of the pallets. The performance was no better than a good cylinder watch but was undoubtedly easier to produce than any previous escapement except the verge, and was popular for cheap watches. An early variant is seen in figure 50 in which the balance has been detached by replacing the rack with a simple roller. The stone impulse pin is fitted to a thinner projection of the roller so that the safety action takes place at the same elevation as the impulse. This device was the subject of a patent by Massey and in its earliest form is seen in figure 51 where the roller is made entirely of steel. It can be seen that both these escapements have curved locking faces with the consequent absence of draw and thus their makers ensured that the rate was little better than the rack lever. The use of the 15-tooth 'scape-wheel necessitated an extra wheel in the train but made the use of a seconds hand convenient. The low lift-angle of the impulse faces and the well proportioned lay-out assured a good rate when eventually their makers overcame their conservatism and introduced the draw.

It is curious to note that with the lever once again detached London makers took a fresh interest in the escapement, and by the middle of the nineteenth century they were producing it in quantity almost to the exclusion of all other escapements except the duplex and the chronometer, which were still used in watches of the highest precision. Exactly when the draw was reintroduced is open to conjecture, for no one actually claimed it as his invention, which is unusual in the history of watchmaking. Possibly anxious to create the illusion that the improvement in rate was due entirely to superior workmanship, the first users felt that they would not be doing themselves justice if they admitted to resorting to a 'dodge'. Examples of 15- and 30-tooth Massey levers can be found with and without draw, but in the experience of the authors, watches with the all steel roller never have draw. Allowing a little time for Massey to get into production with his patent issued in 1814; and presuming that the jewelled roller followed soon after; and with a further short period elapsing to account for the examples without draw; the year 1818 may be acceptable. Most certainly by 1820 it was accepted by the best makers that draw was essential for a steady rate. Its use without sensible alteration was continued into the twentieth century, although towards the end of the nineteenth century the club tooth 'scape-wheel began to replace the pointed or ratchet tooth wheel.

One interesting and successful variant was that of Savage. Figure 52 shows his arrangement in which it can be seen that the safety of the locking action during the supplementary arc is ensured by a pin acting upon the edge of the roller. The unlocking is accomplished by the two pins placed one each side of the impulse notch in the roller, into which the lever guard pin will pass during the unlocking, and the action is then transferred to the guard pin which impulses the balance. The difference in ratio of unlocking to impulsing lever length is small but significant, and results in a most lively action for a comparatively weak mainspring. It also offers the slight advantage that the friction of unlocking, by virtue of the wide notch in the lever, is disengaging, but this is an ancillary advantage and can in any case be achieved by correct proportioning of the escapement and impulse roller. The escapement was not much used, for it required the most careful pitching of the three pins, and any small errors of pitching soon rendered it less reliable than the conventional fork and roller. Variations in rate in these escapements can often be attributed to the widely spaced notch and roller pins occasioning overbanking in excessively long arcs.

In the construction of most of his first series of watches Breguet used the lever. From the outset he showed a most remarkable insight of the requirements of the escapement and figure 53 shows a similar escapement to that used in the watch shown in figure 330. The very high ratio of lever length to pallet radius enabled the use of very shallow lockings for an adequate run to the bankings so that the power absorbed in unlocking was much reduced. The low impulse angles ensure a small escaping angle and the use of the wide impulse stone acting with vertical pins on the lever kept the unlocking frictions to a minimum. The very light thin wheel had broad tips to the teeth with slots for oil retention. Exact poising of the lever was achieved by the counterpoise which also supplied the banking against the 'scape-wheel arbor. The curved lockings show clearly the absence of draw. A later example of his work is seen in figure 34 taken from the watch shown in figure 435. The same ratios of lift and lever are used but the 'scape-wheel now has club teeth so that part of the lift is supplied by the inclined tooth tip. This feature, and the use of the single roller with crescent for the passage of the vertical guard pin, are the earliest examples known to the authors. By using the club tooth wheel it is possible to undercut the back of the tooth to give freedom to the entering pallet stone without the excessive drop required with the ratchet tooth wheel; also, by virtue of the length of face of the tip, its oil retention is superior. Both these factors are beneficial, for the one makes better use of the power of the mainspring and the other ensures greater consistency of rate. All his subsequent levers employed this system but with a greater proportion of the lift transferred to the wheel teeth, which were drilled through from the back below the impulse face with a conical hole just breaking through the locking corner for the further retention of the oil. Figure 55 taken from the watch illustrated in figure 6 and figure 56 taken from the watch shown in figure 490 are two further variants of Breguet's escapements and illustrate his marked propensity for experimenting with the length of the lever. It is interesting to note that the ratios of lever length to lifting angle are arranged to maintain the same escaping arc so that the power required to maintain the balance was always the same irrespective of the length of the lever. That with the 20-tooth wheel is the later example and the positive angle of the pallet stones shows clearly that draw is present. The 14-tooth escapement made shortly before Breguet's death has no draw on the entry stone at the limit of banking, and only a little at the limit of banking on the exit stone. This is occasioned by the recoiling of the wheel during withdrawal of the radial locking surface and is almost absent at the limit of locking. It is surprising that Breguet did not make more positive use of draw. His continuous experiments with the ratios of his levers suggest that he may have considered that a more satisfying solution to the problem than that of introducing what he must have regarded as a bad principle lay in this direction. The straight locking surfaces were used in his escapements after 1814 and when locked are radial to the 'scape-wheel arbor. This shows clearly his reluctance to make use of the draw which he could hardly have been unaware of, for he was inclined to give some angularity to the locking face of his chronometer detents to prevent accidental unlocking of the wheel through careless handling. In the lever the wheel cannot unlock, for the dart will ensure its safety. The power absorbed in unlocking the escapement with draw is considerably greater than that required for the escapement without draw and consequently variations in power cause greater variations in the rate. Breguet no doubt considered that the effect of the dart touching the roller was of less consequence to the rate. The thin repeating watches which he made so fashionable required large diameter barrels to make up the loss of power occasioned by the reduction in height of the barrel, and it was convenient to dispense with the fusee so that power fluctuations were inevitable and this may also have influenced his decision not to use draw. The indications are that he never regarded the lever as a precision timekeeper but only as a good compromise between the relatively inferior rate of the cylinder and the delicacy of the chronometer. On the whole his clients were more concerned with the appearance and novelty of their watches and probably would not be sensible of the small variations found in the performance of the lever. It is worth noting that almost without exception his lever watches used pointed pivots to the balance staff (see 57), running in blind holes, and whilst this system makes for improved reliability in withstanding the many shocks an everyday watch is likely to suffer, it is not conducive to the maintenance of a close rate. The extra run to the banking achieved by his long levers was necessary to allow sufficient clearance for the impulse pin to pass the horns with the watch on edge, in which position the clearance would be continually varying, for with pointed pivots the side shake is proportional to the end shake and some shake is essential to the freedom of the pivot.

A form of lever escapement popular in France for watches beating seconds was that devised by Pouzzait. Figure 58, taken from the watch shown in figure 369, shows the arrangement. The balance diameter almost equals that of the back plate above which, and located in a skeleton cock, it oscillates. The 'scape-wheel of 30 upraised teeth is at the centre of the movement and carries the sweep seconds hand. The impulse is delivered to the balance by the notch, seen between the spokes of the wheel, acting upon the large impulse pin. The safety action is effected by the pin on the exit side of the lever passing through a gap in the large safety ring.

Robin

The necessity for oiling the teeth of the lever escapement no doubt influenced Robin in his development of the escapement bearing his name. In its use of the lever with two locking stones and the impulse delivered to the balance at each alternate vibration via a pallet attached to the balance roller, it utilises the principles of both the lever and chronometer escapements. In this combination its inventor no doubt intended that it should possess the mechanical reliability of the lever with the superior rate of the chronometer. It failed in both respects, for with impulse in one direction only it was prone to setting and, unlike the lever escapement, in which the lever is helped to the banking by the action of the wheel tooth on the impulse face, the Robin lever relies upon the balance to perform this function for it. Thus, depending on the condition of the oil at the pivots and the balance amplitude, the clearance between the notch of the lever and the pin in the roller will, during the approach to unlocking, be a variable factor. Unless made with great precision the rate will be seriously affected by the pin actually striking the corner of the notch during entry. Figures 59 and 60 taken from the watch shown in figure 523 illustrate the escapement, in this instance of straight line arrangement popular with Swiss constructors. The plates show the position of the lockings for alternate vibrations. The small drop to the entry stone in figure 60 allows no impulse to the balance. The large drop to the exit stone seen in figure 59 will allow of an impulse to the balance by the tooth nearest the balance staff acting upon the impulse pallet seen projecting from the roller beneath the unlocking pin. The banking is to the 'scape pinion by the ring formed in the lever. Constructed in this manner during the resurgence of popularity of the escapement during the second quarter of the nineteenth century it was very successful as a timekeeper if kept clean and oiled. The reason for this lies in the extreme angle of draw of the locking faces ensuring firm banking of the lever. This feature was not included by Robin and his contemporaries and their rates suffered badly for the want of it. Breguet made frequent use of the escapement and figure 61 shows his most common arrangement in which he introduced a lifting face to the exit stone so that the balance, being impulsed in one direction by the lever and on its return vibration by the 'scape-wheel, is less inclined to set. This modification necessitated the use of oil to the 'scape-wheel which, being in contact with the balance roller, soon affected the rate. To overcome this fault he introduced a double 'scape-wheel. Figure 404 taken from the watch shown in figure 403 illustrates the arrangement in which the upper wheel teeth impulse the balance. With this arrangement its performance is as good as the lever, but the complex and costly construction prohibited its use to all but the most expensive of his productions in which, quite often, the high cost of the watch was brought about by unnecessarily complicated work.

Debaufre

One of the first practical solutions to the problem of the recoil in the verge escapement was that of Debaufre. He moved the balance axis so that it was tangential to the face of the crown, or escape-wheel, teeth; and with an additional crown-wheel mounted on the same arbor so that the two sets of teeth faced inwards and supplied impulse to the balance by inclined planes cut into a circular roller attached to the staff. During the supplementary arc the tooth-tip rested on the dead face of the roller close to the centre of motion. Figure 63 shows the usual arrangement and is taken from the watch shown in figure 367. It is said that the objection to this arrangement is that the impulse tends always to exert pressure on the end of the top pivot. This may have been objectionable if the staff pivots were unjewelled, as they may have been in the earliest examples, but is not in itself of serious consequence as can be seen from the going of marine chronometers which always run dial up with a heavy balance.

The prime cause of the varying rate associated with this escapement lies in the lack of constancy of the resting friction, which is continuously changing by reason of the freedom of the balance pivots in their holes. With the best workmanship its going was never better than a moderate cylinder watch but it was nevertheless produced spasmodically for over a hundred years by a variety of makers. A variant of this escapement which suffers from the same fault is seen in figure 64, where a single wheel with radial teeth takes the place of the double crown-wheel and impulses a double roller each with an inclined impulse face cut into its edge (Sully's escapement).

So that the 'scape-wheel could run vertically between the plates with sufficient freedom for the wheel teeth, it of necessity had to be small in diameter and as this increased the ratio of resting friction variation was bad for the rate.

Fasoldt

An interesting and rarely seen variant of the lever escapement is that shown in figure 65. The two locking stones engaging the large 'scape-wheel and mounted on the lever serve the same purpose as those of the Robin, but the impulse is delivered to the balance by the smaller impulse-wheel acting upon the stone seen engaged by a tooth of the wheel. Turning the balance anti-clockwise would withdraw the exit stone allowing the impulse to be delivered. The inertia losses in the escapement are high and the action is correspondingly weak. At the time of its production in the last years of the nineteenth century the lever escapement held a position of great supremacy for pocket timekeepers and this position was undisturbed by Fasoldt's escapement. The watches are beautifully made and were a brave if undistinguished attempt to introduce a little variety into escapements which, by that time, had inevitably settled into a pattern of dull uniformity.

J. F. Cole Rotary Detent

Figure 66 taken from the watch shown in 551 shows a remarkable escapement by J. F. Cole that may well be the only example. It is a detached escapement in which an extra mobile is placed between the balance and 'scape-wheel and serves both to unlock the wheel and supply the impulse to the balance. The details of this wheel are more clearly seen in figure 67. The teeth of the 'scape-wheel rotate the smaller wheel by means of the vertical pins, but cannot advance by more than one tooth, for the velocity ratios are so arranged that the next tooth to engage will always butt its inclined tip to the approaching pin whilst the engaged pin is on the face of the preceding tooth. The unlocking stone of the balance when turning clockwise forces the small wheel to rotate as it meets one of the thin wire spokes projecting from the rim of the wheel, which it can do only by recoiling the 'scape-wheel as the locked pin travels down the inclined tip of the tooth. Upon reaching the corner of the face of the tooth the impulse commences, for the small-wheel has now been turned far enough to disengage the pin on the preceding tooth. At this moment the impulse pallet on the balance is presented to a tooth of the star-wheel, seen mounted on the small-wheel above the pins, and the impulse is delivered as in the duplex escapement. The small-wheel continues to turn under the influence of the 'scape-wheel until the next pin butts against the following 'scape-wheel tooth. During the return vibration the unlocking stone causes the wheel to recoil as it brushes past the succeeding spoke. The action is then ready to commence again. This curious escapement, reflecting Cole's ingenuity at its best, has a most lively and convincing action. The recoiling of the wheel by the vertical pins causes wear to the corners of the 'scape-wheel, so that tripping is provoked by variations in power affecting the velocity of the 'scape-wheel. It was not found in wear to be very reliable, although its rate dial up is most precise. It is included for its extreme rarity and because the escapement cannot be seen in detail without dismantling the movement.

So far as the authors are aware the only so-called constant force escapement used in a watch is that of Haley shown in figure 68. The action is as follows. As the balance rotates clockwise the unlocking jewel A draws aside the detent B and releases arm C which impelled by the spiral spring supplies impulse to the balance as arm E, mounted on the same arbor, meets impulse pallet D. On completing the impulse the impulse mechanism continues to rotate until a projection on the arbor lifts detent F by its cranked extension and releases winding wheel I from locking stone G. By means of the vertical teeth on the winding wheel the arm H, also mounted on the arbor, is lifted so that C is returned to the locked position on detent B. The conventional passing spring allows for the return vibration without disturbing the locking. This complex arrangement suffers from the fault that it requires two springs—the mainspring and the constant force-spring—to work in concert. The odds against this happening without variance are too great and, particularly in wear, tripping occurs fairly easily. If adjusted so that the action is more certain the drops are excessive and the balance amplitude is poor. The effects of temperature on the spiral constant force-spring would be to some extent compensated for by the change in viscosity of the oil, but the compensation would be unreliable and cause variety in the rate.

20 Verge

21 Breguet ruby cylinder

22 Breguet ruby cylinder

23 Graham cylinder

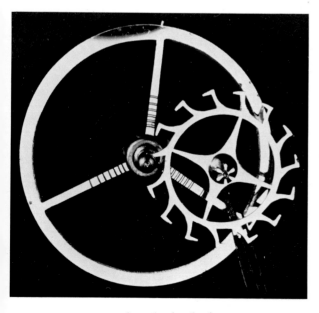

24 Flat wheel cylinder

25 Virgule

26 Double virgule

27 Duplex

28 Double wheel duplex

29 Chinese duplex

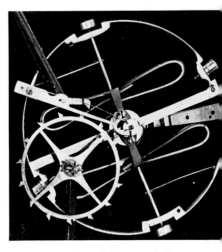

30 Arnold pivoted detent

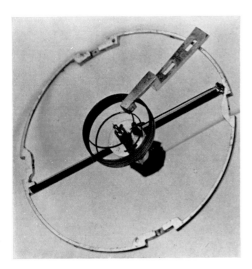

31 Arnold isochronal curb

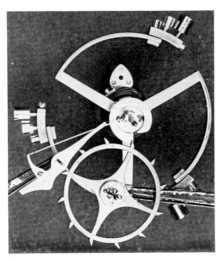

32 Berthoud pivoted detent

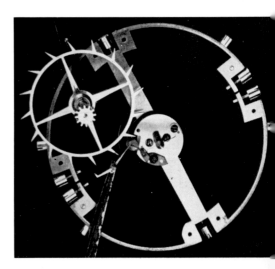

33 Breguet pivoted detent

34 Breguet pivoted detent   35 Kendal pivoted detent   36 Arnold spring detent

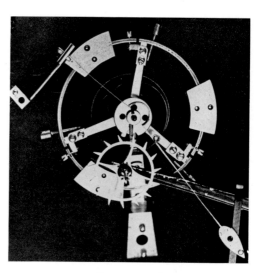

37 Earnshaw spring detent   38 Frodsham spring detent   39 Peto cross detent

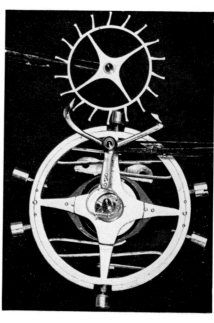

40 J. F. Cole double rotary detached   41 Emery lever   42 Pendleton lever

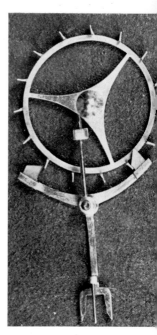

43 Perigal lever

44 Grant lever

45 Grant lever

46 Grant double balance wheel lever

47 Leroux lever

48 Taylor lever

49 Rack lever

50 Massey lever

51 Massey lever

52   Savage two-pin lever   53   Early Breguet lever   54   Breguet Tourbillon lever

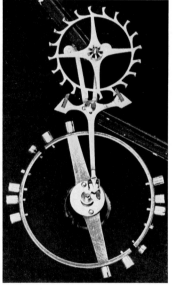

55   Breguet late lever   56   Breguet late lever   57   Breguet pointed pivots

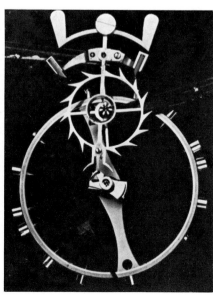

58   Pouzait lever   59   Late robin   60   Late robin

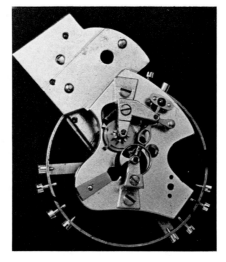

61   Breguet robin   62   Double wheel robin   63   Debaufre

64   Sully   65   Fasoldt   66   J. F. Cole rotary detent

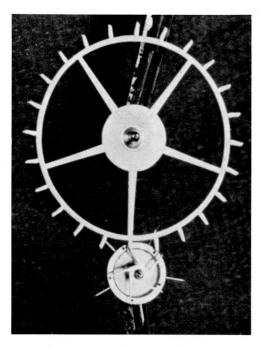

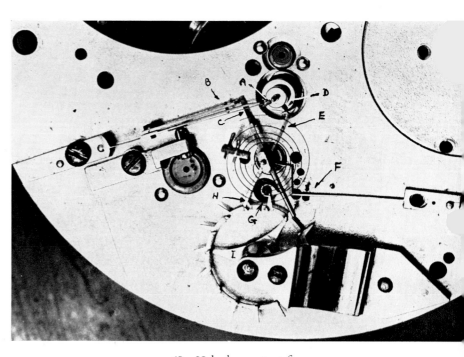

67   J. F. Cole rotary detent   68   Haley's constant force

69–71. Anonymous, probably German. Probably second quarter of the sixteenth century. Verge escapement without balance-spring. Large, thin-rimmed iron balance-wheel with thin flexible S-shaped balance cock. Iron train with long thin fusee and gut. Metal gilt engraved drum-shaped case with 24-hour dial and iron hand, numbers 1 to 12 in Roman numerals, 13 to 24 in Arabic numerals. Touch pieces at the hours. The 2's are written as Z's. It may be that these early watches with fusees show Italian influence as against the more typically German stackfreed.

72–3. Anonymous, probably German. Second quarter of the sixteenth century. Verge escapement without balance-spring. Ratchet set-up regulator. Iron train. Long narrow fusee with gut. Drum-shaped metal gilt and engraved case and dial with iron hand. 24-hour dial, numbers 1 to 12 in Roman numerals and 13 to 24 in Arabic numerals, the 2's as Z's, which is an indication of early date. The skeleton lay-out of the movement is similar to the large drum-shaped clock by Jacob Czech, dated 1525, belonging to the Society of Antiquaries of London and may therefore be of South German origin.

74–6. Jacques de la Garde, Loire, France. Dated 1551. Verge escapement without balance-spring. Set-up regulator. Fusee and gut. Hour-striking clock-watch. Case and dial engraved metal gilt. This is the earliest dated watch. As opposed to all the German watches, the train is entirely of brass. Note the long narrow fusee typical of early French watches. It is believed that the winding key is original. The watch also has its original travelling case.

77–81. Watch with alarum attachment. Anonymous, German. Probably second quarter of the sixteenth century. Verge escapement without balance-spring. Bristle regulator. The train of both watch and alarum are of iron throughout. Stackfreed, unenclosed mainspring. The drum-shaped case and dial are of brass gilt engraved. The dial has touch pieces at each hour and a single iron hand. The alarum has three spring feet by which it is attached to a rim on the top of the case of the watch. Depending from the alarum is the detent and the alarum is rotated until the detent is over the hour at which the alarum is to go off. The hand of the watch trips the detent as it reaches it.

82–4. Anonymous, German. Third quarter of the sixteenth century. Verge escapement without balance-spring. Bristle regulator. Stackfreed with uncased mainspring. Iron train with alarum. Brass gilt case and dial. 24-hour dial, numbers 1 to 12 in Roman numerals, 13 to 24 in Arabic numerals. Movable alarum setting dial in the centre. Single iron hand. The case pierced and engraved with apertures in the lid through which to see the hours. Note the S-shaped balance cock, making for easy adjustment of the depth of the escapement. The drum-shaped case indicates a date not later than the third quarter of the sixteenth century. Note also that 2's are engraved as Z's, indicative of an early date.

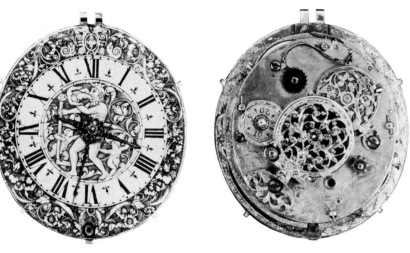

85–8. Silver skull watch, formerly the property of Mary Queen of Scots. Late sixteenth century. An exceptionally important specimen of this type of form watch. The movement, by J. Moysan of Blois, France, has been modified to balance-spring, *circa* 1780. The engraved dial and hands are of the same period.

89–91. Anonymous, but bearing the initials A. R. in a shield. German. End of the sixteenth century. Verge escapement with bristle regulator. Stackfreed. Hour-striking clock-watch. The case which is engraved and pierced and the dial which has touch pieces at the hours are of metal gilt. This is a typical watch of the end of the sixteenth century, at which time curved sides were just beginning to come into fashion. The hinged cover over the dial has apertures pierced in it for reading the hours.

92–3. P. Chappelle. Probably French. *Circa* 1600. Verge escapement without balance-spring. Ratchet set-up regulator. Fusee and gut. The case and dial are of plain brass gilt. Single blued steel hand. This is an unknown maker, but from the style of the signature and the floreate design of the balance-cock it is almost certainly French in origin. The movement does not hinge into the case but is held in by two spring clips disengaged by knobs emerging through the dial at 9 o'clock and 3 o'clock.

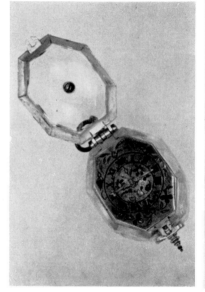 

94–5. Anonymous, German. *Circa* 1600. Verge escapement without spring. Stackfreed with bristle regulator. Chamlevé silver and enamel dial with single gilt hand. Octagonal crystal case. See also colour illustration (A) on Dust Jacket. This is an example of a very rare form of rock crystal case in which the movement is hinged direct to it, and not with a metal rim as is usual.

96–8. Jacques Bulke, London, England. *Circa* 1600. Verge escapement without balance-spring. Ratchet set-up regulator. Fusee and gut. Hour-striking clockwatch. The case, which is flat-sided and pierced, and the dial are of engraved gilt metal. Single steel hand. Jacques Bulke is one of the earliest recorded British watchmakers and this must be one of the earliest surviving British watches. A characteristic English feature is the engraved decorative border round the edge of the watch plate, but in its brass train with fusee and almost all other mechanical and decorative features the watch shows strong French influence.

99–101. C. Cameel, Strasbourg, Germany. *Circa* 1625. Verge escapement without balance-spring. Ratchet set-up regulator. Fusee and gut. Plain silver dial and blued steel hand. Silver case. This is one of the more elaborate form watches of the early seventeenth century. The dial is revealed by hinging back the legs and stomach of the bird whereupon the dial is revealed and the movement will also hinge through the same aperture.

102–3. Robert Grinkin, London, England. First quarter of the seventeenth century. Verge escapement without balance-spring. Ratchet set-up regulator. Fusee and gut. The case and dial plate of engraved gilt metal, chapter ring of silver, blued steel hand. Note engraved border to watch plate, typical of early English work. Foliate design of balance-cock showing French influence, pegged and pinned to the watch plate.

104–5. Robert Grinkin, London, England. First quarter of the seventeenth century. Verge escapement without balance-spring. Ratchet set-up regulator. Fusee and gut. Engraved silver dial with single blued steel hand. Engraved silver oval case with solid dial cover. Note engraved border round the movement plate typical of English work of this period. Balance-cock fitted to a peg on the watch plate and pinned.

106–8. Edmund Bull, London, England. *Circa* 1620. Verge escapement without balance-spring. Worm and wheel set-up regulator. Fusee and gut. Silver engraved dial with single blued steel hand. Silver case of unusual design, being flat-sided and scalloped, reminiscent of the crystal cases of the period. The watch at present has a glass over the dial which is apparently original but may at first have been crystal held in by the earliest method of four tags bent over the edge of the glass. The signature is in a border round the edge of the dial, similar to the English engraved borders which by this time were beginning to go out of fashion.

109–11. Simon Bartram. Unrecorded. England. First quarter of the seventeenth century. Verge escapement without spring. Fusee converted from gut to chain. Dial gilt with silver chapter rings for hours, month, date. Apertures for moon phases, day of the week and zodiac sign. Single steel hand. Rock crystal case with enamel rim to front cover, attached to back without metal rim. Note decorated edge to top plate and balance-cock pinned to stud.

112–13. David Ramsay (Scotus), England. First quarter of the seventeenth century. Verge escapement without spring. Ratchet type set-up regulator. Fusee and gut. Engraved silver dial with single steel hand. Octagonal rock crystal case; the movement hinged to metal rims into which the crystal is fitted.

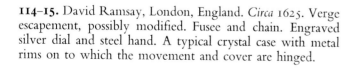

114–15. David Ramsay, London, England. *Circa* 1625. Verge escapement, possibly modified. Fusee and chain. Engraved silver dial and steel hand. A typical crystal case with metal rims on to which the movement and cover are hinged.

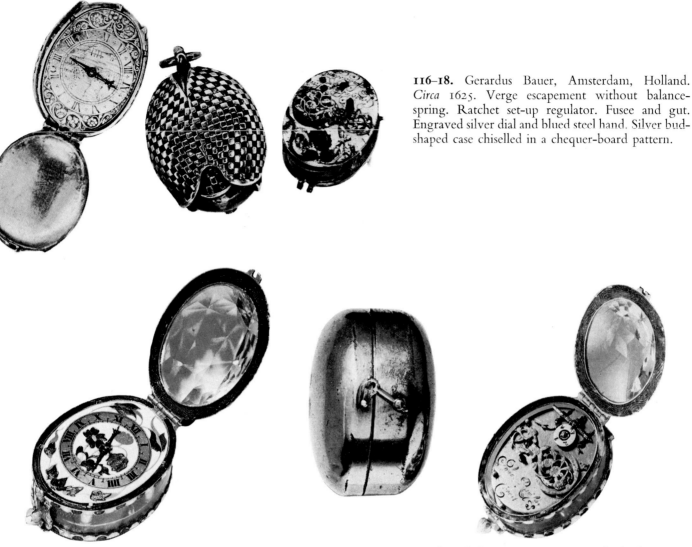

116–18. Gerardus Bauer, Amsterdam, Holland. *Circa* 1625. Verge escapement without balance-spring. Ratchet set-up regulator. Fusee and gut. Engraved silver dial and blued steel hand. Silver bud-shaped case chiselled in a chequer-board pattern.

119–21. David Ramsay, London, England. *Circa* 1625. Verge escapement without balance-spring. Worm and wheel set-up regulator. Enamel dial painted in white with coloured flowers. Silver chapter ring. Blued steel hand. Faceted rock crystal case held in metal rims. Outer silver carrying case.

–3. John Snow, London, England. *Circa* 1630. ge escapement without balance-spring. Worm wheel set-up regulator. Fusee and gut. Plain silver and blued steel hand. Plain silver case with tal. This is probably original as it represents a early method of fixing the crystal, which is held a rim with tags which are turned alternately er the crystal and under the rim of the watch.

124–5. P. Grebauval, Rouen, France. Second quarter of the seventeenth century. Verge escapement without balance-spring. Decorative continental-type ratchet set-up regulator. Fusee and gut. Engraved silver dial with single blued steel hand. Oval-shaped, engraved gilt case with solid front and back covers. The deep engraving is typical of French work as opposed to English engraving which was usually more shallow. The cover of the movement has on its inside a sundial and compass.

126–9. Signed David Ramsay Scottes. England. *Circa* 1625. Verge escapement without balance-spring. Ratchet set-up regulator. Fusee and gut. Balance-cock pegged and pinned. The case and dial, which are in the form of a six-pointed star, are of silver and engraved all over. The single hand is of gold.

130–2. James Vautrollier, London, England. *Circa* 1630. Verge escapement without balance-spring. Ratchet set-up regulator. Fusee and gut. Engraved silver dial. Gilt hand. Engraved silver case. Note the circular window: from the engraving of the case it is evident that there always was such an aperture which was probably originally filled with crystal. The present fixing of the bezel by screws is probably later. The decoration of the movement with engraved band round the edge is typically English. Note also the outer travelling case and original key.

133–5. A. Senebier, Geneva, Switzerland. *Circa* 1630. Verge escapement without balance-spring. Ratchet type set-up with unusually large decorative click. Fusee and gut. Engraved gilt dial with silver chapter ring and steel hand. Eight-lobed crystal case with gilt engraved rims. The watch also has an outer case of wood covered with fish skin. Note the unusual rectangular shaped cock-foot, pegged and pinned to the watch plate.

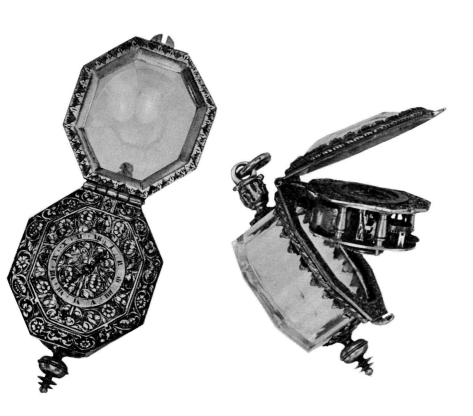

136–7. John Micasius, London, England. *Circa* 1630. Verge escapement without balance-spring. Ratchet set-up regulator. Fusee and gut. Engraved gilt dial with silver chapter ring and steel hand. Octagonal crystal case with gilt rims.

138–9. F. Sermand. Either French or Swiss. *Circa* 1640. Verge escapement without balance-spring. Ratchet type set-up regulator. Fusee and gut. Gilt engraved dial with silver chapter ring and single steel hand. Oval case cast in silver in the form of a cockle shell. Winding hole with shutter.

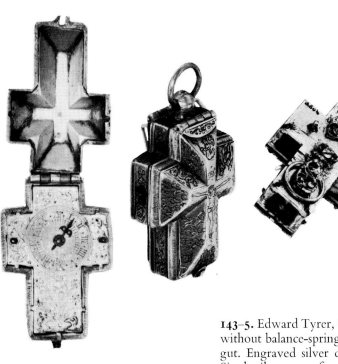

140–2. George Coique, France. Second quarter of the seventeenth century. Verge escapement. Plain balance-wheel probably slightly later, without balance-spring. Ratchet type set-up regulator. Fusee and gut. Engraved silver case with gilt dial plate and silver chapter ring. Single blued steel hand, possibly of later date. A typical form watch of the type popular in the second quarter of the seventeenth century.

143–5. Edward Tyrer, Chester, England. *Circa* 1630. Verge escapement without balance-spring. Worm and wheel set-up regulator. Fusee and gut. Engraved silver dial and chapter ring. Single blued steel hand. Single silver case of oval shape with hinged cover to dial. The movement hinges out of the case. Note the engraved band of decoration round the movement plate typical of English practice at this time; the balance-cock is pegged and pinned to the plate. This is a fairly early specimen of the English 'Puritan' watch.

146–8. Beniamin Hill, London, England. Mid-seventeenth century. Verge escapement without balance-spring. Worm and wheel set-up regulator. Balance-cock attached to plate by screw. Fusee and gut. Silver dial with subsidiary dials for calendar and astronomical work. Blued steel hands. Split bezel for glass. Pair case, the outer case covered in leather decorated with silver pinwork.

149–51. Edward East, London, England. Second quarter of the seventeenth century. Verge escapement without balance-spring. Worm and wheel set-up type regulator. Fusee and gut. Engraved silver dial with single blued steel hand. Silver pair case, the outer case decorated with leather and silver pinwork. Note cock with foliate engraving and piercing and irregular-shaped foot typical of this period, with a late example of fitting the cock to a peg on the watch plate and fixed with a pin. The thinness of the movement is typical of the half-century before the introduction of the balance-spring.

152–4. Daniel Fletcher, London, England. Mid-seventeenth century. Verge escapement without balance-spring. Worm and wheel set-up type regulator. Fusee and gut. Engraved silver dial, the centre part pierced over a gilt background. Single blued steel hour hand; fixed calendar chapter ring with moving annular ring between hour and date chapter rings, with gilt pointer for the date, seen in the illustration pointing to the fourteenth day. Silver pair case, the outer case covered in black leather decorated with silver pinwork. Note irregular shaped cock-foot and an early example of fixing by a screw. Foliate type decoration of the cock plate typical of mid-seventeenth century English design. This is a very early example of what was to become the typical English pair case.

155–6. Sam Aspinwall, England. Early seventeenth century. Verge escapement without balance-spring. Ratchet type set-up regulator. Fusee and gut. Plain silver dial with touch pieces on gilt background; silver blued steel hand. Cast silver oval case. Note the typical balance-cock, pegged and pinned.

157-9. Nicolaus Rugendas, Augsburg, Germany, 1650. Verge escapement without balance-spring. Worm and wheel set-up regulator. Fusee and gut. The case and dial, except for the chapter ring which is of white enamel, is chiselled radially to produce an effect which, 150 years later, was commonly produced by engine-turning, and is covered by a translucent rust-coloured enamel. Single gilt hand.

160-2. Goullons, Paris, France. *Circa* 1650. Verge escapement without balance-spring. Worm and wheel set-up regulator. Fusee and gut. Enamel chapter ring with steel hand. Gold case enamelled with white flowers and foliage in relief with black markings.

163-5. Beniamin Hill, London, England. *Circa* 1650. Verge escapement without balance-spring. Worm and wheel set up regulator. Fusee and gut. Silver dial with matt centre and single steel hand. Silver cast and chiselled case in the form of a pomegranate. Note unusually long oval-shaped cock foot attached to watch plate by a screw.

166–8. Estienne Hubert, Rouen, France. *Circa* 1660. Verge escapement without balance spring. Worm and wheel set-up regulator. Engraved silver dial and steel hand. Chiselled and engraved silver case. Revolving slide to cover winding hole in back of the single case. A typical French watch of the late pre-balance-spring era. It also has an outer case of leather with silver pinwork.

169. Thomas Tompion, London, England. *Circa* 1675. Verge escapement without balance-spring. Worm and wheel set-up regulator (part of the decorative supporting hinges missing). Fusee and gut. This is a movement only and has no dial or case. It is the only known surviving specimen of a Tompion watch movement of the pre-balance-spring era. Note the early type of cock with irregular edge to cock-foot and plate, the cock screwed to the plate. The train is of high quality with no pinion of less than six leaves. Three-wheel train. 15-hour going period.

170–2. Seignior, London, England. *Circa* 1670. Verge escapement without balance-spring. Worm and wheel set-up regulator. Fusee and chain. Matt gold champlevé dial. Single steel hand. Gold inner case, outer case covered in black leather decorated with gold pinwork. This almost mint watch is typical of the period just before the introduction of the balance-spring.

173–5. Ignatius Huggeford, London, England. *Circa* 1670. Verge escapement without balance-spring. Worm and wheel set-up regulator. Fusee and chain. Silver dial, the hour numerals on heart-shaped plaques with a single steel hand surrounded by a revolving silver calendar ring. Silver pair case, the outer case covered in tortoiseshell decorated with silver pinwork. In 1704 this watch was used to oppose Facio de Duillier's application for a prolongation of his patent for jewelling. It was produced by the Clockmakers' Company to show that he had been anticipated in his invention, but in the nineteenth century it was found on examination that what appears to be a ruby end-stone to the balance-staff is purely decorative and does not operate as an end-stone. The watch is additionally unusual in that the balance-cock is made of blued steel.

176–8. Martinot, Paris, France. *Circa* 1670. Verge escapement without balance-spring. Worm and wheel set-up regulator. Fusee and gut. Enamel dial with single steel hand. This is a very early example of a one-piece enamel dial. Gold pair case. The outer case gold filigree.

179-81. Jeremie Gregory, London, England. *Circa* 1670. Verge escapement without balance-spring. Worm and wheel set-up regulator. Fusee and gut. Alarum. Silver dial with engraved centre and rotating alarum set dial. Single steel hand, pierced and engraved silver case and plain silver outer case probably of later date.

182–4. Henry Arlaud, London, England. *Circa* 1665. Verge escapement without balance-spring. Fusee and gut. Gilt dial with silver chapter rings for age of moon, hours and date. Aperture for sign of zodiac, moon phases and day of the week. Silver case engraved with floral pattern and the words 'Richard Baillie at the Aibay'.

185–7. Daniel Carre. Probably English. *Circa* 1670. Verge escapement. Plain steel balance, later converted to balance-spring with later regulator. Fusee and gut. Engraved gilt dial with subsidiary dials for phases of the moon, month, day of the month, day of the week and hours. Pair case, the outer case covered in oxydised iron decorated with silver pinwork. Note the presence on the back plate of the worm and wheel set-up regulator belonging to the pre-balance-spring period. The day of the month indicator is in French but the style of the watch is English, suggesting that it was made for the export market.

188–90. Thomas Tompion, London, England. *Circa* 1675–80. Verge escapement. Fusee and chain. Later enamel dial and steel beetle and poker hands. Silver pair case, the outer case decorated with tortoiseshell and silver inlay. This is a very early balance-spring watch. It is unnumbered, indicating a date earlier than about 1682 when Tompion started numbering his watches. Also, the foot of the balance-cock has an irregular rim and there is no mask engraved at the juncture of the table and foot of the cock. All these are signs of the very early balance-spring period.

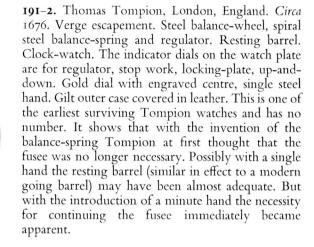

191–2. Thomas Tompion, London, England. *Circa* 1676. Verge escapement. Steel balance-wheel, spiral steel balance-spring and regulator. Resting barrel. Clock-watch. The indicator dials on the watch plate are for regulator, stop work, locking-plate, up-and-down. Gold dial with engraved centre, single steel hand. Gilt outer case covered in leather. This is one of the earliest surviving Tompion watches and has no number. It shows that with the invention of the balance-spring Tompion at first thought that the fusee was no longer necessary. Possibly with a single hand the resting barrel (similar in effect to a modern going barrel) may have been almost adequate. But with the introduction of a minute hand the necessity for continuing the fusee immediately became apparent.

193–5. Henricus Jones, London, England. 1675–80. Verge escapement. Fusee and chain. Silver dial with oval chapter ring for minute divisions, and expanding hand so that the pointer is always pointing to the outer edge of the oval-shaped chapter ring. Silver pair case, the outer case decorated with leather and silver pinwork. This must be one of the earliest surviving watches of the balance-spring period.

196–7. Jonathan Grounds, London, England. *Circa* 1680. Verge escapement. Barrow type regulator. Fusee and chain. Champlevé enamel dial with blued steel hands. Silver pair case. Note the very early type of balance-cock without a mask at the juncture of the table and foot. The barrow regulator is also indicative of the very early balance-spring period. The signature on the dial is spelt Grounds, but that on the movement is spelt Growndes.

198–9. Daniel Quare. No. 441. London, England. *Circa* 1680 or a little earlier. Verge escapement. Spiral steel balance-spring and regulator. Fusee and chain. Silver dial. An unusual combination of the six-hour dial with an outer calendar ring. Blued steel hand. Pair case, the outer case of green leather with gold pins which, judging from the curved ends of the hinge, is probably a little later than the inner case and movement. The watch is undoubtedly of very early balance-spring date, the balance-cock which is of silver having an irregular shaped foot and no mask engraved at the junction of the foot and the plate. See also Fig. 204 for another Quare six-hour dial, Quare's watch No. 699.

200–2. Joseph Windmills, London, England. *Circa* 1680. Verge escapement. Fusee and chain. Champlevé silver dial with blued steel hand. Silver pair case, the outer case decorated with tortoiseshell inlaid with silver. Note irregular shaped foot to the balance cock typical of the earliest balance-spring period.

203–4. Daniel Quare. No. 699. London, England. *Circa* 1680–5. Verge escapement. Fusee and chain. Six-hour silver champlevé dial and blued steel hand. Silver pair case. For a discussion of the six-hour dial, see page 76,

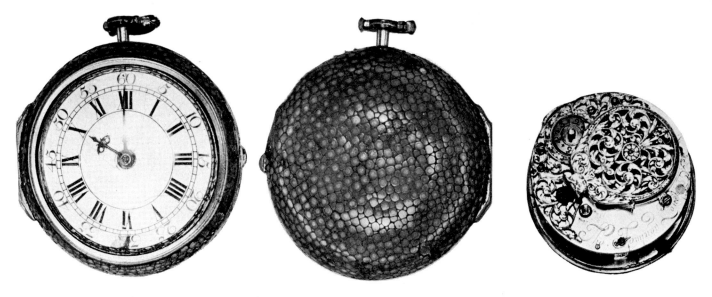

205–7. Thomas Tompion, London, England. *Circa* 1680. Verge escapement. Fusee and chain. Later enamel dial with blued steel beetle and poker hands. Pair case, the inner case gilt, the outer case covered in shagreen. This watch probably dates from the period about 1680 just before Tompion started numbering his products.

208–9. Benjamin Bell, London, England. *Circa* 1690. Verge escapement. Fusee and chain. Champlevé dial with blued steel tulip and poker hands with subsidiary seconds dial. Plain silver pair case with squared hinges. This watch, which is of very high quality, is of exceptionally large size and the presence of a seconds hand in the seventeenth century is unusual.

210–11. Peter Garon, London, England. *Circa* 1695. Spiral steel balance-spring and regulator. Fusee and chain. Champlevé silver dial with blued steel tulip-type hour hand and poker minute hand. Heavily engraved silver pair case with square-ended hinge. This is an exceptionally large watch, 3 inches in diameter and the movement is unusually decorative as to the cock foot, which is of unusually large size. The dial has a day-of-the-month aperture.

212–14. George Lyon. English. Probably last decade of the seventeenth century. Verge escapement. Fusee and chain. Silver 'sun and moon' dial with steel minutes hand and subsidiary seconds dial. Silver pair case, the outer case covered in tortoiseshell with silver inlay. For a discussion of the sun and moon dial see page 77. It was not unusual for the bottom part of these dials to be used for a seconds dial. The movement of this watch is highly decorative, even the rim of the contrate wheel being engraved.

215–16. Francisco Papillion, Florence, Italy. Late seventeenth century. Verge escapement. Resting main spring barrel without fusee. Alarum. Silver champlevé dial with rotating alarum set-dial in centre, single steel hand. Pierced silver case. Italian watches of this period are extremely rare. This watch is of fairly typical French lay-out, and it is rare but not unique to find such watches without a fusee. Note the irregular shape of the cock-foot typical of late seventeenth century design, and stopwork above the plate to both going and alarum spring-barrels.

217–18. Henry Poisson, London, England. *Circa* 1700. Verge escapement with spiral steel balance-spring and regulator. Fusee and chain. Engraved silver dial with eccentrically mounted chapter ring. Subsidiary dial for regulator and mock pendulum swinging in aperture at the bottom of the dial. In this form of mock-pendulum watch with the pendulum showing through the dial, the back plate of the watch is usually engraved all over as in this example.

219–20. Christoff Schöener, Auxburg, Germany. *Circa* 1700. Verge escapement with spiral steel balance-spring and regulator. Fusee and chain. Metal gilt sun and moon dial with subsidiary dial for seconds in the lower half of the dial, the whole surrounded by a calendar ring with a rotating pointer. Continental watches with unusual dials such as the sun and moon, fashionable at the end of the seventeenth century, are not very frequently found. It is however not unusual for sun and moon dial watches to have a seconds dial in the lower part of the dial. Note the all-over pierced decoration of the watch plate sometimes found in Continental watches but rarely or never in English watches of the period.

221–2. Langley Bradley. Code No. HYY. London, England. *Circa* 1710. Verge escapement with spiral steel balance-spring and regulator. Fusee and chain. Champlevé silver dial with beetle and poker blued steel hands. Silver pair case. This watch is unusual in that the dial is in mint condition, showing that the matt background of the silver champlevé dials were almost white in colour. This shows clearly in the illustration. Note also the unusual type of decorative pillars in which this maker seems to have specialised.

223–5. Christopher Egleton. No. 375. London, England. *Circa* 1700. Verge escapement. Fusee and chain. Champlevé silver dial with tulip hour hand and minute poker hands. Silver pair case, the outer case decorated with tortoiseshell and silver pinwork.

226–8. Langley Bradley. Code No. DBB. London, England. *Circa* 1700. Verge escapement. Fusee and chain. Silver dial with concentric calendar ring. Gilt pointer for hours and blued steel poker hand for minutes. Silver pair case. Fig. 228 is of the view under dial. The watch, which is in Sir John Soane's Museum, Lincoln's Inn Fields, is said to have belonged to Sir Christopher Wren and to have been presented to him by William and Mary. The Royal monogram W & M is worked into the plate pillars, Fig. 227. Note the curved ends to the hinges of the outer case, which came in at about 1700.

229–30. Gaudron, Paris, France. *Circa* 1700. Verge escapement. Spiral steel balance-spring and regulator. Fusee and chain. Gilt metal dial with separate enamel plaques for each hour and a white enamel ring for the hour divisions. Blued steel hand. Plain gilt case. This is a typical example of a single-handed oignon watch with bridge cock. The watch is wound through the centre of the dial. The case is unusual as these are usually engraved all over. It is interesting that this winding through the centre of the dial was later employed by Breguet for his souscription watches.

231–2. Brounker Watts, London, England. *Circa* 1700. Verge escapement. Fusee and chain. Hour-striking clock-watch on a bell. Silver repoussé dial with blued steel hands. Silver pair case, both cases pierced and engraved. Note squared ends to hinges of outer case. Note also brass gilt dust-cap with revolving steel catch of which this is a very early example.

233-4. Daniel Quare. No. 4465. London, England, 1713. Verge escapement. Fusee and chain. Gold champlevé dial, blued steel tulip-type hour hand and poker minute hand. Gold pair case. The plain loose-fitting loop-type pendant typical of the third and early fourth quarters of the seventeenth century was retained by Quare long after it had been abandoned by most other makers.

235-6. John Knibb, England. *Circa* 1700. Verge escapement. Fusee and chain. Champlevé silver dial with blued steel beetle and poker hands. Plain silver pair case. The square-shaped hinges of the outer case are typical of the late seventeenth century. The signature on the dial is Knibb, London, but on the watch plate is engraved John Knibb at Oxford; the word 'Oxford', however, has been erased as far as possible by being over-engraved with a foliate design. The inference may be that the watch was made by John Knibb for his brother Joseph in London.

237-9. John Finch. No. 135. London, England. *Circa* 1700. Verge escapement. Fusee and chain. Silver differential dial (see page 77). Pair case, outer case decorated with engraved tortoiseshell. Note Royal Arms engraved on balance cock.

240–2. Charles Gretton, London, England. 1702. Verge escapement. Fusee and chain. Champlevé gold dial with blued steel beetle and poker hands. Gold pair case. The pair case is decorated in a form which appears to anticipate engine turning but was probably done by punching with a dividing engine.

243–4. Daniel Quare. No. 3720. London, England. *Circa* 1705. Verge escapement. Fusee and chain. Gold dial with blued steel tulip hour hand and minute hand cranked to clear winding square at 3 o'clock. Regulator, dial and operating square at 12 o'clock. Gold pair case. Quare made several watches of this kind in which evidently the emphasis was upon being able to wind and regulate the watch without hinging the movement out of the case. Some of his watches of this type have original enamel dials. In the picture of the movement, note also the early use of a diamond end-stone to the balance staff.

245–8. Tompion & Banger. No. 233. London, England. *Circa* 1710. Verge escapement. Steel balance-wheel. Spiral steel balance-spring with regulator. Fusee and chain. Quarter repeater on a bell. Gold champlevé dial. Steel hands. Gold pair case, the outer case pierced, engraved and repoussé.

249–50. John Lanais, signed London, England, but see below. *Circa* 1720. Verge escapement, spiral steel balance-spring with regulator. Fusee and chain. Silver champlevé dial. Pierced gilt hands. Plain silver pair case. This watch is typical of a large number of this period, ostensibly London made, but in fact produced in Holland. Most of them, as in this case, have a bridge cock and an almost sure indication of Dutch manufacture in the arcaded minute ring round the edge of the dial. The pierced Continental-type gilt hands are also typical. These watches may be nevertheless of quite high quality, as is this example.

251–2. Joseph Banks, Nottingham, England. First quarter of the eighteenth century. Spiral steel balance-spring and regulator. Fusee and chain. Ornate silver differential-type dial with military and musical trophies, repoussé, chiselled and engraved. Plain silver pair case. For an explanation of this rare type of dial, see page 77. Provincial makers of this period were quite rare and work by Joseph Banks is usually characterised by ornate dials and the unusual position of the maker's signature on the balance-cock. The Banks family seem to have been active in Nottingham from the end of the seventeenth throughout the eighteenth century.

253–4. Belliard, Paris, France. First quarter of the eighteenth century. Verge escapement. Fusee and chain. Metal gilt dial with enamel cartouches for each hour and enamel hour ring. Blued steel hands wound through the dial with a male key. Metal gilt cast and engraved case. A typical French oignon of the early eighteenth century with typical French bridge-type cock. The hands have no motion work and thus have to be set independently.

255–6. John Bushman, London, England. Early eighteenth century. Verge escapement. Fusee and chain. Silver wandering hour dial. Silver pair case. The wandering-hour type of dial is found in the late seventeenth and early eighteenth century. For reasons not known nearly all these watches have one or more Royal emblems. In this case the Royal Arms are found engraved on the cock and a portrait of Queen Anne is found in the lower part of the dial surrounded by a pierced gilt fret. For an explanation of the workings of the wandering hour dial, see pages 76–7.

257–9. F. Bertrand, Paris, France. First quarter of the eighteenth century. Verge escapement. Bridge-type balance-cock. Alarum. Enamel dial with gilt hands and rotating alarum set-dial in centre. Silver pair case, both inner and outer cases pierced and engraved.

260–1. Simpton, London, England (but see note below). *Circa* 1720. Verge escapement with spiral steel balance-spring and regulator. Fusee and chain. Silver repoussé dial ornamented with semi-precious stones. Hands also decorated with semi-precious stones. Gold pair case, the outer case repoussé with free-standing decoration applied in two layers, the whole contained in a third outer case of shagreen. This watch is similar to that shown in Fig. 249, being made in Holland despite the London attribution. The arcaded minute chapter ring is typical of this type of watch. This form of free-standing repoussé decoration was only fashionable for a short period.

262–5. John Elicott. No. 2700. London, England, 1742. Cylinder escapement with spiral steel balance-spring and regulator. Fusee and chain with bolt and shutter maintaining power. Complicated calendar and astronomical trains. Equation work. Seconds dial on the back of the watch. Gold case. For a picture of the complicated dial, see colour plate, Fig. 15.

266–7. Archambo. No. 1623. London, England. *Circa* 1740. Verge escapement. Steel balance-wheel, spiral steel balance-spring and regulator. Fusee and chain. Quarter repeating clock-watch playing music (choice of two airs) on five bells, at each hour. Enamel dial. Steel hands. Movement only.

268–70 (*below*). George Graham. No. 883. London, England, 1745. Cylinder escapement. Fusee and chain. Quarter repeater on a bell, operated by depressing the pendant. Enamel dial, blued steel beetle and poker hands. Gold pair case, the outer case covered in leather decorated with gold pinwork. Note diamond end-stoned balance staff universally used by Graham, and solid engraved foot to the balance cock, introduced by him in about 1725 and subsequently used in all his watches. The dust-cap is gilt.

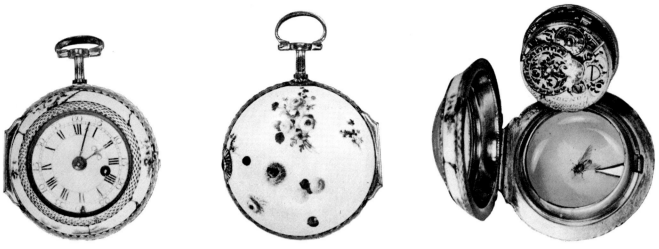

271–3. G. Grantham. No. 2980. London, England. *Circa* 1750. Verge escapement. Fusee and chain. Enamel dial, blued steel beetle and poker hands. Pair case, the outer case painted enamel. The decoration is painted on a white background and a fly is painted on the inside of the back case.

274–5. Julien le Roy, Paris, France. *Circa* 1750. Verge escapement. Fusee and chain. Gold dial with ring of white enamel plaques for hour figures. Small plaque for minute figures. Two enamel plaques for name and Paris. Diamond shaped inserts of green translucent enamel between minute plaques. Note typical mid-eighteenth century French type of bridge cock with steel coqueret as end bearing for balance-staff.

276–8. Conyers Dunlop. No. 3383. London, England. 1750. Cylinder escapement with ruby end-stones to balance staff. Fusee and chain. Dumb quarter repeater. Enamel dial with blued steel beetle and poker hands. Gold case, the back enamelled with a classical subject signed G. M. Moser.

279–81. Julien le Roy, Paris, France. *Circa* 1750. Verge escapement. Steel balance-wheel, spiral steel balance-spring with regulator. Fusee and chain. Enamel dial, gold hands. Inner case gold, outer case enamel with pierced and repoussé gold appliqué decoration. This is a very rare form of case decoration. The movement, almost certainly by Julien le Roy, is also unusual in having steel pillars and a silver cock.

282. Julien le Roy. No. 4757. Paris, France. *Circa* 1755. Lever escapement. Steel and gold balance. Spiral steel balance-spring with gridiron type compensation curb. Fusee and chain. Movement only. For a discussion of this movement, see pages 44–6.

283–4. Benjamin Gray. Code No. XON. London, England. *Circa* 1760. Cylinder escapement. Spiral steel balance-spring and regulator. Fusee and chain. Enamel dial, steel hands. Single gold case. Benjamin Gray may have specialised in watches of this shape as at least one other example is known to exist.

285–6. Laurence, Bath, England, 1763. Cylinder escapement. Fusee and chain. Enamel dial with blued steel beetle and poker hands. Silver gilt case. A typical, if fairly rare, eighteenth century skeleton movement.

287–9. Mudge & Dutton. No. 580. London, England. 1764. Cylinder escapement with spiral steel balance spring and regulator. Enamel dial. Blued steel hour and minute hands. Polished steel sweep centre seconds hand. Gilt dust-cap. Plain gold pair case. This watch is virtually identical with the cylinder watches made by George Graham from before 1730.

290–1. Ferdinand Berthoud. No. 417. Paris, France, 1764. Verge escapement with spiral steel balance-spring. 'Gridiron'-type compensation curb with regulator. Fusee and chain. Enamel dial. Gold hour and minute hands. Steel sweep centre seconds hand. Plain gold case. With the exception of the Jeffreys-Harrison watch of 1753 and possibly the Julien le Roy lever watch (see Fig. 282 and pages 44–6), this is the oldest surviving pocket watch with temperature compensation.

292–4. Barrow, London, England. *Circa* 1685. Verge escapement with spiral steel balance-spring and regulator. Fusee and chain. Hour-striking clock-watch. Champlevé silver dial, blued steel hands. Pierced and engraved gold pair case. A typical clock-watch of the last quarter of the seventeenth century. Note design of balance cock typical of early balance-spring period without mask and with irregular edge to cock-foot. Note also locking plate on the back plate of the watch.

295–7. Richard Carrington. No. 326. London, England. *Circa* 1770. Verge escapement. Fusee and chain. Enamel dial with blued steel beetle and poker hands. Gold pair case, the outer case decorated with translucent enamel and an heraldic shield.

298–9. John Arnold, London, England. No. 21. *Circa* 1782. Spring detent. Helical steel spring with terminal curves. Free-sprung. Fusee and chain. Later (1797) enamel dial with blued steel hands. Signed Arnold and Son. Silver case HM 1797. In 1797 Arnold added his final type of bimetallic compensation balance. Probably in substitution for an original 'S' balance.

300. English. *Circa* 1780. No movement, illustrated solely on account of the unusual case which is of Battersea enamel.

301–2. Recordon. No. 157. London, England. Probably 1780–90. Duplex escapement. Going barrel. Self-winding. See weight in illustration of movement. Enamel dial with gold hands and steel seconds hand. Plain silver case. Recordon took out a patent in this country for the self-winding watch in 1780, of which this is probably the earliest surviving English example.

303–4. J. Leroux, London, England, 1785. Lever escapement. Plain brass balance with two affixed bimetallic rims, with stops to limit outward movement. Conical shaped steel balance-spring, free sprung. Fusee and chain. Enamel regulator-type dial with gold hands. Gold pair case. For illustrations of this very unusual escapement, see Fig. 47, described in the technical section on page 116.

305–7. Breguet à Paris. No. 128$\frac{5}{85}$. Paris, France, 1785. Cylinder escapement with spiral steel balance-spring with regulator. Fusee and chain. Minute repeater. Enamel dial, gold hands. Plain gold case. This is one of the earliest surviving Breguet watches. The fractional number $\frac{5}{85}$ indicates the date, May 1785. At this date Breguet always added 'à Paris' to his signature. The cylinder is of steel and not of Breguet's later pattern.

308. Josiah Emery. No. 1123. London, England. *Circa* 1786. Ruby cylinder escapement. Four-arm brass balance. Steel tapered helical balance spring with regulator incorporating a compensation curb consisting of two bimetallic strips. Movement only. While this movement bears no great resemblance to the lever watches of Emery, it bears a very close resemblance to the lever watch by Francis Perigal, see Fig. 309. Emery's watches, on the other hand, bear a close resemblance to those of Pendleton and Mudge & Dutton. The inference may be that all these makers used a common source for their ébauches.

309–10. Francis Perigal. No. 1053. London, England. Probably late 1780's. Lever escapement. Plain four-arm brass balance with spiral steel balance-spring and regulator carrying sugar-tong-type compensation curb with two bimetallic arms. Fusee and chain. Enamel dial and gold hands with subsidiary dials for seconds and temperature. Plain silver case (recased). For illustration of escapement, see Fig. 43, described in the technical section on pages 113–14.

311–12. Recordon. No. 180. London, England. Probably 1784. Duplex escapement. Regulator operated through the dial. Going barrel self-winding. See illustration of movement. See remarks in caption to Fig. 301 regarding Recordon and self-winding watches.

313–14. Larcum Kendall. Code No. B + Y. London, England, 1786. Pivoted detent escapement. Three-arm brass balance; spiral steel balance-spring with reverse curve at end for regulator, mounted on spiral bimetallic compensation curb which can be adjusted for mean time by a square seen in the illustration between the cock-foot and the cock of the compensation curb. Fusee and chain. Enamel regulator type dial with blued steel hands. Silver case. For illustration of escapement, see Fig. 35, described in the technical section on page 104.

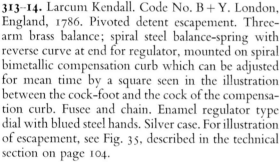

315–18. Breguet. No. 19. Paris, France. *Circa* 1787. Lever escapement. Three-arm bimetallic compensation balance. Helical steel balance spring with terminal curves and regulator. Two going barrels. Quarter repeating. Engine-turned silver dial with blued steel hands. Subsidiary dials for up-and-down and seconds. Engine-turned gold case with the arms of the Prince Regent. This is one of the first 30 watches appearing in Breguet's books which started in 1787. All were perpetuelles—this is the simplest type. For a further discussion of the escapement, see technical section, pages 119–20.

319-20. A. L. Breguet. No. 12. Paris, France, 1789. Escapement pivoted detent. Two-arm bimetallic compensation balance. Helical steel balance-spring without end-curves, free sprung, the balance-staff supported at each end by three friction rollers. Fusee and chain. Engine-turned silver dial with sweep centre minutes hand, subsidiary dials for hours and seconds. Plain silver case. This is the only example known of a watch by Breguet with friction rollers, and the lay-out of the movement is in every way more typical of Ferdinand Berthoud.

321-2. John Arnold. No. 64. London, England, 1789. Pivoted detent. Two bimetallic affixes. Helical spring with terminal curves and unusual attachment to balance to quicken the rate during excessively long arcs. Enamel dial with extra large seconds dial overlapping minute divisions. For illustration of escapement, see Fig. 30. For illustration of isochronal attachment to balance, see Fig. 31.

323-4. Richard Pendleton, Pentonville. No. 180. London, England. Late eighteenth century. Lever escapement, plain brass balance with S-shaped bimetallic compensation affixes. Helical steel balance-spring with end-curves free sprung. Fusee and chain. Enamel regulator type dial with blued steel hands. Silver case. Pendleton is known to have made all or most of Emery's lever escapement watches which this watch greatly resembles, especially as to the bridge-type balance-cock and balance-wheel. The escapement, however, is quite different. For illustration of escapement, see Fig. 42, described in the technical section on page 118.

325–7. Jaquet Droz, marked London, but in fact Swiss; the firm had branches in several capital cities. *Circa* 1790. Cylinder escapement. Quarter striking clock-watch on one bell. Self-winding with separate weights for going and striking trains. Enamel dial with gold hands and sweep centre seconds hand. Case decorated round the dial with half pearls and green stones with painted enamel back. This watch is one of a pair and is also illustrated in colour, Fig. H.

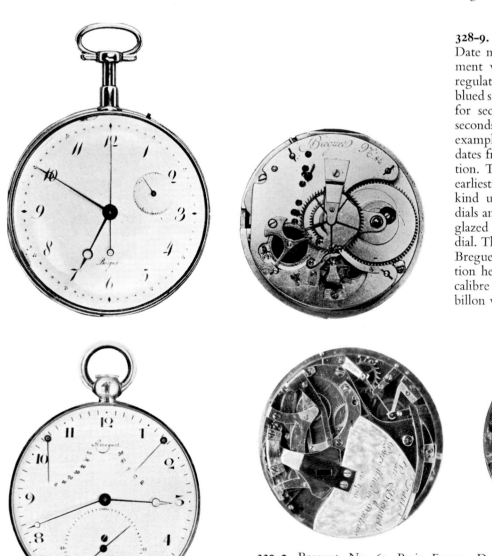

328–9. A. L. Breguet. No. 84. Paris, France. Date not later than 1790. Cylinder escapement with spiral steel balance-spring and regulator. Going barrel. Enamel dial with blued steel hands. Subsidiary dial at 2 o'clock for seconds and also sweep centre jump seconds. Plain gold case. This is a very early example of Breguet's work and certainly dates from well before the French Revolution. The script signature is typical of this earliest period. The seconds dial is of the kind usually used by Breguet on enamel dials and was formed by grinding away the glazed surface to form a recessed subsidiary dial. The plated movement is also typical of Breguet's earliest work. After the Revolution he almost universally used the Lepine calibre except for chronometer and tourbillon watches.

330–2. Breguet. No. 62. Paris, France. Date, see below. Lever escapement. Three-arm compensation balance. Helical steel balance-spring without end-curves, with regulator. Two going barrels. Self-winding. Minute repeater. Enamel dial with blued steel hands. Subsidiary dials for thermometer, up-and-down, and seconds. Gold engine-turned case. The platinum weight of this watch bears the inscription 'Faite par Breguet pour Mr le Duc d'Orleans en 1780', but for a discussion of the date of this watch, see page 48.

333. French. *Circa* 1790. The movement is by Gide but is illustrated solely on account of the unusual case which is of painted porcelain.

334–5. Brockbanks. No. 3499. London, England, 1791. Spring detent escapement of Earnshaw type. Three-arm bimetallic compensation balance of typical Brockbanks type with heavy weights. Helical steel balance-spring with end-curves, free sprung. Fusee and chain. Enamel dial with gold hour and minute hands and steel seconds hand. Silver case.

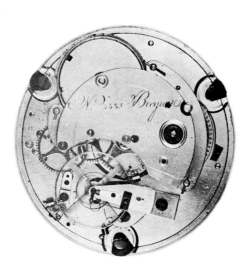

336–7. A. L. Breguet. No. 153/4570. Paris, France. Date either just before or after the French Revolution, 1793 or 1795. Pivoted detent escapement, four-arm bimetallic compensation balance, helical steel balance-spring with end-curves, free sprung, fusee and chain. Engine-turned silver dial, blued steel hands, subsidiary dials for seconds and up-and-down indicator. Engine-turned gold case. This very early specimen of Breguet's work, dating from the French Revolution, was taken back into the works, modernised with a new dial and probably new case, some time about 1825. It was then given the new number 4570 which appears on the cuvette. See also page 60 about Breguet's numbering.

338–9. Josiah Emery. No. 1289. London, England, 1792. Lever escapement. Brass balance with bimetallic S-shaped compensation affixes. Steel tapered helical balance-spring, free sprung. Fusee and chain. Enamel regulator-type dial with blued steel hands. Plain gold case. This is an early example of Emery's second type of lever escapement with a pivoted impulse pin or cranked roller. The escapement is without draw.

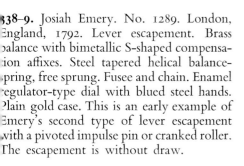

340–1. Brockbanks. No. 3711. London, England, 1793. Peto cross-detent escapement. Three-arm bimetallic compensation balance, helical steel balance-spring with end-curves free sprung. Fusee and chain. Enamel dial, gold hands, plain silver case. For illustration of escapement see Fig. 39, described in the technical section on page 111.

342–3. Breguet. No. 147. Paris, France. *Circa* 1792. Spring detent escapement of Arnold pattern. Three-arm bimetallic compensation balance, helical steel balance spring with end-curves free sprung, fusee and chain. Enamel dial, with sweep centre minutes hand and subsidiary dials for seconds and hours. Plain gold case. This watch is an important and unusual specimen of Breguet's pre-Revolution style; the script signature on the dial is rarely found after the Revolution.

345-6. Taylor. No. 1143. London, England. *Circa* 1795. Lever. Pointed pallet without draw. Two spiral balance-springs, one above balance and one below with regulator. Fusee and chain. White enamel dial, gold hands. Silver recase. Nothing is known of Taylor. There is in the British Museum a watch movement made from the same ébauche as the movement shown in Fig. 346 but this is a cylinder with single balance-spring. Taylor certainly had access to the work of Leroux, Pendleton and Grant, for this watch embodies in its escapement the principal features of their work. Thus the pallet stone arrangement is as used by Grant, the 'scape wheel is an exact copy of Leroux and the fork of the lever is carried round to the opposite side of the balance staff in the manner of Pendleton. For illustration of escapement, see Fig. 48.

344. Pedometer by Ralph Gout. *Circa* 1800. For use on horseback. Patent No. 2351 of November 4th, 1799. The gilt metal base is attached to the saddle and the rest of the 'watch' bounces up and down at each pace of the horse.

348-9. Anonymous, French. *Circa* 1795. Verge escapement with spiral steel balance-spring and regulator. Fusee and chain. Enamel dial with decimal or Revolutionary time with subsidiary dials for days of the month and twelve-hour time. Gold hands to Revolutionary dial, steel hands to calendar and 12-hour dial. Silver case. A typical late eighteenth century French verge movement.

347. The Mudge lever replica watch made in 1795, see page 36.

350–1. John Grant. No. 1479. London, England, 1795. Lever escapement. Four-arm bimetallic compensation balance. Helical balance-spring with end-curves, free sprung. Fusee and chain. Enamel regulator type dial, blued steel hands. Gold case. For illustration of escapement, see Fig. 44, described in the technical section on page 114.

352–4. Breguet. No. 217. Paris, France. Date probably just after the French Revolution. Lever escapement. Two-arm bimetallic compensation balance with two additional arms containing screws to prevent excess outward movement of the compensation arms. Helical steel balance-spring with end-curves and regulator. Self-winding. Two going barrels. Equation work. Calendar. Quarter repeater. Engine-turned silver dial with gold hour and minute hands. Blued steel hands to subsidiary dials for equation, up-and-down, month, and seconds; the last two concentric, the date appearing through an aperture. Engine-turned gold case. This watch represents Breguet's highest level of workmanship with considerable complications.

355–7. Alexander Hare. No. 440. London, England. Last quarter of the eighteenth century. Cylinder escapement. Fusee and chain. Enamel dial with gold beetle and poker hands. Gold pair case, the outer case enamelled with a scene of cupid, surrounded by a band of transparent maroon-coloured enamel. The band of the case is of blue enamel with white spots.

358–9. Vaucher. No. 10971. French. *Circa* 1800. Verge escapement. Fusee and chain. Quarter repeat on two gongs operated by pressing pendant. Enamel dial with blued steel hands, gold engine-turned case. This watch is typical of late eighteenth century French verge watches. Typical bridge-type cock and winding through dial.

360–3. Anonymous, Swiss. Third quarter of the nineteenth century. Cylinder escapement. Barred movement, going barrel. Enamel dial with blued steel hands. Gold case, a good example of very small Continental work in the middle of the nineteenth century. To give scale the movement is shown illustrated beside an English sixpence; the diameter of the case is 15 mm.

364–6. J. Herbert, Brighthelmstone (i.e. Brighton), England. Third quarter of the eighteenth century. Verge escapement. Mock-pendulum balance-wheel. Enamel dial with Continental-type pierced gilt hands. Gilt pair case, the outer case covered in tortoiseshell. A fairly typical cheap watch of the third quarter of the eighteenth century and a late example of the mock-pendulum balance. The bridge-type balance-cock has been later engraved with initials and a crest.

367-8. Du Bois et fils. Marked 'London' on the plate but certainly French or Swiss. *Circa* 1800. Debaufre type, dead beat escapement with two parallel escape wheels acting on one pallet on the pallet arbor. The balance is geared up. Brass balance-wheel, spiral steel balance-spring and regulator. Fusee and chain. Enamel dial with sweep centre seconds beating seconds. Steel seconds hand, gold hour and minute hands. Aperture for mock-pendulum attached to pallet arbor. Silver-gilt case. For illustration of escapement, see Fig. 63, described in the technical section on page 122.

369-70. Breguet à Paris. France. *Circa* 1800. Pouzzait type detached lever. Very large brass balance. Spiral steel balance-spring with regulator. Fusee and chain. Enamel dial with sweep centre seconds beating seconds. Subsidiary dials for hours, minutes and date. Steel hands for date and seconds, gold hands for hours and minutes. Silver case. Pouzzait's version of the lever escapement was invented in about 1785, but the style of the case of this watch suggests a date not earlier than 1800, by which time Breguet had ceased using the signature 'à Paris'. For an illustration of this escapement, see Fig. 58, described in the technical section on page 120.

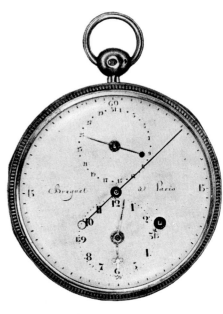

371-2. Berthoud, Paris, France. *Circa* 1800. Cylinder escapement. Going barrel. Self-winding. Gold hands with sweep centre seconds. Silver case. The square visible above the 12 is for the regulator.

373. Richard Comber, Lewes, England. 1776. Verge escapement with spiral steel balance-spring and regulator. Fusee and chain. Enamel differential dial and gold hand. Plain silver case. This is an extremely late example of the differential dial which was very rarely employed after 1710. It is also unusual in coming from a provincial maker.

374–5. Mudge & Dutton. No. 1571. London, England, 1800. Lever escapement, similar to that of Pendleton No. 180 (Fig. 42 and technical section, page 113). Two-arm bimetallic compensation balance, helical steel balance-spring with terminal curves, free sprung. Fusee and chain. Enamel dial, gold beetle and poker hands and steel seconds hand. Plain gold case. Note bridge-cock very similar to those used by Emery.

376–7. J. Grant. No. 2315. London, England. *Circa* 1800. Lever escapement. Three-arm brass balance with two bimetallic compensation affixes. Helical steel balance-spring with end-curves free sprung. Fusee and chain. Enamel regulator-type dial, steel seconds hand, gold hour and minute hands. Plain silver case (recased). For illustration of the escapement, see Fig. 45, described in technical section on page 114.

378–9. Breguet et Fils. No. 898. Paris, France. *Circa* 1802. Verge escapement with jewelled pallets. Elastic suspension for verge. Reversed fusee and chain. Enamel dial, and blued steel hands; Turkish numerals; secret signature 'Breguet et mixte No. 898', together with a Turkish signature. Engine-turned silver case. For Breguet mixte watches, see page 58.

380–1. J. R. Arnold. No. 1869. London, England, 1802. Spring detent escapement. Two-arm bimetallic compensation balance, gold helical balance-spring with end-curves, free sprung. Fusee and chain. Enamel dial with blued steel hands. Silver case. Note blued steel mainspring ratchet set-up on the watch plate. The escapement is what is generally known as the Earnshaw type. J. R. Arnold made both Arnold and Earnshaw types of spring-detent escapement.

382–5. Breguet. No. 1410. Paris, France. *Circa* 1804. Lever escapement. Three-arm compensation bi-metallic balance, the helical steel balance-spring without end-curves with regulator. Elastic suspension to the balance arbor. Two going barrels. Quarter repeating. Days of the month, phases of the moon. Self-winding. Engine-turned silver dial with blued steel hands, with auxiliary dials for moon work, up-and-down, seconds and day of the month. This represents Breguet's highest level of perpetuelle watch and incorporates all his improvements except for a few perpetuelles of somewhat different type made after 1820, see Fig. 485.

386–8. Breguet. No. 1225. Paris, France. *Circa* 1804. Cylinder escapement with spiral steel balance-spring and compensation curb. Going barrel. Quarter repeating with pendant push. Enamel dial with Turkish numerals. Blued steel hands. Gold pair case, the inner engine-turned and the outer decorated with red translucent enamel and gold shell pattern over engine-turning.

389–90. J. Hovenschöld. No. 586. Stockholm, Sweden. Early nineteenth century. Sully escapement. Fusee and chain. Enamel dial with Arabic numerals and cut steel brilliants between each pair of hours. Gilt hands. Single brass gilt case. This watch is fairly typical of Swedish and Danish design at about 1800. The bridge-type balance-cock has the initials of the maker J. H. woven into the piercing of the cock. This also is fairly typical of Swedish makers. Sully's escapement is very rarely found in watches, as opposed to the Ormskirk escapement widely used by the British Preston watch manufacturers at this time, which has a double escape wheel and a single pallet on the balance staff. Sully's escapement has a single escape wheel with double pallets on the balance staff. For illustration of escapements, see Fig. 64, described in the technical section on page 122.

391–2. Recordon (late Emery). No. 7392. London, England, 1807. Lever escapement, converted probably from Duplex. Two-arm bimetallic compensation balance also of later date. Spiral steel balance-spring with regulator. Fusee and chain. Enamel dial and Breguet-type blued steel hands. Gold case.

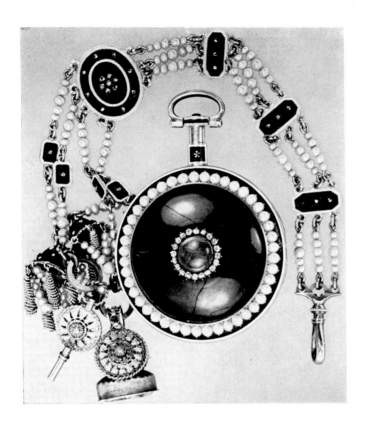

393-4. Wightwick & Moss, London, England, 1807. Verge escapement. Fusee and chain. Enamel dial with gold hands. Gold case, back of translucent blue enamel with ring of pearls; in centre plaited hair under glass with ring of diamonds. Bezel with blue enamel and ring of pearls. The chatelaine has blue enamel bars with white borders, studded diamonds joined by triple pearl strings, with fob hook.

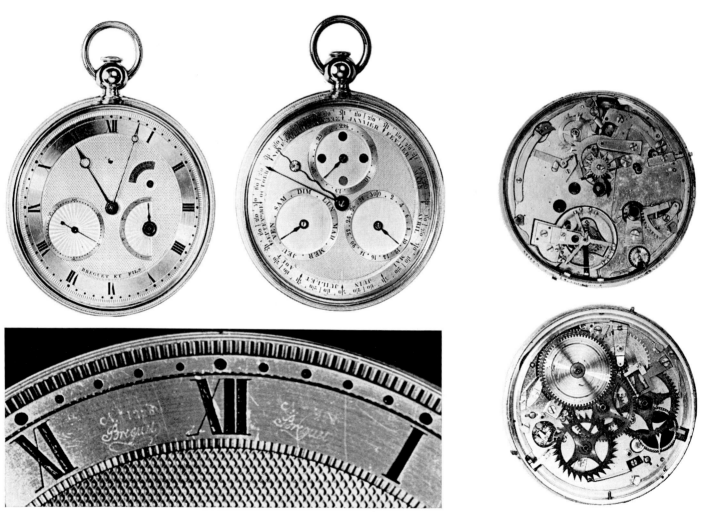

395-9. Breguet. No. 1226. Paris, France, 1807. Double-wheel Robin escapement. Three-arm bimetallic compensation balance. Spiral steel balance with overcoil. Regulator operated below the band of the dial. Going barrel. Quarter repeating. The watch has a dial on both sides. A gold engine-turned dial has normal concentric hours and minute hands, subsidiary dial for seconds at 8 o'clock, up-and-down indicator and a set-square for the calendar. This dial has secret signatures illustrated in large scale in Fig. 398. The other dial is of engine-turned silver, has two sweep centre hands indicating equation of time, and subsidiary dials for phases of the moon, the day of the month, and day of the week. The escapement is of a very unusual kind with only five teeth on the escape wheels.

400–2. A. L. Breguet. No. 1619. Paris, France, 1808. Double-wheel duplex escapement, three-arm bimetallic compensation balance, spiral balance-spring with overcoil and regulator, elastic suspension for balance-staff, going barrel; quarter repeater operated by plunger in the band of the case at 11 o'clock. Engine-turned gold dial with blued steel hands and subsidiary dials for calendar and seconds. Engine-turned gold case. For illustration of escapement, see Fig. 28, described in the technical section on page 105.

403–4. Breguet. No. 1890. Paris, France, 1809. Échappement naturel. Two-arm bimetallic compensation balance. Spiral steel balance-spring with overcoil, free sprung. Four-minute tourbillon. Reversed fusee. Engine-turned gold dial. Blued steel hands. Subsidiary dials for seconds, stop seconds, and up-and-down. Concentric central subsidiary dial for hours. This watch represents Breguet's highest achievement in the tourbillon watch. Only one other example of the échappement naturel in a pocket watch with tourbillon is known. This watch has the added and unique peculiarity that in addition to the normal Breguet secret signature it has signed in secret between the hour numerals 4, 5, 6, 7, 8, the name of the owner, the Comte Alexis de Razzoumofski. Fig. 403 shows the tourbillon carriage with the balance-wheel removed. The general lay-out and appearance of the movement is almost identical to other Breguet tourbillions.

405–6. Breguet et Fils. No. 2555. Paris, France. *Circa* 1811. Spring detent escapement with Peto-type cross-detent and six-minute tourbillon. Three-arm bimetallic compensation balance, spiral steel balance-spring with overcoil, free sprung. Fusee and chain. Engine-turned silver dial and blued steel hands. Engine-turned silver case.

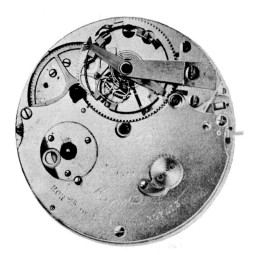

407-8. Breguet et Fils. No. 2329. Paris, France. *Circa* 1811. Spring detent escapement with Peto-type cross-detent and four-minute tourbillon. Two-arm compensation balance with four bimetallic compensation arms. Spiral steel balance-spring with overcoil free sprung. Fusee and chain. Engine-turned silver dial with blued steel hands. Stop, sweep centre seconds, subsidiary dials for hours, minutes and seconds. Engine-turned silver case.

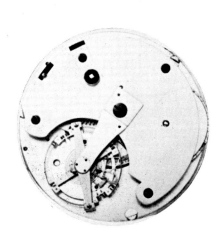

409-10. Breguet et Fils. No. 2571. Paris, France. *Circa* 1812. Double roller lever escapement with minute tourbillon. Two-arm balance with four bimetallic compensation arms. Spiral steel balance-spring with overcoil, free sprung. Fusee and chain. Enamel dial and blued steel hands. Silver case. The dial signature in script is fairly late for a Breguet. Signatures in script are usually restricted to watches made before the Revolution. The dial also carries a secret signature.

411–13. Brockbanks. No. 700. London, England, 1812. Spring detent escapement. Earnshaw pattern. Three-arm bimetallic compensation balance. Helical steel balance-spring, free sprung. Fusee and chain. Quarter repeating on two gongs operated by depressing the pendant. Gold dial with engine-turned centre covered with translucent red enamel. Serpentine gold hands. Hunter case in three-colour gold.

414–15. Anonymous. Swiss or French. First quarter of the nineteenth century. Virgule escapement. Decorative four-armed steel balance-wheel showing through the dial. Spiral steel balance-spring and regulator. Going barrel. Grande sonnerie clock-watch. Enamel dial with blued steel Breguet-type hands surrounded by half pearls. Plain gold case. This must be one of the earliest watches designed to be worn as a wrist watch. It is also of exceptionally small size to include grande sonnerie striking, the dimensions of the movement being 25 × 15 mm.

416–17. Ralph Gout. No. 267. London, England. *Circa* 1800. Verge escapement. Fusee and chain. Skeleton dial. Gilt metal case. In addition to the watch train the watch contains a pedometer mechanism which, being strapped to the wearer's leg, would indicate the distance walked in units of 10. The watch plate is engraved 'by the King's letters patent'. Gout patented his pedometer in 1799.

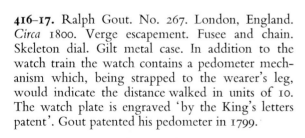

418. For other views of this watch, see colour plate, Fig. 19 and Dust Jacket (F). Chinese Duplex escapement, probably by Ilbury, made for the Chinese export market, with typically decorated case, and devils (for frightening away the evil eye) fixed to the balance-wheel. *Circa* 1800.

419–21. Anonymous. No. 4993. French or Swiss. Early nineteenth century. Verge escapement. Fusee and chain. Enamel dial with gold hands. Gold spherical case faceted all over and enamelled with a scene of a bird feeding young ones. [Slightly enlarged.]

422–4. Breguet. No. 1310. Paris, France. First quarter of the nineteenth century. Steel cylinder escapement with steel escape wheel. Plain steel balance with spiral steel balance-spring and regulator. Going barrel. Enamel dial with blued steel hands. Engine-turned silver case. This is a typical example of the Breguet Mixte watch. The cuvette is signed 'No. 1310. Etabl mixte de Breguet'. It is difficult to date Breguet mixte watches as it appears likely that they had a different numbering series to the ordinary Breguets.

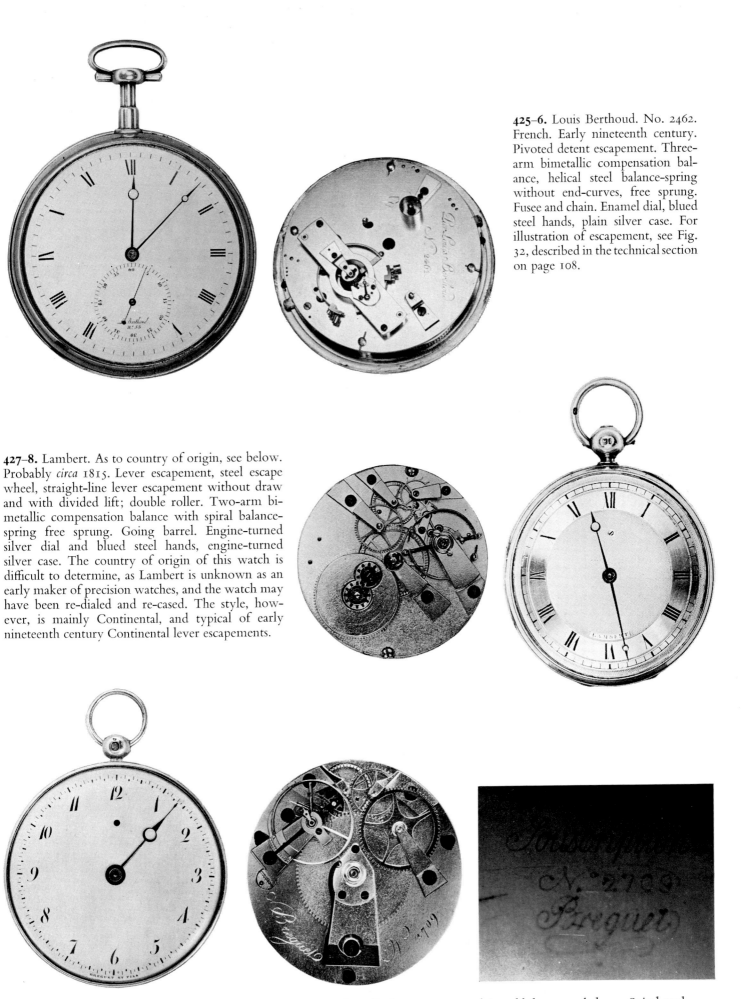

425-6. Louis Berthoud. No. 2462. French. Early nineteenth century. Pivoted detent escapement. Three-arm bimetallic compensation balance, helical steel balance-spring without end-curves, free sprung. Fusee and chain. Enamel dial, blued steel hands, plain silver case. For illustration of escapement, see Fig. 32, described in the technical section on page 108.

427-8. Lambert. As to country of origin, see below. Probably *circa* 1815. Lever escapement, steel escape wheel, straight-line lever escapement without draw and with divided lift; double roller. Two-arm bimetallic compensation balance with spiral balance-spring free sprung. Going barrel. Engine-turned silver dial and blued steel hands, engine-turned silver case. The country of origin of this watch is difficult to determine, as Lambert is unknown as an early maker of precision watches, and the watch may have been re-dialed and re-cased. The style, however, is mainly Continental, and typical of early nineteenth century Continental lever escapements.

429-31. Breguet et Fils. No. 2709. Paris, France, 1815. Ruby cylinder escapement, plain gold three-arm balance. Spiral steel balance-spring with regulator and elastic suspension to balance staff. Going barrel. Enamel dial with blued steel hand and secret signature. Engine-turned case, the band and back of silver and the rims and pendant of gold. This is Breguet's 'montre à souscription', see pp. 56, 57. Fig. 431 is of the secret signature, greatly enlarged.

432-3. Breguet. No. 2732. Paris, France, 1815. Plain gold balance. Spiral steel balance-spring with regulator. Bimetallic compensation curb, elastic suspension to balance arbor. Going barrel. A small silver dial with blued steel hands. Montre à tact, the tact lever in gold on an engine-turned gold case covered with transparent blue enamel and pearl touch pieces. Short Breguet chain and key. [Slightly enlarged.]

434-5. Breguet et Fils. No. 2572. Paris, France, 1811. Single roller lever escapement with minute tourbillon. Two-arm compensation balance with four bimetallic compensation arms, spiral steel balance-spring with overcoil, free sprung. Fusee and chain. Engine-turned silver dial and blued steel hands. Silver hunter case added in 1823, replacing an original gold case. For illustration of escapement, see Fig. 34, described in the technical section on page 119.

436-8. Breguet. No. 2614. Paris, France. *Circa* 1815. Cylinder escapement. Plain brass balance with spiral steel balance-spring and regulator with bimetallic compensation curb and elastic suspension to the balance-staff. Going barrel. Gold engine-turned dial engraved with Turkish numerals. Subsidiary dials for month and days of the month. Single gold hand. Second hand in blued steel for equation of time, mounted on a loose fitting collar over the canon pinion; its differential movement is operated by a segmental rack mounted on the loose collar and whose position is determined by the equation lever. Engine-turned gold case.

439–40. D. & W. Morice. No. 5788. London, England, 1815. Duplex escapement. Spiral balance-spring and two-arm bimetallic balance. Fusee and chain. Enamel dial with gold hands. Silver engine-turned case.

41–2. Urban Jürgensen. No. $\frac{24}{58}$. Copenhagen, Denmark. *Circa* 1815. Spring detent escapement of Arnold type, three-arm bimetallic compensation balance, helical gold balance-spring with end-curves free sprung. Fusee and chain. Enamel dial with separate subsidiary dials for hours, minutes and seconds. Silver case.

443–5. Viner, No. 456. London, England. *Circa* 1816. Duplex escapement, two-arm bimetallic balance, spiral steel balance spring free sprung. Fusee and chain; alarum and minute repeater; repeater operated by depressing pendant. Alarum set by rotating button at between 5 and 6 o'clock in the band of the case (Viner's patent). Matt gold dial with polished gold hour numerals and gold hands. Heavy cast gold case typical of English work towards the end of the first quarter of the nineteenth century. Note the very advanced design of the repeating work.

446–7. Rundell, Bridge & Rundell, Ludgate Hill, London, England, 1817. No number. Cylinder escapement. Fusee and chain. Matt gold dial with polished raised Arabic numerals and gold hands. Embossed and engraved two-colour gold case.

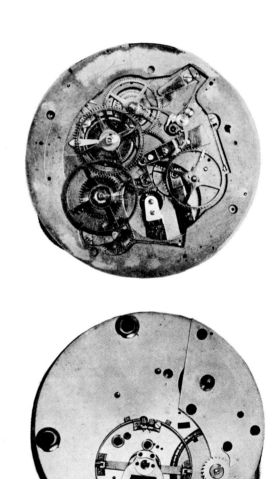

448–50. A. L. Breguet. No. 2894. Paris, France. *Circa* 1817. Pivoted detent escapement with passing spring on the balance-roller (see technical section, page 108). Two-arm balance with four bimetallic compensation arms, helical steel spring with end-curves free sprung, engine-turned silver dial with sweep centre seconds, subsidiary dials each with hour and minute hands for mean time and sidereal time and subsidiary dial for calendar. The hands of the mean-time and seconds dials are blued steel. The hands of the sidereal time and calendar dials are gold. Plain silver case. Fig. 449 is of view under dial. For illustration of escapement, see Fig. 33.

451–2. Breguet et Fils. No. 3261. Paris, France. *Circa* 1819. Ruby cylinder escapement. Three-arm brass balance. Bimetallic compensation curb with elastic suspension to the balance-arbor. Going barrel. Quarter repeater on one gong. Engine-turned silver dial with blued steel hands. Engine-turned gold hunter or savonette case. Note lay-out typical of most Breguet watches with cylinder escapement. Note also, plunger for operating repeater in the band of the case, and Breguet key with ratchet to prevent winding backwards. The hand-set is through a hole drilled in the glass, which is a common arrangement with Breguet savonette watches.

453–4. Vulliamy. Code No. UOAM. London, England, 1825. Duplex escapement, plain steel balance, spiral steel balance-spring with regulator and compensation curb, fusee and chain. Silver dial with matt centre, gold hour and minute hands, blued steel seconds hand. Engine-turned gold case. Note the pierced gilt decoration to the watch plate typical of this type of Vulliamy duplex watch, which was made throughout the first quarter of the nineteenth century.

455–6. Thomas Earnshaw, London, England. *Circa* 1811. Spring detent escapement. Plain steel balance-wheel. Spiral steel balance-spring with regulator carrying 'sugar-tong' bimetallic compensation curb. Fusee and chain. Enamel dial and gold hands. Silver case. For a discussion of Earnshaw's compensation curb, see page 27. It is interesting that in this watch the balance-spring stud has been moved so as partly to obscure the watch number which is 574. Earnshaw's watches also sometimes have a second number which in this case is 3017. The meaning of these numbers is not at present understood. This type of dial with radially disposed Arabic numerals is one fairly commonly employed by Earnshaw. For illustration of escapement, see Fig. 37.

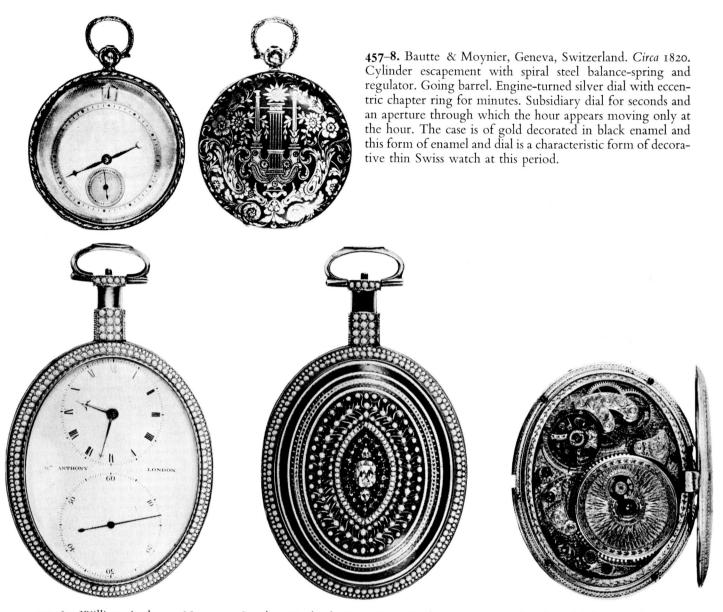

457–8. Bautte & Moynier, Geneva, Switzerland. *Circa* 1820. Cylinder escapement with spiral steel balance-spring and regulator. Going barrel. Engine-turned silver dial with eccentric chapter ring for minutes. Subsidiary dial for seconds and an aperture through which the hour appears moving only at the hour. The case is of gold decorated in black enamel and this form of enamel and dial is a characteristic form of decorative thin Swiss watch at this period.

459–61. William Anthony. No. 1931. London, England. *Circa* 1820. Duplex escapement. Spiral steel balance-spring and regulator. Going barrel. Enamel dial with separate dials for concentric hours and minutes and for seconds. Highly engraved and decorated movement. Oval gold case decorated with red and blue enamel and pearls.

462–3. F. L. Fatton, Paris, Fran Circa 1820. Cylinder escapem with spiral steel balance-spr with regulator and Breguet-ty bimetallic compensation cu Elastic suspension to barrel arb Going barrel. Quarter repeati Engine-turned silver dial, blu steel hand. Engine-turned sil case with gold bands and penda Fatton was a prominent pupil Breguet's. This watch is alm identical to Breguet's souscript watches with the addition o repeating train, seen in one cor of the movement.

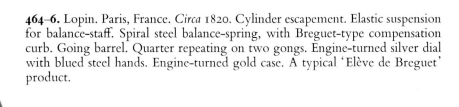

464–6. Lopin. Paris, France. *Circa* 1820. Cylinder escapement. Elastic suspension for balance-staff. Spiral steel balance-spring, with Breguet-type compensation curb. Going barrel. Quarter repeating on two gongs. Engine-turned silver dial with blued steel hands. Engine-turned gold case. A typical 'Elève de Breguet' product.

467–8. Thomas Earnshaw. No. 581. London, England, 1811. Spring detent escapement. Two-arm bimetallic compensation balance with heavy weights. Helical steel balance-spring, free sprung. Fusee and chain. Enamel dial and blued steel hands. Silver case. It is interesting that the number of this watch is only 7 later than the watch in Fig. 455, showing that Earnshaw used compensation balances and compensation curbs at the same period on his spring detent watches. For a discussion of this, see page 27. For a discussion of the escapement, see pages 110–11.

469–71. J. R. Arnold. No. 47. London, England, 1821. Cylinder escapement. Bimetallic compensation curb consisting of a strip fixed to the regulator and carrying one curb pin. Going barrel with Prest keyless winding. Silver dial with blued steel hands with centre square for hand setting. Gold case. Prest's patent was the earliest effective system of keyless winding, but it made no provision for setting the hands, which was done in the old way by a square on the centre arbor.

472–3. Breguet et Fils. No. 3679. Paris, France. *Circa* 1822. Spring detent escapement of Earnshaw type. Two-arm bimetallic compensation balance. Helical steel balance-spring without end-curves. Two going barrels wound separately. Matt silvered dial with eccentric sweep minutes overlapping with the second dial, and subsidiary dial for hours. Plain silver case. This is a favourite lay-out for Breguet for deck watches, although this watch could be worn in the pocket. Breguet regarded two going barrels as a satisfactory substitute for the fusee and several such watches are wound from a single square mounted between the two barrels.

474-5. Richard Webster. No. 5479. London, England, 1823. Lever escapement. Plain gold balance with spiral steel balance-spring and regulator. Fusee and chain. Engine-turned silver dial with gold hour and minute hands and blued steel sweep centre seconds hand. Engine-turned silver case. This watch is a very rare example of the transition from the full plate English movement to the three-quarter plate. This has a full plate movement, but the plate below the balance is recessed so that the balance-wheel itself is on the level of the plate, thus producing the effect of the three-quarter plate movement.

476-7. R. Hornby. No. 5537. Liverpool, England, 1823. Single roller lever escapement. Fusee and chain. Matt gold dial with polished engraved decoration in centre and raised Roman numerals. Gold hands. Heavily decorated gold case. This is one of the earliest recorded examples of the English use of the single roller lever escapement.

478-9. Breguet. No. 4196. Paris, France. *Circa* 1824. Spring detent escapement, Earnshaw type. Two-arm bimetallic compensation balance. Helical steel balance-spring with end-curves free sprung. Elastic suspension to the balance arbor. Going barrel. Silvered dial with overlapping chapter rings and steel hands. Silver case. This watch dates from just after the death of Abraham Louis Breguet and the use of a single going barrel in a chronometer watch of Breguet's is quite unusual. The going barrel is of exceptionally large size.

480–1. Waight. No. 440. England, 1816. Massey-type lever escapement. Steel balance wheel, spiral steel balance-spring with regulator. Fusee and chain with pump wind. Gold dial and hands. Plain gold case. The under-dial illustration shows the operation of the pump-wind, which is Massey's patent No. 3854 of November 17th, 1814.

482–4. Breguet. No. 4764. Paris, France. *Circa* 1826. Lever escapement. Two-arm bimetallic compensation balance, spiral steel balance-spring with overcoil and regulator. Going barrel. Half-quarter repeater. Silver engine-turned dial. Gold hands. Plain gold case. The watch is keyless wound by a flat, un-knurled button. A smaller button concentric with the winding button is pulled out and then turned in order to set the hands. The repeater is operated by a slide in the band of the case.

485–7. Breguet. No. 4548. Paris, France. *Circa* 1826. Lever with draw. 20-tooth pierced 'scape wheel. Two going barrels. Perpetuelle. Silver engine-turned dial with eccentric chapter ring for hours and minutes. Apertures for date and sectors for up-and-down indicator and regulator. Gold hands. This watch represents the final development of Breguet's perpetuelle. Extra thinness is achieved by setting the weight below the top plate. There is provision for winding the watch by hand.

488–9. T. Cummins. No. 17-27. London, England, 1826. Lever escapement. Two-arm bimetallic compensation balance. Helical steel balance-spring, free sprung. Fusee and chain. Gold engine-turned, regulator-type dial. Steel hands. Gold engine-turned case. The escapement is a refined version of Massey's, and has resilient banking. There is no motion work and no square for setting the hands. For a discussion of Cummins' work, see page 42.

490–2. Breguet. No. 4938. Paris, France. *Circa* 1829. Straight-line lever escapement with divided lift and draw, two-arm bimetallic compensation balance, spiral steel balance-spring with overcoil and regulator, elastic suspension to balance staff. Going barrel, half-quarter repeater on one gong. Enamel dial with secret signature and gold hands. Engine-turned gold case.

493–4. Delage et Cie. France. *Circa* 1830. Straight-line lever escapement with divided lift. Breguet-type bimetallic compensation curb with Breguet-type elastic suspension to the balance staff. Fusee and chain. Enamel dial, blued steel hands. Engine-turned gold case. Nothing is known of the maker of this fairly high-grade, fairly early, Continental lever escapement watch.

495–6. Anonymous. Swiss. No. 4212. Second quarter of the nineteenth century. Cylinder escapement, spiral steel balance-spring and regulator. Going barrel. Engraved silver dial and blued steel Breguet-type hands. Heavily chiselled and engraved gold case. The unusual feature of this watch is its form of winding which is by a lever pivoted to the main-spring arbor and projecting through the side of the case. On being moved backwards and forwards it winds up the spring. The hands are set by turning a milled disc which projects through the cuvette.

497–8. L. Golay, Switzerland. Second quarter of the nineteenth century. Cylinder escapement. Bi-metallic compensation curb. Going barrel, quarter-striking grande sonnerie clock-watch. Silver engine-turned dial with blued steel hands, gold engine-turned case.

499–500. George Cowle, No. 34: London, England. *Circa* 1830 Spring detent escapement, Earnshaw type; two-arm bimetalli compensation balance, helical stee balance-spring with termina curves, free sprung; fusee an chain. Matt gold dial with raise polished Turkish numerals, gol hands. Cast gold case with crescen incorporated in pendant.

501–2. Barwise. No. 4791. London, England, 1829. Rack lever escapement. Fusee and chain. Enamel dial with gold hands. Plain gold case. A late and particularly finely finished example of the rack lever escapement. A watch of typical lay-out and appearance of the 1830 period.

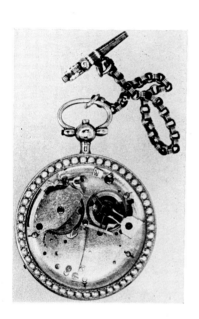

503–5. Anonymous, probably Swiss. *Circa* 1830. Cylinder escapement. Going barrel. Gold dial and hands. Painted enamel case surrounded by a circle of half pearls. The figures in the painting are automata; a young man pushes a girl on a swing and another lady seated at the bottom left-hand corner of the picture plays a guitar. The Breguet-type key is enamelled to match the watch.

506–7. Anonymous. French or Swiss. *Circa* 1830. Lever escapement. Breguet-type bi-metallic compensation curb. Going barrel. Engine-turned gold dial and blued steel hands. Engine-turned gold case. This is a remarkably thin watch for the period, especially as applied to a lever escapement. The thickness of the movement is 3 mm. and that of the entire watch is 6 mm.

508–9. Anonymous, Swiss. First quarter of the nineteenth century. Verge escapement with spiral steel balance-spring and regulator. Fusee and chain. Enamel dial, steel hands. The dial is surrounded by a ring of pearls and is set in a finger ring. [Slightly enlarged.]

510–11. Tavernier. No. 868. Paris, France. *Circa* 1830. Cylinder escapement. Two dials at front and back of the watch. The dial for hours, minutes and seconds is enamel and has steel hands. The other dial is silver. The outer ring is a table giving equation of time for the day; it has no equation mechanism. The subsidiary dials are for days of the week (centre); regulator; month; date; setter to determine at what time of day the date indicator shall change; phases of the moon.

512–13. Courvoisier et comp. No. 509 Swiss. *Circa* 1830. Verge escapement. Fuse and chain. Enamel dial with painted monochrome classical figures. Silver hunter ca with no glass to dial. This watch is typical middle grade Swiss work at about this tim

514–15. Hunt & Roskell. No. 10514. London, England, 1836. Earnshaw-type spring-detent escapement with one-minute tourbillon. Two-arm bimetallic compensation balance. Spherical steel balance-spring, free sprung. Fusee and chain. Enamel dial, steel hands. Sweep centre minute hand. Subsidiary dials for hours, minutes and thermometer. Gold engine-turned case. This watch was almost certainly made for Hunt & Roskell by Sylvan Mairet (compare the very similar dial in Fig. 537).

516–18. Robert Roskell. No. 10030. Liverpool, England, 1832. Rack lever escapement. Spiral steel balance-spring and regulator. Fusee and chain. Engine-turned gold dial and blued steel serpentine hands. Engine-turned gold case. This watch is unusual for its system of quarter repeating which is effected by turning the pendant to the left to obtain the hours and to the right to obtain the quarters. J. A. Berrollas's patent No. 3174 of October 31st, 1808.

519–22. Breguet. No. 5009. Paris, France, 1836. Lever escapement. Two-arm bimetallic compensation balance. Spiral steel balance-spring with overcoil and regulator. Going barrel. Half-quarter repeater on one gong operated by a slide in the band of the case. Silver engraved dial with gold hands and subsidiary sectors for up-and-down and regulator. Gold case. This is the final development of Breguet's 'montre sympathique' and is here shown with the 'parent' clock (No. 128) which not only sets the watch to time but also winds it. As this is a precision watch the parent clock does not move the regulator, as was done with the earlier type of sympathique watch, which had no temperature compensation.

523-4. L. F. Audemars, Brassus, Switzerland. *Circa* 1840. Robin escapement, two-arm compensation balance, spiral steel balance-spring and regulator. Going barrel. Enamel dial and blued steel hands. Engine-turned gold case. The straight-line lay-out is unusual for the Robin escapement; the lever has the counterbalance arms popular in Swiss work at this time.

525-6. Hunt and Roskell. No. 10413. London, England. *Circa* 1840. Lever escapement with divided lift, two-arm compensation balance, spiral steel balance-spring with overcoil and regulator. Going barrel. Enamel dial with blued steel hands, sweep centre minutes hand, subsidiary dials for phases of the moon, hours concentric with days of the month, thermometer, seconds dial with two hands, one of which may be started and stopped at will. Plain gold case with à tact.

527-8. Hunt and Roskell. English, but an imported movement. Probably *circa* 1840. Lever escapement with divided lift, two-arm balance with bimetallic rim but uncut, spiral steel balance-spring with regulator and Breguet-type bimetallic compensation curb, Breguet-type elastic suspension for the balance-staff. Two going barrels, one for the independent jump seconds train. Engraved gold dial with blued steel sweep centre seconds hand. Two subsidiary dials each for hours and minutes, one with steel and one with gold hands, driven off the same train but able to be set independently. Engraved gold case.

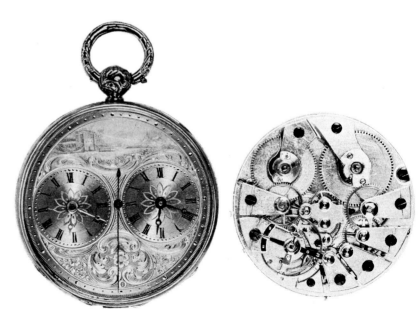

529–31. Viner, No. 4913. Regent Street, London, England, 1840. Lever escapement, two-arm bimetallic compensation balance; going barrel with pump wind. Enamel dial with blued steel hands. Engine-turned gold hunter case with à tact attached to back cover.

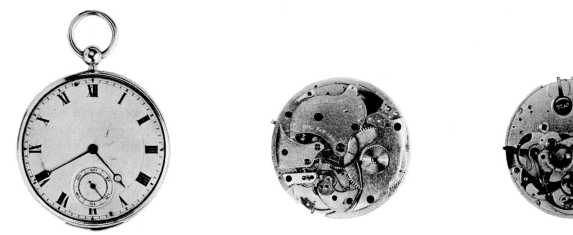

532–4. J. Ferguson Cole, London, England. No number. January 1844. Escapement double rotary detached chronometer. Two-arm bimetallic compensation balance. Spiral steel balance-spring with overcoil and regulator. Going barrel. Half-quarter repeater. Engine-turned silver dial and blued steel hands. Plain gold case. For illustration of escapement, see Fig. 40, described in the technical section on page 111.

535–6. Anonymous. No. 40757. English, 1845. Verge escapement. Fusee and chain. Painted enamel dial with gold hands. Silver pair case. This watch is typical of what is generally described as a Farmer's watch of the mid-nineteenth century. While the verge escapement continued to be made until the end of the century, this watch represents about its final appearance with classical lay-out and a pierced and decorated balance-cock.

537–8. Hunt & Roskell, London, England, 1846. Lever escapement. Two-arm bimetallic compensation balance. Spiral steel balance-spring with overcoil and regulator. Going barrel. Engine-turned gold dial with subsidiary dials for minutes and seconds. The hours appear through an aperture and pass a fixed pointer. Large segmental auxiliary dial for Fahrenheit temperature. Plain gold case. Although the watch is signed Hunt & Roskell, the movement is stamped S.M. indicating that the movement was in fact made by Sylvan Mairet, the pupil of Breguet who worked for a time for Hunt & Roskell. It has his special form of lever escapement in which all the lift is on the escape wheel. This is clearly shown in the illustration. Note also the unusual form of fixed pendant. No photograph can do justice to the quite exceptional elegance of this watch.

539–40. Anonymous. No. 224890. Swiss. Probably mid-nineteenth century. Lever escapement, two-arm uncut bimetallic balance. Going barrel. Enamel dial, blued steel hands and sweep centre seconds hand. Chinese numerals with inner 24-hour chapter ring with European Roman numerals. Silver case.

541–3. Anonymous. Japanese. Mid-nineteenth century. Verge escapement. Brass balance, spiral steel balance-spring. No regulator. Fusee and gut. Clock-watch with locking-plate and no warning. Gilt and painted dial with movable chapters for the varying length of day and night-time hours in the ancient Japanese time-system. Inro watch with Netsuke and Ojime.

544–5. Anonymous. Swiss. *Circa* 1860. Cylinder escapement. Going barrel. Engraved gold dial, blued steel hands, painted enamel case.

546–7. Richard Dover, Statter & Thomas Statter, No. 1. Liverpool, England, 1862. Lever escapement. Two-arm bimetallic compensation balance. Fusee and chain. Enamel dial with blued steel hands. Gold case. This is a very late example of the decimal dial. In the centre of the dial is marked 'Decimal timekeeper'. Ordinary 12-hour time is shown on a subsidiary dial. There is a sweep centre seconds, the minute being divided into 100 parts.

548–50. Breguet. No. 931. Paris, France. *Circa* 1864. Lever escapement. Two-arm bimetallic compensation balance. Spiral steel balance-spring with overcoil and regulator. Going barrel. Gold engine-turned dial. Gold hands. Engine-turned gold case. This is an early example of keyless winding with pull-button for hand-setting. The watch number is of a later series than any used in A. L. Breguet's lifetime.

551–2. J. Ferguson Cole. No. 1848. London, England, 1867. Rotating detent escapement. Two-arm bimetallic compensation balance. Spiral steel balance-spring with terminal curve. Fusee and chain. Enamel dial and blued steel hands. Plain gold case. For illustration of escapement, see Figs. 66, 67, described in the technical section on pages 123–4.

553–4. Anonymous, Swiss, 1850. Cylinder escapement, spiral steel balance-spring and regulator, barred movement, going barrel. Engine-turned silver dial with gold hands. Gold case with painted enamel on black background, a typical decorated lady's Swiss watch of the mid-nineteenth century.

555–6. G. F. Roskopf. Swiss. *Circa* 1875. Pin-wheel lever escapement with spiral steel balance-spring with regulator. Going barrel. Enamel dial. Gilt hands. Nickel-plated case. Roskopf was the first successful manufacturer of a really cheap watch, which he introduced in 1868.

557–8. J. & H. Jump. No. 516. London, England. *Circa* 1875. Single roller lever escapement. Two-arm bimetallic compensation balance, spiral steel balance-spring with overcoil and regulator. Going barrel. Silver dial with matt centre, steel hands. Gold engine-turned case. Jump generally worked in the style of Breguet, and his watches are almost invariably of most elegant appearance.

559–60. Charles Frodsham. No. 01378. London, England, 1859. Spring detent escapement, two-arm bimetallic compensation balance, helical steel balance-spring with end-curves, free sprung. Fusee and chain. Enamel dial with blued steel hands, subsidiary up-and-down dial. Plain gold case. This watch is typical of the highest grade of English work throughout the second half of the nineteenth century. For the interpretation of the inscription AD. FMSZ on the dial and movement, see page 134.

561–3. James McCabe. No. 08400. London, England. Date: probably one of the last products of the firm, which closed in 1883. Lever escapement, two-arm compensation balance, helical steel spring with overcoil, free sprung, going barrels for going train and for minute repeating grande sonnerie clock-watch train. Enamel dial with gold hands. Plain gold case.

564–5. Girard Perragaux, Switzerland. Pivoted detent escapement. Two-arm bimetallic compensation balance. Spiral steel balance-spring with overcoil and regulator. Going barrel. Barred movement with tourbillon. Enamel dial also signed 'Tourbillon by Ernest Guinand'. Plain gold case with glass back and front. The movement is signed on the spring barrel 'Patent March 25th 1884', but the date of the watch is certainly somewhat later. It is also an exceptionally small watch for a tourbillon, the diameter of the case being 36 mm. Note also the elegant form of keyless winding pendant.

566–8. Waterbury Watch Company, Connecticut, America. *Circa* 1890. Duplex escapement with spiral steel balance-spring and regulator. The mainspring is contained in the barrel and occupies the whole diameter of the movement. Enamel dial with steel hands. Nickel-plated case. The Waterbury watch was a pioneer in the production of a cheap watch. They were notorious for the extremely long time they took to wind up. In some of them the entire movement revolved, thus producing in effect a tourbillon.

569–70. Jules Jürgensen. No. 8573. Copenhagen, Denmark (but in fact made by the firm then working in Switzerland). *Circa* 1890. Lever escapement with divided lift, two-arm bimetallic compensation balance, spiral steel balance-spring with overcoil and regulator, going barrel and separate barrel for independent jump seconds train. Enamel dial with blued steel hands. Plain gold case. This watch was probably made by the second Jules Jürgensen. The slender figuration of the dial and slender hands are typical of late Jürgensen work. These watches frequently had gold trains.

571–2. Jules Jürgensen. No. 15172. Signed Copenhagen but see below. Lever escapement. Two-arm bimetallic compensation balance. Spiral steel balance-spring with overcoil and regulator. Going barrel. Split seconds chronograph. Enamel dial with steel hands. Gold hunter case. Jules was one of the two sons of Urban Jürgensen. He moved to Switzerland in 1834 but continued to sign his work Copenhagen. The firm continued until 1912 and this is a fairly late example of its work.

573–4. Albert H. Potter & Co. No. 4. Geneva, Switzerland. *Circa* 1900. Pivoted detent escapement, spiral steel balance-spring with overcoil, free sprung, going barrel. Enamel dial with blued steel hands. Plain gold hunter case. Albert Potter was an American working in Geneva, he patented his pivoted detent escapement in 1875 and was known for his very high grade precision work.

575–7. Dent. No. 58621. London, England. *Circa* 1910. Spring detent escapement. Duo-in-uno steel balance-spring, free sprung. Keyless-wound fusee with chain. Enamel dial, steel hands, up-and-down dial. Plain gold case. A very late example of the pocket chronometer.

578-9. American Waltham Watch Company, No. 3006260. Waltham, Mass., U.S.A. *Circa* 1910. Lever escapement, two-arm compensation balance, spiral steel balance-spring with overcoil and regulator going barrel. Enamel dial and blued steel hands. Gold case. The words 'Riverside Maximus' on the movement indicate that this is the highest quality work of the Company.

580-1. Charles Frodsham. No. 09551. London, England, 1913. Lever escapement. Two-arm bi-metallic compensation balance. Spiral steel balance-spring with overcoil and regulator. Going barrel. Engine-turned silver dial with gilt chapter ring to the seconds dial and gilt plaque for the signature. Blued steel Breguet-type hands. Engine-turned gold case. This is a remarkably late date for a watch externally almost completely of Breguet design. Note also the elegant form of keyless winding not unlike earlier forms of repeater pendants. Note also typical three-quarter plate English lay-out. The watch bears the stamp ADFMSZ, characterising Frodsham's highest grade work from 1850 onwards. The movements of Frodsham's watches at this time were made by Nicole Nielson and while this example retains the English single roller escapement the escape wheel has divided lift. See also colour plate, Fig. 17.

582-3. Hunt & Roskell. London. Late nineteenth century. Swiss ébauche. Lever escapement. Spiral spring with terminal curve. Going barrel. Keyless wind. Enamel dial. Steel hands. Minute repeat. Fly-back chronograph. Perpetual calendar. This represents the final development of the Swiss precision complicated watch. Inner bezel opened to show calendar setting levers.

584-6. Frodsham. No. 09655 and the additional code No. A. D. FMSZ (see page 134). London, England, 1913. Lever escapement and one-minute tourbillon. Two-arm, bimetallic, Guillaume-type compensation balance. Spiral steel balance-spring, free sprung. Keyless-wound fusee and chain. Silvered dial, with up-and-down regulator. Steel hands. Plain gold case. This watch has on four separate occasions between 1913 and 1946 taken a Kew certificate.

587-9. Anonymous. First quarter of the twentieth century. Lever escapement; two-arm bimetallic compensation balance-wheel, spiral steel balance-spring and regulator, going barrel. Simple calendar with moon work; fly-back sweep centre seconds; minute repeater on gongs, operated by a plunger in the band of the case. Enamel dial with blued steel hands, plain gold hunter case. This watch is typical of complicated Continental work in the first quarter and a little later of the twentieth century.

590-1. Rotherham. No. 250024. London, England, 1923. Lever escapement and karrusel. Two-arm bimetallic compensation balance. Spiral steel balance-spring with overcoil and regulator. Going barrel. Enamel dial and blued steel hands. Gold case. For a discussion of the karrusel watch, see page 100; for a discussion of the invention of the karrusel by Bonniksen, see page 63. This example is the last karrusel watch made by Rotherham.

592–3. Breguet. No. 3356. Paris, France, 1939. Lever escapement. One-minute tourbillon: two-arm bimetallic compensation balance, spiral steel spring with overcoil, free sprung. Going barrel. Engine-turned silver dial with blued steel hands, subsidiary up-and-down dial. Plain gold case. The movement of the watch is of Swiss manufacture, finished and adjusted by Breguet.

594–5. Ulysse Nardin. No. 124082. Locle, Switzerland. *Circa* 1950. Two-arm bimetallic Guillaume-type compensation balance. Spiral steel balance-spring with overcoil and regulator. Lever escapement. Sweep centre seconds driven through an idler pinion off the third wheel of the train. Enamel dial and blued steel hands. Plain silver case. This watch was prepared for service use and represents the highest development of the Swiss precision watch.

596–7. Breguet. No. 5026. Paris, France. *Circa* 1960. Lever escapement, two-arm compensation balance, spiral steel balance-spring with overcoil and regulator, going barrel. Engine-turned silver dial with blued steel hands with subsidiary dials for phases of the moon, months, days of the month, up-and-down indicator, equation of time. Plain gold case. The movement of this watch is of Swiss manufacture, finished and adjusted and cased by Breguet and is an example of the latest work of the firm.

4 Biographical Notes

Biographical Notes

The following selection of biographical notes is in no way exhaustive. It is confined to makers or men who in some way advanced or influenced the progress of watch-making; and mostly to facts which are likely to be of assistance in identifying or dating their work. Their watchmaking exploits only are described; clocks are not mentioned.

For more numerically complete lists the reader is referred to *Britten's Old Clocks and Watches and their Makers* (up to the current, 7th edition, by Baillie, Clutton and Ilbert, published in 1956 by E. & F. N. Spon Ltd.) and *Watchmakers and Clockmakers of the World* (by G. H. Baillie, the second edition published in 1947 by N. A. G. Press Ltd.). Baillie's immense list of 37,000 names is practically confined to dates and town of origin, with only occasional references to specimens in well-known collections. Britten's list, only about a third as long, gives a good deal more information, including addresses in a large number of cases. The book also includes about two dozen fairly full biographies of the most famous makers.

ARNOLD, JOHN and JOHN ROGER. John, the father, was born in 1736 and apprenticed to his father in Bodmin. In about 1760 he moved to London and established himself in Devereux Court. In 1764 he presented to George III a half-quarter repeating watch set in a ring. The whole movement was only $\frac{1}{3}$ inch in diameter and the diameter of the ruby cylinder, probably the first of its kind, was only $\frac{1}{54}$ inch. He started work on marine timekeepers in about 1770 and in 1775 patented (No. 1113) a bimetallic compensation balance and helical balance-spring. A patent for terminal end curves followed in 1776. All early chronometers had the pivoted detent escapement, but between 1780 and 1782 Arnold developed his spring detent and patented it in 1782 (No. 1328).

At some time before 1776 he left Devereux Court for Adelphi Buildings and in about 1785 he moved to 112 Cornhill. He also had a chronometer factory at Chigwell. He took his son, John Roger, into partnership in 1787 and the work was then signed 'Arnold & Son' until John's death in 1799. Curiously, John was not admitted to the Clockmakers' Company until 1783.

John's son, John Roger, was admitted to the Clockmakers' Company in 1796 and was Master in 1817. In 1820 he moved from Cornhill to 27 Cecil Street, and in 1830 to 84 Strand, where he continued until his death in 1843, although latterly he took little active part in the business. In 1830 he entered into partnership with E. J. Dent with power to break in 1840, which Dent then did (Arnold having been almost inactive) and set up on his own at 82 Strand. Products of the partnership are signed 'Arnold & Dent'.

John Arnold's system of numbering is not much guide in dating his work. He often used fractional numbers and in his marine chronometers there is always a difference of 90

BIOGRAPHICAL NOTES

between the numerator and denominator. But this does not apply to fractionally numbered watches which are all early, and apparently numbered quite erratically. John
Roger started a new series of numbering after his father's death.

For further details of the Arnolds' work see pp. 25, 27–30.

BARRAUD. Of the several makers of this name the most famous was Paul Philip, Clockmakers'
Company 1796–1813 and Master 1810 and 1811. He traded at 86 Cornhill.

His sons, John and James, traded as 'Barraud & Sons' from 1813–36 and at 41 Cornhill until 1838 after which the firm became known as Barraud & Lund.

BARROW, NATHANIEL was the most famous of several makers of this name. He was among
the pioneers of the balance-spring and invented a form of regulator called after him. This
was a worm- and straight-line sector operating on the end of the balance-spring for which
purpose the end section of the spring had to be straight (*195*). He was apprenticed to Job
Betts in 1653, admitted to the Clockmakers' Company in 1660 and was Master in 1689.

BEATSON, 32 Cornhill. The name engraved on McCabe's lowest grade of watches.

BERTHOUD, FERDINAND and LOUIS. Ferdinand was born in 1729. He moved to Paris in 1745
and in 1762 was appointed Horloger de la Marine. He did much experimental work on
marine timekeepers and from crude beginnings arrived independently at the spring
detent escapement between 1780 and 1782. A fine collection of his marine timekeepers is
in the Musée des Arts et Métiers in Paris. Although he made fine watches they were
almost without exception conventional in design and so far as is known he never made a
pocket chronometer. He died in 1807 and was succeeded by his nephew Louis (1754–
1813) who made both pocket and marine chronometers. The craftsmanship and elegance
of Louis' work is second to none, and although he adhered to such out-of-date features
as the pivoted detent escapement and cylindrical balance-springs without end-curves,
his chronometers nevertheless had the reputation of an excellent performance (*425*). He
made about 150 chronometers in all and was succeeded in his business by two sons as
Berthoud Frères.

BONNIKSEN, BAHNE (1859–1935) was a Dane who moved to England and was naturalised as
a British subject in 1910. In 1890 he began to develop a type of watch intended to combine the timekeeping qualities of a tourbillon with the robustness of an ordinary lever
watch. The resulting watch he called a karrusel which he patented in 1894 and brought
out an improved pattern in 1903. The mechanism of this revolving escapement is explained on p. 63 and illustrated in figure 590.

For many years Bonniksen's karrusels carried all before them in the Kew Certificate
trials, but with the growing impact of mechanisation he turned his attention to other
activities, and died in 1935.

Other makers were permitted to use Bonniksen's karrusel under licence, including

128

Hector Golay, a Swiss who settled in 1870 at Spencer Street, Clerkenwell, where he made very high quality watches. Golays had their ébauches made in Switzerland but did the finishing themselves; but they also supplied unfinished movements, largely to Rotherhams, who then finished them and sold many karrusel watches. The firm of Golay continues in business in Hatton Garden as sole agent for Cyma watches.

BOOTH, EDWARD (1636–1716) changed his name to BARLOW after his godfather. He invented Rack-striking for clocks, followed by repeating mechanism, in 1676, which he applied to watches in 1686 and applied for a patent. In this he was defeated by Daniel Quare on the grounds that Barlow's repeater had two push-pieces, for hours and minutes respectively, whereas Quare operated the whole mechanism with a single push-piece. Barlow, in conjunction with William Houghton and Thomas Tompion, devised a precursor of the virgule escapement in 1695 (patent number 344). He died in 1716.

BREGUET, ABRAHAM-LOUIS was born in 1747. In 1762 he moved to Paris, but the details of his early career are obscure and it is likely that after completing his articles he worked for a time for Berthoud. His earliest identifiable work dates from 1782 and at any rate up to 1787, and to some extent into the early 'nineties, he used a system of fractional numbering: thus $17\frac{10}{85}$ would be watch number 17 completed in October 1785. In 1787 the books of the firm start and have all survived. These have a straightforward system of numbering which continued up to Breguet's death in 1823 and subsequently and by which, with some exceptions, his watches may be fairly closely dated (see p. 60). Any number higher than 5999 is a fake.

In 1791 Breguet was forced to leave France to escape the Revolution, living first in Switzerland and then in England, and he returned in 1795. Up to 1791 his work is almost, if not quite universally, signed 'Breguet à Paris' but practically never after 1795. All or nearly all watches manifestly later than 1795 and signed 'à Paris' are fakes. In 1807 Breguet took his son Louis Antoine into partnership after which the work is signed 'Breguet et fils'. Soon after 1813 he was appointed Horloger de la Marine in succession to Louis Berthoud after which important work is so signed.

After Breguet's death in 1823 the style of the firm continued but for a short time in about 1830 the work was signed 'Breguet et Neveu'.

The firm continues at 28 Place Vendôme, Paris.

BROCKBANK. Of the several clockmakers of this name, the most important were the brothers John and Myles who traded at 6 Cowper's Court, and were among the pioneers of chronometer making. Myles was admitted to the Clockmakers' Company in 1776 and John in 1779. Earnshaw claimed to have revealed his version of the spring detent escapement to them and that they passed on the information to Arnold. One of their principal workmen, Peto, invented the cross-detent escapement which combined the theoretical advantages of Arnold's and Earnshaw's escapements, and several examples by the Brockbanks survive, coupled with an overbanking device which limits the expansion of the helical spring. Myles died in 1821 and the brothers were succeeded by two nephews, also John and Myles, who traded as 'John Brockbanks & Company'. From 1815–35 the style of the firm was 'Brockbank & Atkins', still at 6 Cowper's Court.

BULL, RAINULPH or RANDOLPH, is the earliest identifiable British watchmaker. A large oval watch by him, dated 1590, is in the British Museum. The dates of his birth and death are not known, but he was certainly alive as late as 1617.

CARON, PIERRE AUGUSTIN (1732–99) won early fame as a watchmaker and invented the double virgule escapement. He was a brother-in-law of Lépine (*q.v.*). He soon abandoned watchmaking for a varied and successful court career and changed his name to Beaumarchais.

COLE, JAMES FERGUSON (1798–1880) was a most prolific inventor of escapements, some of them practical, but others of the wildest improbability. His work is nearly always of the highest order and elegance. In addition to the experimental or one-off pieces he produced many ordinary pocket watches of high grade and mostly with the lever escapement. He also made fine and elegant travelling clocks.

CUMMING, ALEXANDER (*c.* 1732–1814) improved the cylinder escapement, including curved teeth on the escape wheel. He was also a famous chronometer maker and in 1766 published *The Element of Clock and Watch Work*. He was at the 'Dial and 3 Crowns' in Bond Street until 1777; then 12 Clifford Street until 1794; and finally had a shop in Fleet Street until his death, after which it was occupied by his nephew John Grant (*q.v.*). Cumming was a Fellow of the Royal Society.

CUMMINS, T. This virtually unknown maker was almost certainly the first English maker to use the lever escapement in watches of the highest quality, when this escapement was revived after its almost complete neglect in England from 1800-20. He appears to have started using the lever escapement soon after 1820, with a highly sophisticated form of Massey's escapement. About four of these watches survive (*488*). He used a form of double numbering thus: 17–27. The 27 almost certainly refers to the year of manufacture, and 17 is probably the watch number in that year. The earliest recorded specimen was made in 1822. Another name and address, presumably that of the owner of the watch, sometimes appears on the balance-cock.

DEBAUFRE, PETER. Church Street, Soho. Clockmakers' Company 1689–1722 and previously in Paris. In 1704 he was associated with Nicholas Facio (*q.v.*) in obtaining a patent for watch jewelling. He also invented a dead-beat escapement with two parallel-mounted escape-wheels, often called after him. It did not become popular until revived by Litherland and the Preston makers at the end of the century. Sir Isaac Newton spoke favourably of his escapement and Sully used a variant of it, with one wheel and two pallets, in his marine timekeeper of 1724.

DENNISON, AARON (1812–95) (not to be confused with E. B. Denison, later Lord Grimthorpe) is sometimes known as the 'Father of American Watchmaking'. He started business on his own as a repairer and retailer, in 1839, and in 1849 he interested E. Howard and D. P. Davis in setting up a watch factory at Roxbury, where he was the superintendent until 1861. After varying vicissitudes it became the Waltham Watch Company, but by this time Dennison had left it. After a period in Switzerland he settled in England and in 1874 set up a successful case-making industry at Handsworth, Birmingham, where he continued until his death. He formed a superb collection of watches which his son bequeathed in 1937 to the Waltham Watch Company. There it was brutally neglected and ill-treated until the mangled remains were returned to this country and auctioned at Christies in 1961.

DENT, EDWARD JOHN (1790–1853). After starting life as a tallow chandler, Dent went over to watchmaking, and from 1815–29 he was employed by the Vulliamys and the Barrauds. In 1830 he went into partnership with John Roger Arnold and in 1840 set up on his own at 33 Cockspur Street. The year before his death he secured the contract for making 'Big Ben'. He made many fine chronometers and watches as well as others of a high commercial grade. The firm, as E. Dent & Co. Ltd., survives at 41 Pall Mall, London S.W.1.

DUTTON, WILLIAM. Clockmakers' Company 1746–1794. He was apprenticed to Graham and afterwards in partnership with Mudge, as 'Mudge & Dutton' from 1759–90, at 148 Fleet Street. Mudge's name was dropped at his death in 1794 and after Dutton's death the business was carried on by his son Matthew at the same address. He made fine watches including at any rate one before 1800 with the lever escapement (374); was master of the Clockmakers' Company and continued in business until shortly before his death in 1843.

EARNSHAW, THOMAS (1749–1829). On coming to London he first worked for the trade. In about 1781, simultaneously with Arnold and Berthoud, he devised a spring detent escapement. The first examples were unsuccessful, and all his detent escapements were subject to rapid cutting of the impulse pallet, so that very few of his marine chronometers, and relatively few of his pocket watches have survived. Nevertheless, it is Earnshaw's form of the spring detent escapement, subject only to minor development, which has survived to this day in universal use. He also devised the modern method of fusing together the brass and steel laminae of the compensation, as opposed to the earlier methods of riveting or soldering them together. In pocket watches he employed either compensation balances and helical springs, or alternatively, flat steel balances with a spiral-spring and a pincer-type compensation curb, commonly known as 'sugar tong compensation' (*456*). His superficial finish is generally perfectly plain, and he only engraved the watch plates and jewelled throughout to special order.

As he could not afford a patent for his spring detent one was taken out for him by Thomas Wright, and early examples were stamped '*Wright's Patent*'. However, Wright was very dilatory in taking out the patent after Earnshaw had approached him, and in the meantime Arnold had patented his own. Earnshaw always claimed that the Brockbanks had told Arnold of Earnshaw's design; but no real evidence was produced, and Arnold's design was completely different, as also was Berthoud's.

Earnshaw was perhaps the first leading maker to make quite cheap, single-roller, lever-escapement watches in the last year or two of his life.

In 1794 or 1795 Earnshaw took over the business of Wm. Hughes at 119 High Holborn. He died in 1829 when the business was carried on until 1842 by his son, also Thomas, first at High Holborn, and subsequently at 87 Fenchurch Street.

EAST, EDWARD (1602–97) had such a long life that it has been suggested that he was really two people of the same name, but the researches of Alan Lloyd have shown fairly conclusively that there was only one of him. In 1631 he was a founder member, and junior Assistant of the Clockmakers' Company. He was Master in 1645 and 1652. He was clockmaker successively to Charles I and II. His work was of an extremely high order, both mechanically and decoratively (*150*). Particularly beautiful is the tall, sloping script signature which he put on all his work until about 1670. After about 1670, his later work is coarser in design, partly following the fashion, but suggesting that he had pretty well retired at the age of 70, and was no longer directly responsible for the work sold under his name. Balance-spring watches, even nominally by him, are exceedingly rare.

ELLICOTT, JOHN. The first John Ellicott was a creditable maker. He was admitted to the Clockmakers' Company in 1696 and died in 1733. He was an enterprising watchmaker, having been one of the first to use a centre-seconds hand, and he made one very thin watch, dating from soon after 1700, which measured only $\frac{1}{5}$ inch between the plates. He often signed his name under the cock or balance.

But his son John was much more famous. Born in 1706, he set up in business in Sweeting's Alley in about 1728. Also about this time he began to use the cylinder escapement, very little later than Graham. In some of his later watches he used a ruby cylinder. All his watches are finely made and some are in highly decorated cases.

He seems to have used only one series of numbers and Baillie gives the following sequence of dates and numbers

Year	1728	No.	123
	1730		400
	1740		1800
	1750		3250
	1760		4770
	1770		6435
	1780		7620
	1790		8450
	1800		8760
	1810		9074

Special watches, however, were not numbered.

Until about 1750 watches were signed '*Jno Ellicott*' but thereafter '*Ellicott*' or '*John Ellicott & Son*'.

Ellicott was a Fellow of the Royal Society and clockmaker to the King. He died in 1772, being succeeded by his son Edward who died in 1791. He in turn was succeeded by his son, also Edward, at about which time the style of the firm became '*Edward Ellicott & Sons*'. The second Edward went into partnership with one Taylor, when their work was signed '*Ellicott & Taylor*', from about 1811–30. Subsequently the signature was '*Ellicott & Smith*', up to 1840, Edward Ellicot having died in 1835.

EMERY, JOSIAH was a Swiss, born in about 1725. He settled in England and carried on business at 33 Cockspur Street, Charing Cross. He was made an honorary freeman of the Clockmakers' Company in 1781. He made fine watches, mostly with the cylinder escapement, but he is most famous for his pioneering of the lever escapement from 1782, being the first maker to use this escapement after Mudge (and perhaps Julien le Roy—see page 45). His lever escapements are described fully on page 38. He made about 30 lever watches from 1782 to about 1795. Before taking up the lever he made a few precision watches with a pivoted detent escapement and spiral compensation curb. Emery died in 1797 and was succeeded in business by Louis Recordon (*q.v.*).

FACIO DE DUILLIER, NICHOLAS was born at Basle in 1664, settled in England in 1687 and died in Worcester in 1753. He was the first to succeed in piercing jewels for watch pivots, a method which he patented jointly with Debaufre (patent No. 371 for May 1704), although the patent was later defeated by the Clockmakers' Company. For the next 80 years jewelling was an entirely British monopoly, to the great advantage of home trade. Facio was a Fellow of the Royal Society.

FASOLDT, CHARLES was born in Germany in 1818 and emigrated to New York in 1849 where he made high-quality watches with a curious form of lever escapement, having two concentric escape-wheels. The larger wheel was concerned only with locking the two ordinary pallets of the lever, and gave no impulse. However, the lever was continued towards the escape-wheel pivot and ended in an impulse jewel, which was impulsed by the second, smaller escape-wheel. Impulse therefore was given only on alternate swings of the balance and generally operated very much like the Robin escapement, except for impulse being delivered via the lever, and not by the escape-wheel direct. The escapement therefore combined most of the disadvantages of the lever and chronometer escapements. Fasoldt called his watches chronometers, and made about 50 of them before moving in 1861 to Albany, in the state of New York, where he set up a factory for making watches and clocks, employing some 50 men. He died in 1898.

FATTON, FREDERICK LOUIS was one of Breguet's most eminent pupils. He settled in New Bond Street, London and made many fine watches and clocks in the Breguet style, frequently signed 'Fatton élève de Breguet' (462). He is best known for his ink-recording chronograph watches, patented in 1822.

FRODSHAM. The numerous members of the Frodsham family were in business from some time before 1780. William Frodsham, the second generation of watchmakers, married Alice, a grand-daughter of John Harrison. Charles, the last member of the family to be active in watchmaking, died in 1871 but the firm still continues. From some time before the middle of the last century they began making lever escapement and chronometer escapement watches of the very highest quality, and continued to do so until the outbreak of war in 1939. For the 1851 Exhibition they introduced a three-quarter plate calibre which they marked *AD.FMSZ*, which continued subsequently to be put on all their highest grade work. The significance of FMSZ is said to be found by putting the name Frodsham against numbers thus

$$
\begin{array}{ccccccccc}
F & R & O & D & S & H & A & M & Z \\
1 & 2 & 3 & 4 & 5 & 6 & 7 & 8 & 0
\end{array}
$$

Thus FMSZ gives the date 1850.

During the first part of this century the firm was closely connected with Nicole Nielsen, who made most of the movements, including some of the most perfect tourbillons ever made, which can still perform with almost unrivalled accuracy (584). When other watches became increasingly ugly during the nineteenth and twentieth centuries, Frodsham watches are almost always elegant and well proportioned, and even as late as 1914, some of them, with engine-turned silver dials, were worthy of Breguet (580).

GRAHAM, GEORGE was born in 1673 or 1674. In 1688 he was apprenticed to Henry Aske and was admitted to the Clockmakers' Company in 1695. He then worked for Thomas Tompion whose niece Elizabeth he married in 1696. In about 1711 Tompion took Graham into partnership and from then until Tompion's death in 1713 some or all of the work was signed '*Tompion & Graham*'. Graham was elected a Fellow of the Royal Society in 1721 and Master of the Clockmakers' Company in 1722. In about 1726 he developed and rapidly almost perfected the cylinder escapement, and thereafter very seldom used any other for watches. These nearly all have an elegant enamel dial with blued-steel beetle and poker hands (*268*). The plain watches frequently have a polished steel centre-seconds hand, but this is not found on the repeaters, which also are somewhat smaller. Graham continued Tompion's numbering, No. 4369 being a '*T. Tompion & G. Graham*'. Baillie gives the following dates and numbers.

Plain Watches		Repeaters	
1715	No. 4660	1720	No. 480
1725	5260	1730	620
1735	5610	1740	790
1745	6180	1750	960
1750	6480		

The number is stamped on the pillar plate and the underside of the balance-cock.

Apart from Graham's earliest work, he always used a solid, engraved cockfoot and the balance staff is jewelled with a big diamond end-stone (*270*). There are many faked Grahams, but the genuine watches are of such standardised design that, having seen one, any fake is easily detected.

Graham died in 1751 and was succeeded in business by Thomas Mudge.

GRANT, JOHN & SON. John Grant senior was apprenticed to his famous uncle, Alexander Cumming, and became an honorary freeman of the Clockmakers' Company in 1781. He was probably the last of the band of English experimenters with the lever escapement and his work is of the very highest quality. He used a helical balance-spring and a variety of complicated compensation balances. Working without draw, he evidently set great store on deep locking of the lever pallets and it was perhaps this that induced him, in about 1800 or a little later, to arrange the escape-wheel with its arbor at right angles to the lever and escape-wheel arbors. There are examples of this lay-out, commonly known as Grant's 'chaff-cutter', in the Ilbert and Guildhall Collections, but none is known elsewhere and indeed, outside of these collections very few of his lever watches survive at all. The chaff-cutter escapement is well-illustrated on page 75 of Chamberlain's *It's About Time*.

In the Guildhall is a movement with his earlier, more normal lever escapement, with two balances geared together (*46*).

Grant died in 1810 when he was succeeded by his son John who was also a fine maker,

BIOGRAPHICAL NOTES

and was five times Master of the Clockmakers' Company between 1838 and 1867. Both father and son traded at 75 Fleet Street.

GRIGNION. Successive members of this family did fine work from about 1690 to 1825. Thomas, 1713–84, introduced improvements to the cylinder escapement and prolonged the life of the cylinder by arranging the teeth of the escape-wheel at different levels.

GUILLAUME, CHARLES-EDOUARD (1861–1938) was not primarily an horologist, but his metallurgical researches brought him in contact with the problem of middle temperature error, which he finally eliminated by the nickel alloy 'Invar' for pendulums and balance-wheels, and 'Elinvar' for balance-springs, which keep constant strength under different temperatures.

HALEY, CHARLES was admitted to the Clockmakers' Company in 1781 and died in 1825. He was a pioneer chronometer maker and made fine watches with duplex or detent escapements. In 1796 he patented a remontoir, or constant-force escapement which, despite its complication, he contrived to compress into a watch movement of normal size, of which there is an example in the Guildhall Museum. The escapement is illustrated on page 167 of Chamberlain's *It's About Time*, copied from a drawing by Berthoud, and in this book on figure 68. Impulse is imparted to the balance by a helical spring which is rewound at every beat by the train. The escapement, which was the first of several of this kind devised by contemporary and later makers, was never reliable.

HARRISON, JOHN (1693–1776), despite his achievements in the field of marine timekeepers, is memorable in connection with watches only for the prototype of the successful 'Number four' made for him in 1753 by John Jeffreys, which has what is almost certainly the first compensation curb ever applied to a watch.

HAUTEFEUILLE, JEAN (1647–1724), was a physician and mechanician, and not primarily an horologist. Nevertheless, he made early experiments with the balance-spring, and devised a straight-line spring similar to Hooke's. With it he was able to defeat Huygen's application for a French patent for his spiral-spring. In 1722 Hautefeuille also invented the forerunner of the rack lever escapement, but it did not become popular until taken up by the English Peter Litherland and the Preston makers over 60 years later.

HELE or HENLEIN, PETER is the first recorded maker of pocket watches, in about 1520. He worked in Nürnberg and died in 1542.

HOOKE, ROBERT (1635–1703) worked for Robert Boyle and from 1662 was curator of the Royal Society. He was also Professor of Geometry at Gresham College. From about 1658 he experimented with balance-springs, probably in the form of a straight spring. In 1675 he was prominent in contesting with Huygens for the priority of invention of the balance-spring. He also claimed the invention of the anchor escapement for pendulum clocks, but in neither case does there seem to be much solid evidence to support his claims. He did much to assist Tompion, with whom he co-operated in making the first English balance-spring watches.

HOURIET, JACQUES FRÉDÉRIC (1743–1830) was one of the finest Swiss makers and he also worked for the foremost French makers, including Breguet. He made fine chronometers and tourbillons and in 1814 devised the spherical balance-spring.

HOWARD, EDWARD (1813–1904) was a pioneer of high-quality watchmaking in America. He was apprenticed to the famous American clockmaker Aaron Willard, but in 1849 he went into partnership with A. L. Dennison to found the company which eventually became the Waltham Watch Company (*see also* A. L. Dennison).

HUYGENS, CHRISTIAN (1629–95). Although primarily a mathematician and optician, Huygens made more important contributions to horology than probably any other man, before or since. Huygens was Dutch and was sometimes referred to (particularly by Hooke) as 'Zulichem', this being his home town. In 1657 he successfully applied a pendulum to the verge escapement and the first examples were made by Samuel Coster. In 1675 he brought the spiral balance-spring to a practicable stage of development, the first examples being made in Paris by Jacques Thuret. Thus, although he actually invented neither, he was nevertheless the first man to bring to a practical form the pendulum and the balance-spring, upon which two all precision timekeeping for the next 250 years was to be based.

INGOLD, PIERRE-FRÉDÉRIC (1787–1878), a pupil of Breguet, was a pioneer of interchangeability of parts in watch manufacture and invented the Ingold milling tool.

JAPY, FRÉDÉRIC (1749–1813) effectively founded the modern methods of mass-produced watch manufacture. He manufactured ébauches by machine tools as early as 1776.

JEANRICHARD, DANIEL (1665–1741) was the leading pioneer in setting up the Neuchâtel watch-making industry.

JUMP, JOSEPH was articled to Benjamin Lewis Vulliamy in 1827 and on Vulliamy's death in 1854 continued on his own account in Bond Street, and later Pall Mall, until his death in 1899. He made very fine watches with typical English three-quarter plate movements, but externally in a style fully worthy of the Breguet tradition.

JÜRGENSEN, URBAN and JULES. Urban Jürgensen was born in Copenhagen in 1776. After preliminary training in his father's workshop, in 1796 he was sent to Houriet at Le Locle. In 1800 he moved to Paris and continued his training with Berthoud and Breguet. In 1800 or 1801 he moved to London where he studied with Arnold. Later in 1801 he married Houriet's daughter, Sophie Henriette. Urban then returned to Copenhagen and began to train his brother Frédéric. He also began to make the marine and pocket chronometers for which he is famous. It seems certain that he carried out a very much higher proportion of the work himself than did his contemporaries and with such a catholic training, coupled with his own genius, it is natural that his work should be of a very high order.

He made 73 chronometers and about 800 watches. The chronometers have double numbers, the first being the chronometer series and the later the watch series. Nearly all have silver cases (*442*).

Urban made very fine balances and often made the weights of oval shape to reduce air resistance. In view of his practical experience of both types it is interesting to find him say: 'from my own experience I know very well that a soldered balance is just as good if not better than a cast balance and has all the desired sensitiveness and regularity of action'. He sometimes employed Arnold's type of gold helical balance-spring and escape-wheel and in general, the style of his work resembles the English more closely than the French. He died in 1830 and was succeeded by his sons Louis Urban and Jules Frederick. The latter was the better business man. He moved to Switzerland in 1834 and opened a factory at le Locle, although his watches continued to be signed '*Jules Jürgensen, Copenhagen*'. On his death in 1877 he was succeeded by his sons Jules Urban and Jacques Alfred. Jules Urban died in 1894, but Jacques Alfred lived, and continued in business, until 1912. After 1912 the business was carried on by David Golay and after passing subsequently through several hands, still survives in America. The Genealogy of the clock-making members of the family is as follows:

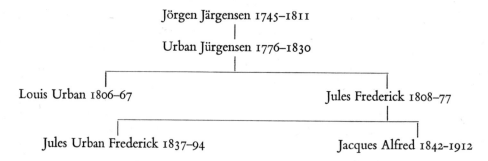

KENDALL, LARCUM (1721–95) is best known for his duplicate of Harrison's marine timekeeper No. 4 and two subsequent variants on the same theme. Watches by him are rare, but there is a very fine pivoted detent watch by him, hallmarked 1786, in the Guildhall Museum (*314*).

KULLBERG, VICTOR (1824–90) was a Swede. After working for the trade he moved to England in 1851 and set up on his own in 1856. He was overwhelmingly successful as a maker of marine chronometers, at first with a form of flat-rimmed balance and subsequently with a more normal pattern with auxiliary compensation. He also specialised in keyless-wound fusee, chronometer watches. To minimise the position errors to which spring detents are specially subject he arranged his pocket watches so that the detent spring is vertical in the 12-up position. His work was all of a very high order.

LEPAUTE, JEAN-ANDRÉ (1720–89) is best known as a clockmaker of great merit, and as a watchmaker his fame rests upon his invention of the virgule escapement in 1753. He retired from business in 1774, being succeeded by two nephews and the firm continued far into the nineteenth century under a variety of names, including '*Lepaute et fils*' and '*Henry Neveu Lepaute*'.

LEPINE, JEAN-ANTOINE (1720–1814). Although Lepaute invented the virgule escapement its development and wider use was attributable to Lepine. But his greatest importance as a watchmaker rests on his introduction of the barred (as opposed to the plated) movement, often known as the 'Lépine calibre' in about 1770. The firm continued long after his death.

LEROUX, JOHN (1744–1808). Nothing is known about Leroux's personal history but he was an important and very early pioneer of the lever escapement in England, and differed from his contemporaries in putting all the lift on the teeth of the escape-wheel. His lever spans only $1\frac{1}{2}$ teeth of the escape-wheel. He used a compensation balance and a conical shaped balance-spring. Only two examples of his lever escapement are known; a movement in the Ilbert collection and a watch, hallmarked 1785, in the Guildhall Museum (*303*).

LE ROY, JULIEN and PIERRE. Julien Le Roy was born in 1686 and died in 1759. He was a very fine maker and raised French watch and clock making to a level at which it could successfully challenge the supremacy which British makers had established in the last quarter of the seventeenth century. In this he was much assisted by the English Henry Sully, and perfected the oil-sinks invented by Sully. In about 1725 he introduced the adjustable potence for the escape-wheel in verge watches and in 1727 obtained from George Graham an example of his cylinder escapement, which he subsequently often used himself. It is thought that Julien was the first to use wire gongs, instead of bells, in repeater watches, thus paving the way for Breguet's thin repeaters. He also used a small anchor escapement (also used later by Breguet) to regulate the speed of striking in a repeater and this may be considered as evidence corroborating the likelihood of his having invented the lever escapement (discussed at length on pp. 44–45).

Julien's son Pierre (1717–85) was almost entirely taken up with the invention of a marine timekeeper. As early as 1748 he invented a detached detent escapement of a sort, and by 1766 he had brought it to a considerable stage of perfection, in the instrument now preserved in the Musée des Arts et Métiers in Paris. Thus, although Pierre took little direct interest in watchmaking his influence upon it, as the inventor of the detent escapement, was great. The firm still exists in Paris.

BIOGRAPHICAL NOTES

LITHERLAND, PETER (1756–1804) was born at Warrington, and in 1791 took out his first patent for the rack lever escapement, which had been dormant since its invention by Hautefeuille in 1722. Litherland's form of it is so different from Hautefeuille's that he may well not have known of the latter. The rack-lever as made by Litherland came to be made in great numbers in Lancashire. Despite its complete non-detachment it performed remarkably well, and probably paved the way for the introduction of Massey's detached lever escapement in 1815 and subsequently the development, mostly in Lancashire, of the single-roller lever, from the early 1820's.

Dr. Vaudrey Mercer has done much research into the work of the Litherlands, which is set out in *Antiquarian Horology* (the proceedings of the Antiquarian Horological Society), Volume 3, No. 11, for June 1962. He gives the following list of the successive styles of the firm, with dates:

1796	Peter Litherland,			21 Mount Pleasant
1800–3	Peter Litherland,			12 Commutation Road
1800–7	Litherland Whiteside & Co.,			Ranelagh Street
1810–3	,,	,,	,,	Church Street
1816–35	Litherland, Davies & Co.,			Church Street
1837–76	,,	,,	,,	Bold Street.

McCABE, JAMES came of a Belfast clockmaking family, but moved to London and was admitted to the Clockmakers' Company in 1781. He made many fine watches, with a variety of escapements, and in particular brought the duplex escapement to a high level of perfection. His best watches were signed '*James McCabe*', the second graded '*McCabe*' and it is said that common watches were signed '*Beatson*'. He died in 1811 but the firm continued until 1883, and Britten gives the following dates, styles and addresses:

James McCabe was first at 11 Bell's Buildings Fleet Street in 1778; 34 King Street Cheapside in 1783; 8 King Street Cheapside in 1788; 97 Cornhill Royal Exchange in 1804.

After James's death the business was carried on by successive members of the family as McCabe & Son, at 99 Cornhill, until 1820. McCabe & Strahan, 1825–6; J. McCabe, 97 Cornhill until 1838 and then 32 Cornhill until 1883 when Robert Jeremy McCabe retired and closed the business.

However, the signature of James McCabe seems also to have persisted long after his death, as there survives a movement with the Savage two-pin escapement, which must be later than 1820, and by the style more like 1830, which is signed 'Jas McCabe, Royal Exchange London'.

MAIRET (alternatively JEANMAIRET), SYLVAIN (1805–90) was one of the finest Swiss watchmakers of the nineteenth century, alike on account of the quality of work, the technical interest of his escapements (particularly the lever) and the external elegance of his watches. Between 1830 and 1840 he lived for five years in London, working largely for B. L. Vulliamy, and also Hunt and Roskell (537). Most of his lever watches have all the lift on the escape-wheel teeth.

MARGETTS, GEORGE was born in 1748, admitted to the Clockmakers' Company in 1779 and died insane in 1808. He was an early chronometer maker, but so far as is known he made no pocket chronometers. In the watch field he made a number of very complicated and decorative astronomical watches, and was also among the pioneers of the lever escapement in England, employing a fairly straightforward form of cranked roller with separate safety roller. His trains are finely cut and high-numbered, but the superficial finish is remarkably rough and the movements are seldom even signed. It is thought that no specimen of his lever escapement has survived. One was said to be in the Dennison collection, but this was so badly catalogued as to be most unreliable, and it certainly did not appear in the sale of the collection at Christies in 1961.

MARTINOT. This prolific family were watchmakers to the French court, on and off, for two centuries from about 1570 to 1770. As watchmakers they introduced no special innovations, but are mentioned because of their long history and the large number of watches by them, especially fine oignons, which have survived.

MASSEY, EDWARD (1772–1852) was a Coventry maker. He patented a form of pump-wind and, in 1815, a form of detached lever escapement. This is of great importance, being the first introduction of a simple, cheaply-made lever escapement into England, as opposed to the very complicated work of the earlier experimenters from Mudge to Grant. It is doubtful if any lever watches were made in England during the decade before Massey's patent in 1815 (and very few even then before 1820). Massey is said by many authorities to have invented the crankroller escapement, but this he certainly did not (either Emery or Margetts may have done so, or possibly even Julien Le Roy) and anyway his escapement is not cranked at all. The essence of a cranked roller is that it should be quite detached from the balance-staff and supported by cranks at one or both ends. Massey's impulse roller is integral with the staff and has vertical grooves cut into the balance-staff on each side of it, through which the pointed extremities of the lever fork pass, constituting the safety action (51). It is thus very simple, and certainly as made by Cummins was capable of very accurate timekeeping. It is best described as 'Massey's escapement' which is the name for it used throughout this book. Examples of it by Massey himself are now exceedingly rare.

MOINET, LOUIS (1758–1853) was Breguet's business secretary and later set up in business on his own account, making fine watches in the Breguet style. Breguet never published anything except what amounted to catalogues in his lifetime, but it was known that he had compiled a lot of notes, and when these could not be discovered after his death, Moinet was widely thought to have purloined them. This became a certainty in 1848 when Moinet published his *Nouveau Traité Général Astronomique et Civil d'Horlogerie Théoretique et Pratique*. The Breguet family successfully applied to the courts for the return of the original notes, which still exist. Moinet's *Traité* is a most valuable work, finely illustrated.

MOTEL, JEAN FRANÇOIS HENRI (1786–1859) was one of Breguet's most eminent pupils and made watches of the highest quality, especially with a form of pivoted detent escapement. He used Houriet's spherical-shaped balance-spring, and a cylindrical spring with conical-shaped ends, of his own.

MUDGE, THOMAS was born in 1715 and apprenticed to George Graham. Although Thomas Colley was legally Graham's successor at his death in 1751, Mudge was so effectively. For the King of Spain he made a watch, set in the top of a walking stick, which showed true and apparent time, struck the hours, and was a minute repeater. In the Guildhall Museum is the movement of another Mudge watch which reputedly belonged to the King of Spain, but the evidence for this is obscure. It has a very sophisticated form of verge escapement, from which it may be supposed that it dates from not much after 1760; a spiral bimetallic compensation curb (which suggests that it is not much earlier than 1760) and a remontoir wound once every minute. This is almost certainly the first time a remontoir was fitted to a pocket watch and indeed, it has very rarely been done at any time.

For his ordinary watches Mudge used the cylinder escapement and in almost every way, including the dial, hands and case, closely followed the design laid down by Graham (*287*). In about 1755 he entered into partnership with William Dutton, another apprentice of Graham, and the work was then signed '*Thos Mudge Wm Dutton*'.

During the 1760's Mudge had been experimenting with the detached lever escapement and probably the bracket clock with lever escapement in the Ilbert Collection dates from this decade. But in 1770 he succeeded (with great difficulty on his own admission) in compressing it into the famous pocket watch which was sold to George III and is still in the Royal ownership. Apart from the somewhat speculative possibility that Mudge was anticipated by Julien le Roy, this was the first lever-escapement watch from which all modern watches have been developed. In 1771 Mudge retired from active business and moved to Plymouth to concentrate on the development of his remontoir escapement, marine timekeeper, but the name of the firm continued unchanged to the time of his death in 1794. Mudge, or Mudge & Dutton cylinder watches are of very fine workmanship and appearance and are now moderately rare.

NOUWEN, MICHAEL (alternatively NOWE, NOWAN, NEUWERS) was active from about 1580–1613 as one of the first English watchmakers of the highest quality. Several specimens of his work survive, including a superb crystal watch in the British Museum.

OUDIN, CHARLES was one of Breguet's best pupils and was in business on his own account from 1807–25. He produced a close copy of Breguet's souscription watch and frequently signed himself 'Oudin, élève de Breguet'. He invented a form of keyless work.

PENDLETON, RICHARD was active from about 1780 and died in 1808. He worked first for Emery and was generally known to have made Emery's lever escapement watches. Two lever watches under his own name survive, but unfortunately neither is in its original case so that it cannot be determined whether they were made in Emery's lifetime or subsequently. One, in the Ilbert collection, closely follows the Emery pattern, but the escapement of the other is quite different (42). The balances and cocks are hardly distinguishable from Emery's. In about 1794 he became one of the team employed by Thomas Mudge junior to make marine timekeepers on his father's plan. It is therefore difficult to know at what period he was working on his own; but from his own two lever watches, and his work for Emery, he must be accounted as a watchmaker of the front rank. The lever watches are signed 'Richd Pendleton, Pentonville, London'.

PENNINGTON, ROBERT, was active in Camberwell from about 1780–1816 as a chronometer maker, and with Pendleton was one of the team got together by Thomas Mudge junior to make marine timekeepers on his father's plan. He made pocket watches of very high quality, including chronometers, and employed a much lighter and more modern form of bimetallic compensation balance than most of his British contemporaries. At his death he was succeeded by his son, also Robert, who continued in business at 11 Portland Row, Camberwell until 1842.

PERIGAL, FRANCIS was active from about 1770 to the time of his death in 1794. He was admitted as honorary freeman of the Clockmakers' Company in 1781. A fine maker, he is particularly important by virtue of the very early lever watch by him which survives, certainly made before 1790 (unfortunately it cannot be dated by the hallmark as the case is not original) (310). Since he was appointed watchmaker to the King in 1784 he may well have had an opportunity of examining the Mudge lever watch, which to some extent his resembles. He was succeeded in business by his son, also Francis, and there were several other makers of the same family.

PERRELET, ABRAM-LOUIS (1729–1826) worked at le Locle and was described by Breguet as 'un homme si bon et tout plein de talent'. In La Montre Automatique Ancienne by Alfred Chapuis and Eugène Jaquet (Editions du Griffon, 1952) it is proved at considerable length, and pretty conclusively, that the self-winding watch was invented by Abram-Louis Perrelet. The experiments went on during the 1770's and had attained to a satisfactorily reliable result by 1780. The first examples of these are said to have been bought by Breguet and Recordon. Unfortunately no example of Perrelet's own work can be identified since the Neuchâtel makers did not sign their watches; but there are good grounds for supposing that a very ancient self-winding watch in the Le Roy collection may be by Perrelet. If so, it has the peculiarity that, unlike Breguet's and Recordon's oscillating weights, this one is centre-pivoted and revolves through 360 degrees.

PETO, —— even his Christian name is not known, but he was active from about 1780 to 1800 and worked for the Brockbanks. He is remembered by his cross-detent variant of the spring detent escapement which he may have arrived at to combine the theoretical advantages of Arnold's and Earnshaw's lay-outs; but possibly only to evade Earnshaw's patent (334). Several pocket watches with Peto's escapement were made by Brockbanks, and long after the British makers had given it up, Breguet thought so well of it as to introduce it into at least two of his finest tourbillons made after 1810.

PHILLIPS, EDOUARD (1821–1889) was a mechanical engineer and mathematician. From 1860 he also carried out investigations into the mathematics and properties of balance-springs. Although terminal end-curves to helical springs had been used empirically by Arnold from 1776, and Breguet introduced his overcoil for flat spiral springs some time around 1800, it remained for Phillips to lay down their mathematically correct formation. His best-known treatise is *Le Spiral Réglant* published in 1861.

POUZAIT (or POUZZAIT) JEAN MOÏSE (1743–93) was a capable maker at Geneva where he was put in charge of the first school of horology in 1788. He experimented with the lever escapement and produced a model in 1786 which has no resemblance to the English types, so it may well have been arrived at quite independently. The escape-wheel teeth project vertically from the face of the wheel and have chamfered impulse faces, as also have the anchor pallets. Pouzzait was thus certainly the first to introduce divided lift, which was not taken up by Breguet, nor probably any other maker, until well after 1800. His escapement was, however, defective in having no true safety action, and he seems generally to have used very large, seconds-beating balance-wheels the full diameter of the watch (369). It is believed that Pouzzait did work for Breguet.

PREST, THOMAS was John Roger Arnold's foreman and probably made most of his best watches. In 1820 he patented (No. 4,501) a form of keyless wind which was occasionally used by Arnold (469). It is applicable only to a going barrel and the hands have to be set by a key on the usual square on the cannon pinion. Prest died in 1855.

QUARE, DANIEL (& HORSEMAN) (c. 1648–1724). Quare was admitted to the Clockmakers' Company in 1671 and was Master in 1708. He was second to none in his day as a watchmaker, and his work is always handsomely proportioned, especially his early work, and six-hour dials (*203*). He was conservative in case design, keeping a loose ring pendant, and square-ended hinges long after others had gone over to ringed pendants and curve-ended hinges (*9*). He is said to have introduced motion-work, whereby the hour and minute hands are permanently geared together, whereas previously they had to be set independently. In 1680 he made a quarter repeating watch with which he successfully opposed the Rev. Barlow's application to James II in 1686 for a patent. Barlow's had two push-pieces, one for the hours and another for the quarters, but Quare operated both trains with a single push-piece. In 1718 he went into partnership with Stephen Horseman, after which their work is signed '*Quare & Horseman*' and Horseman continued it un-altered after Quare's death in 1724, until 1733, when he became bankrupt. Known watches signed by Quare have numbers 233 to 4989, and known watches by Quare & Horseman have numbers 4677 to 5503 (indicating some overlap). Quare repeaters are known from 109 to 257 and Quare & Horseman repeaters are known from 843 to 1129. Quare was much faked in his lifetime, but some watches signed Quaré are of such high quality, quite consistent with his own work, that they may be genuine, the accent having been added by him on export pieces.

RAMSAY, DAVID (*c.* 1590 to *c.* 1654) was born in Scotland but worked both in France and London. He was watchmaker to James I and, apparently, Charles I, at any rate until the royal appointment of Edward East. He was the first Master of the Clockmakers' Company, in 1632. He made watches of high quality, a few of which survive, including a particularly fine example which is part of the insignia of the successive Masters of the Clockmakers' Company (*126*).

RECORDON, LOUIS (active 1778–1824) worked in Greek Street, Soho and in 1797 succeeded Emery at No. 33 Cockspur Street. He also acted as Breguet's London agent and in 1780 took out for him an English patent (No. 1249) for self-winding watches (*311*). He made fine watches with a variety of escapements, in a style standing somewhat between English and Breguet's. At some time about 1796 he entered into partnership with Paul Du-pont when their work was signed '*Recordon & Dupont*'. Recordon retired in 1796, but the name continued unaltered until about 1816 when the business was taken over by Peter Des Granges who continued at 33 Cockspur Street until 1842.

ROBIN, ROBERT (1742–1809), a very fine maker, and clockmaker to Louis XV and XVI, and subsequently to the Republic. He devised a pinwheel lever escapement for watches and also, in 1791, the escapement still known by his name. In this, a lever is used for locking only and impulse is given direct by the escape wheel to the balance. Impulse can there-fore only be given on alternate swings of the balance. The escapement was used a good deal by Breguet, including in some of his perpetuelles, while his '*échappement naturel*' is really only a double Robin. Robert Robin is not to be confused with a later Robin who operated in the Rue de Richelieu from about 1790–1825 and was clockmaker to Louis XVIII.

ROSKELL, ROBERT (Active 1798–1830) worked both in Liverpool and London. He made many good quality rack-lever watches and, later, watches with Massey's lever escapement. Many of his watches have dials decorated in multi-coloured gold and he frequently used a small escape-wheel to which was fixed a seconds hand revolving once in 15 seconds. Other members of the family also operated in Liverpool.

SAVAGE, GEORGE (Active about 1808–55). He was born in Huddersfield where in 1808 he patented a remontoir. He later moved to London and in about 1820 invented a lever escapement which was used by a few makers until late in the nineteenth century, and is known as the 'Savage two pin'. In it, a very wide pallet on the balance arbor engages with two pins on the lever, but all or most of the impulse is given by the safety pin which engages with a very narrow slot on the roller (52). The escapement works well with a very brisk action, but it is difficult to make and never came into wide use. It is nevertheless important for the part it played in the revival of the lever escapement after 1820. Savage later emigrated to Canada where he founded a successful retail business in Montreal and died in 1855.

SULLY, HENRY (1680– 1728) had a career of continuous failure, both in France and England. Soon after completing his apprenticeship with Charles Gretton he travelled abroad, where Julien Le Roy recognised his abilities, and he was persuaded by Law, a Scottish Speculator living in Paris, to obtain the services of a number of skilled English watch and clockmakers and set up a factory at Versailles. This venture failed, but it did introduce to France a standard of craftsmanship which had a profound effect upon the whole French industry. Sully's most important single contribution to watchmaking was the invention of oil sinks, later perfected by Julien Le Roy.

After his unsuccessful French venture he returned to England bringing some of his staff with him, but here he was equally unsuccessful and eventually returned to France where he became slightly more prosperous and in 1721 turned his attention to the problem of marine timekeeping. In this he was not successful either, but one of his attempts survives in the Guildhall Museum, with an escapement similar to Debaufre's (but having one escape-wheel and two pallets, as opposed to Debaufre's two escape-wheels and one pallet) which has, though very rarely, been applied to watches.

In 1714 he published in Vienna an important horological work *Règle Artificielle du Tems*.

TAVAN, ANTOINE (1749–1836) worked in Geneva where he came to be considered the most skilled and inventive watchmaker; he was also much admired for his character and amiable personality. He invented a number of escapements of considerable ingenuity and complexity, at a time when the lever and chronometer escapements had not yet established themselves in their position of unchallenged supremacy. Several of these are illustrated in Chamberlain's *It's About Time*. In 1806 he was commissioned by Melly Frères to make models of ten escapements. These survive in the museum of the horological school at Geneva. They all measure 4 inches in diameter and are of great beauty. The escapements, including some of Tavan's own, are: verge, virgule, lever, 'Arnold' (pivoted and spring detent), Constant-force (Tavan); Pin-escapement for watches, Lobster-claw (Tavan, a form of Robin escapement) and *'Brise et à Surprise'* (Tavan, a variant of the lobster-claw, with less drop). Only one watch signed by Tavan is known to survive, and formed part of the Chamberlain collection. It has the *'brise et à surprise'* escapement and may well be the actual watch which won for Tavan the gold medal at the Geneva Competition in 1819.

THURET, JACQUES. Thuret's dates are not known, though he succeeded his father as 'Horloger du Roi' in 1694. His horological importance is that in 1675 Christian Huygens, then living in Paris, selected Thuret to execute a watch with his newly invented spiral balance-spring. The first examples had a gearing between the verge and the balance-wheel with its spring, whereby the vibrations of the balance were amplified. But this complication was soon given up. Several fine oignon watches with normal verge and balance-spring escapements, by Thuret, survive.

TOMPION, THOMAS (1639–1713) is thought to have been brought up by his father as a blacksmith, in Northill, Bedfordshire, where he was born. It is not known what influenced him to take up watch and clockmaking, nor to whom he was apprenticed. But he was admitted to the Clockmakers' Company in 1671 and became Master in 1704. While Tompion made some outstandingly fine clocks, his watches are no better than the best of his contemporaries. He was, however, much assisted by Robert Hooke in co-operation with whom—however unwillingly at times—he developed a practicable form of balance-spring, although not in time to be able to claim the priority over Huygens and Thuret. Nevertheless, the superiority of his wheelwork, in conjunction with the new balance-spring, attained an accuracy in portable timekeeping far exceeding anything that had been known or contemplated previously. And this in turn benefited the whole British industry, giving it a clear pre-eminence over other Continental artists which it enjoyed for at least 80 years. Only one watch by Tompion without a balance-spring, and therefore made before 1675, has survived, and that as a dial-less movement only. It is in the Guildhall Museum of the Clockmakers' Company (*169*).

In 1701 Tompion took Edward Banger (who had married his sister's daughter) into partnership and their work was then signed *'Thos Tompion Edwd Banger'*; but the partnership seems to have been an uneasy one and it broke up in 1707 or 1708. He then took

George Graham into partnership, who had worked for him since 1695, married his brother's daughter, and took over his business after he died in 1713. Pieces signed 'T. Tompion & G. Graham' are, for some reason, very rare, and the joint signature does not seem to have been used before about 1711.

Tompion started to number his watches in about 1682. The number was stamped under the balance-cock and this is a useful point in establishing authenticity, since Tompion was much faked, both in his lifetime, and long afterwards; although the fakes are usually not difficult to recognise. He seems to have had three series of watch numbers. Baillie gives the following dates and numbers:

Signature	Year	Plain Watches	Repeaters
Thos Tompion	1701	No. 3292	No. 203
Thos Tompion Edwd Banger	1701–8	Nos. 3252–4119	Nos. 196–290
Thos Tompion	1709–13	Nos. 4265–4312	Nos. 359–392
T. Tompion & G. Graham	1711–13	Nos. 4369–4543	

George Graham continued the series after Tompion's death and the earliest recorded number with his name alone is No. 4669 (plain) and 393 (repeater). There is a very early repeater by Tompion, in the Ilbert Collection, dating from about 1690, with the number 63. In addition to the above two series Tompion seems to have had a third series for special watches of one kind or another, in which the number was prefixed by an O.

Tompion had a nephew, also Thomas, his brother's son, who was apprenticed to Charles Kemp and admitted to the Clockmakers' Company in 1702, but he does not seem ever to have worked with his uncle and was evidently a bad character, as in 1720 he was sent to prison for pickpocketing.

TYRER, THOMAS, of Red Lion Street, Clerkenwell, did not invent the duplex escapement, but he brought it more or less to its established form and in 1782 took out a patent (No. 1311) in respect of it, described as a 'horizontal escapement for a watch to act with two wheels'. Apart from this nothing, and not even his dates, is known.

VACHERON & CONSTANTIN. The Vacheron family were watchmakers from 1785 and the Constantins were in business by about the same date. They amalgamated in 1819 to form the firm which still flourishes under that name. Early work was of no more than average quality, but in 1839 they took into partnership George Leschot who introduced a large measure of machine-tooling and interchangeability. Since this date the products of the firm have been uniformly of high quality.

VULLIAMY. Three successive members of this family were active from 1730 to 1854 and although they are most famous for their unsurpassed regulator clocks they also made some excellent watches.

Justin Vulliamy was in partnership with Benjamin Gray from 1730 to 1775. His son Benjamin, of Pall Mall, was active from 1775 to 1820 and his son Benjamin Lewis, of 68 Pall Mall continued the business up to his death in 1854.

The most characteristic Vulliamy watches have the duplex escapement and the whole top plate is covered with a decorative pierced fret. These watches were made with little or no variation over a surprisingly long period, from before 1800 until well after 1820. Another, rarer class of Vulliamy watch could almost be taken for a Breguet lever repeater, except that the centre of the gold or silver dial is matted and not engine turned. It is highly probable that these were made for Vulliamy by Sylvan Mairet.

WRIGHT, THOMAS, was admitted to the Clockmakers' Company in 1770 and died in 1792. He is only of importance in having taken out for Thomas Earnshaw a patent (in 1783, No. 1354) for his spring detent escapement and compensation balance, as Earnshaw could not afford to do so for himself. Earnshaw's earliest watches with this escapement were stamped '*Wright's Patent*'.

Index

The numerals in heavy type refer to the *figure numbers* of the illustrations

INDEX

INDEX

INDEX

INDEX